MW00610386

ISBN-13: 978-0-9886768-8-6

To My Father,

Who Taught Me to Love America

Table of Contents

PART I – Free to Act

PART II – Bound by Duty

ACKNOWLEDGEMENTS

Criticizing our forbearers is all the rage these days. But my father grew up in a different era. In the 1950s and early '60s, Americans were taught to love their country, not hate it. The mood changed in the late '60s. It became chic to spell 'America' with a "k" (to associate it with Nazi Germany), to denounce the U.S. as irredeemably racist, and to regard it as an imperialist oppressor of non-white peoples around the world.

In this environment, Arthur Morse published *While Six Million Died: A Chronicle of American Apathy*. Until then, most Americans – particularly American Jews – had held President Franklin D. Roosevelt in high esteem. He had, after all, led the United States to victory over Adolf Hitler and provided desperately-needed leadership during the Great Depression. But Morse presented his readers with a different Roosevelt. This Roosevelt knew six million Jews were being slaughtered in Europe during World War II and did little to save them. Morse's book was the first of many that would paint Roosevelt in this light, and many Americans – already prone to disliking their country – lapped it up.

By the time I grew up in the 1980s, practically everyone I knew accepted this portrayal of Roosevelt. My father, Dr. Lawrence Resnick, was an exception. He believed the State Department and Roosevelt's Jewish advisors were to blame, not the president himself for the U.S.'s failure to do more to save Jews during the Holocaust. He also didn't understand (if I recall correctly) why an *American* president should be excoriated for not taking a special interest in saving *European* Jews – especially in wartime when the lives of millions of American servicemen were in peril.

My father – a brilliant renaissance man – passed away in 2004, but his passionate defense of this country's war record (and, by extension, all those

Jews who adored Roosevelt in the 1930s and '40s) has remained with me. Without it, I don't think I would have written this book, so I must first thank my father.

Other people responsible for this work include Professor Jeffrey Gurock, my PhD advisor, who spent many hours with me reviewing the initial draft and helped give it its original unifying theme; the other members of my doctoral dissertation committee, Daniel Rynhold, Marc Lee Raphael, and David Dalin; historians Rebecca Erbelding and Rafael Medoff, who e-mailed me numerous helpful documents from their research files; Rabbi Aaron Reichel, who allowed me to read several important pages from the unpublished autobiography of his grandfather, Rabbi Herbert S. Goldstein; authors and scholars Thomas J. Campanella, Lynne Olson, Warren Kimball, David Nasaw, Jonathan Schapiro, Zalman Alpert, and Rabbi Dovid Reidel, who kindly answered my e-mail inquiries; librarians Mary Ann Linahan and Rebekah Shoemake, who processed my numerous interlibrary requests at Yeshiva University; and the helpful staff at places like the New York Public Library, the Central Zionist Archives, the Center for Jewish History, the Library of Congress, and the Franklin D. Roosevelt Presidential Library and Museum.

For providing blurbs, I would like to thank historians Michael Berenbaum and Edward Shapiro; Rabbis Berel Wein and Gil Student; and Newsweek editor Josh Hammer. I'm also grateful to venerable historians Henry Feingold and Gerhard Weinberg for reading and praising the book, even if they ultimately declined to write blurbs for it (the latter because it doesn't discuss the origins of America's restrictive immigration policy and the former because of the Appendix). Finally, I wish to thank my mother who, for a long time – as per the old quip about PhD dissertations – was just one of three people in the world who read the book you're holding. She liked every chapter except one – the introduction (it was too academic) – so I complete rewrote it.

INTRODUCTION

Sol Bloom (1870-1949) saved the life of the Gerrer Rebbe. He introduced the Ferris Wheel to the world. He helped draft the founding charter of the United Nations. He put George Washington's visage on the quarter. He successfully combatted a movement that would have introduced an eight-day week into the calendar.

Bloom sat in Congress for 26 years and wielded more power during the Holocaust than any other Jew in America's legislative body.[1] He chaired the House of Representatives' Foreign Affairs Committee and thus manned the gates through which all crucial foreign policy bills passed. Lend-Lease – legislation by which President Franklin D. Roosevelt sent arms to England to fight the Nazis – first had to clear Bloom's committee. So did a 1943 resolution calling for the creation of a government commission to save Europe's endangered Jews. And so did a 1944 resolution favoring the establishment of a Jewish state.

Before the late 1960s, prominent American Jews generally tried to keep their Jewishness under wraps. Bloom didn't. A *mezuzah* graced the door of his congressional office and a large picture of a Yom Kippur service hung inside it. "Sol Bloom is what many in public life today are not. He's mighty proud that he's a Jew!" declared the author of a 1939 profile on the congressman.[2] Shortly after Bloom's passing, one non-Jewish colleague recalled that Bloom "was a Jew, and he was not afraid of being a Jew, or ashamed of it, or sensitive about it."[3] Bloom actually once spoke about Jewish affairs so confidently at a congressional hearing that another colleague responded by jokingly calling him "Rabbi Bloom."[4] Bloom also apparently made a point of not smoking at Friday night social events despite the attention this practice drew to himself.[5]

Bloom's unabashed Jewishness is also evident in his autobiography. He proudly testifies, for example, to reciting the ritual blessings over wine and bread every Sabbath – he even reproduces the text of these blessings in the book – and describes some of Judaism's kosher laws to his readers without a hint self-consciousness (e.g., "No true orthodox Jew would ever...eat meat from a plate on which any food containing milk or butter had *at any time* been served"). He also openly acknowledges that the Democratic Party asked him to run for Congress in 1922 because he was an "amiable and solvent Jew."[6] And then there's this story:

> A number of years ago a group of Protestant and Catholic clergymen came to my office in Washington to consult with me...about a practical means for "solving the Jewish problem."
>
> "Gentlemen, I know of no Jewish problem," I responded. "I must ask you to elaborate."
>
> They elaborated.
>
> "What you refer to is not the Jewish problem," I told them, "but the *non-Jewish problem*."
>
> The clergymen now asked me to explain.
>
> "I mean that the problem we are discussing was created by people who are not Jews. Thus, it is a non-Jewish problem. We Jews do not discriminate against the Catholics and the various Protestant denominations; we Jews do not teach our children to be intolerant of your children; we Jews do not build ghettos. And so it seems to me that those who have made the 'problem' are the only ones who can solve it."[7]

Bloom showed similar gumption on another occasion; a 1932 magazine profile on Bloom reports the following from his tenure as co-director of the George Washington Bicentennial Commission:

> Descendants of three American presidents were gathered in Bloom's office not long ago looking over the portraits of the first President, and discussing Bicentennial plans

with the associate director. The conversation of the three after a while diverted itself to their illustrious forbears.

"I suppose, Mr. Bloom," said one of the group, with the superiority of tone of a proprietary family, "you must get bored hearing us talk about our ancestors."

"Oh, I don't know," replied Sol. "How about Abraham, Isaac and Jacob?"[8]

In short, Bloom was a proud Jew. But you would never know that from the scholarly literature on the Holocaust. In this literature, Bloom is depicted, almost without fail, as a timid, insecure Jew par excellence. One Holocaust historian writes that Bloom "had a reputation among Jews and non-Jews as fearful of rocking the State Department boat." Another claims that Bloom was "widely regarded as a cat's-paw for [Assistant Secretary of State] Breckinridge Long." A third writes that Bloom was "more interested in personal recognition within executive and State Department circles than in championing Jewish causes."[9]

And so, Bloom did little to save Jews during World War II, claim Holocaust historians. David Wyman, for example, in his famous work *The Abandonment of the Jews*, has this to say about Bloom:

> Sol Bloom, despite his influential position in Congress, attempted next to nothing for the Jews of Europe. True, he arranged for several individual Jewish refugees to enter the United States. And he assisted the Orthodox rescue agency, Vaad Hahatzala, in some small ways. But when possibilities for major action arose, he consistently allied himself with the State Department. He seemed most of all concerned to use his post as chairman of the Foreign Affairs Committee to win the esteem of the State Department elite. Three decades later, [Rep. Emanuel] Celler concluded that "Sol Bloom did a great deal of harm because of his attitude. He was a mere sycophant of the State Department."[10]

These assessments of Bloom are untenable. Not only do they

contradict what we know about Bloom's character, they also render incomprehensible the solid reputation Bloom enjoyed among his contemporaries. No fewer than 17 different Jewish organizations honored Bloom by placing "In Memoriam" notices in The New York Times when he died on March 7, 1949.[11] (In contrast, not a *single* Jewish organization placed a death notice in the Times following the passing of Bloom's most prominent Jewish colleagues, Rep. Samuel Dickstein and Emanuel Celler.) One major American Jewish organization, Agudath Israel, even held a dinner in Bloom's honor in 1947. Surely, these organizations wouldn't have feted Bloom in this manner if he had turned his back on his co-religionists during the Holocaust.[12]

And yet, Bloom's Holocaust record is clearly mixed. He saved, as we shall see, many individual Jews whose relatives or friends approached him for assistance, but he never challenged the Roosevelt administration's restrictive immigration policy that barred so many Jews from escaping Europe. He also failed to advance bold rescue plans for Europe's endangered Jews at a critical 1943 conference on refugees in Bermuda and obstructed a congressional resolution later that year that called for the creation of a government commission to save these Jews.

But if Bloom wasn't a timid or insecure Jew, what explains his behavior during the Holocaust? And what explains the behavior of so many American Jews in the 1940s who seemingly did little to save their relatives being slaughtered by the Nazis in Europe? Why didn't they pressure President Roosevelt to come to their brethren's rescue?

The answer to these questions is multifaceted, but a large part of it boils down to patriotism: The Jews of this era loved America and felt indebted to it for permitting them to emigrate from Europe and giving

Rep. Sol Bloom (1870-1949)

them a fresh chance at life, free of persecution. Many modern-day critics assume these Jews were too scared to publicly castigate the Roosevelt administration, but it's more likely they believed it wrong to do so.[13] The United States, after all, was at war. American soldiers were dying in the battlefields of Europe. How could they attack their commander-in-chief at such a moment? How could they place their interests above those of the country?

These questions likely lurked in Bloom's mind as well. Additionally, as a sitting member of Congress and chairman of the House Foreign Affairs Committee, he presumably regarded it as his primary duty to help Roosevelt confront the Nazi threat. That explains why from 1939-1941 he braved a wave of anti-Semitic hostility and isolationism to ensure passage of key legislation in Congress to keep Hitler from conquering Europe and ultimately threatening America. At the same time, however, he didn't challenge America's popular restrictive immigration policy as doing so, in his view, would've undermined Roosevelt's efforts to unite the country for war. Bloom's allegiance to the administration's aims also explains why he largely adhered to the onerous restrictions placed upon him by the State Department at the Bermuda Conference. It explains further why he hindered an effort by activist Peter Bergson – whom the administration regarded as a thorn in its side – to quickly secure a congressional resolution calling on Roosevelt to create a government rescue commission. This same factor was at play in early 1944 when Bloom disappointed Zionist leaders who sought a congressional expression of approval for the establishment of a Jewish state as the administration feared that such an expression would harm the war effort.

No doubt, some will cling to the theory that American Jews were just too timid to protest the government's behavior during the Holocaust. I believe this assessment mistaken. But even if it isn't, it clearly doesn't explain Bloom behavior. For Bloom was not a "sick-souled, scared and tied-in-knots Jew."[14] Indeed, he was uniquely *uninhibited* about his Jewishness for a man of his era. In fact, his personality was almost the antithesis of inhibited and timid. If a historian were to look solely at Bloom's Holocaust activities, he could be excused for thinking him an insecure, timid Jew eager to do the bidding of the State Department. But judging a person's deeds out of context is neither prudent nor fair. So before we examine Bloom's behavior during the Holocaust, we must first survey the first six decades of his life – an exercise that will demonstrate that timidity is not a viable explanation for Bloom's war-time conduct. Once that is established, we will explore a more likely explanation: Bloom's sense of duty as a prominent American congressman.

Part I – Free to Act

~ CHAPTER 1 ~

BRASH AND BOLD BEGINNINGS

S
ol Bloom was born in early 1870 in Pekin, Illinois,[1] to Gershon and Sarah, penniless immigrants who arrived on American shores "some time before 1860" from the Polish town of Szyrpcz.[2] Sol's father operated a small clothing store but lost it in the Panic of 1873, prompting the family to move two years later to San Francisco where economic conditions were more favorable.[3]

San Francisco at this time was home to approximately 15,000 Jews,[4] constituting the second largest Jewish community in the United States.[5] It also was an unusual community, producing perhaps the least timid Jews in America. Established during the California Gold Rush, this community differed from its counterparts in the East or Midwest. The latter were established in developed regions with pre-existing social structures and hierarchies; the former was established in their absence. (Indeed, San Francisco didn't even formally exist until January 30, 1847; before then, it was a "quiet Mexican village" known as Yerba Buena with fewer than 500 people.[6]) The first Jews arrived in San Francisco alongside tens of thousands of adventurers and fortune-seekers of all races and nationalities, an influx that made "San Francisco the most ethnically diverse city on the continent, a nineteenth-century Babel. Along with Southerners, New Englanders, and New Yorkers, virtually every European country was represented. There were [even] Chinese and Latin Americans, Polynesians and South Africans, Australians and Moroccans."[7] Since Jews lived in San Francisco from its very founding and played "a key role in transforming a crude frontier outpost into a thriving center of commerce and culture,"[8] they didn't see themselves as outsiders, nor were they regarded as such by their neighbors. San Francisco was just as much "theirs" as anyone else's.[9] The city's history – along with the "ethos of individualism" and "adventurous, free-for-all spirit"[10] pervading the frontier – begat a place where anti-Semitism was "extremely rare,"[11] with Jews enjoying "unprecedented" social and political acceptance.[12] In fact, as early as 1852, two members of the State Assembly were San Franciscan Jews, and San Francisco elected its first Jewish mayor, Adolph Sutro, in 1894.[13]

Not surprisingly, the unusual conditions prevailing in San Francisco produced an atypical Jewry – one brimming with "self-confidence," "brash sensibility," and a sense of "audacious freedom."[14] Jews out West – the Jews among whom Bloom grew up – possessed a certain confidence and self-assurance. In modern parlance, they felt "comfortable in their own skin" and more at home in the world. They saw themselves, not just as Jews, but as equal members of society, "interacting fully with non-Jews."[15] Historian Fred Rosenbaum argues that out West "Jewish behavior was less constrained than it was in the East" and "the age-old question 'What will the goyim think?' was asked less frequently and less anxiously." Indeed, he writes that "Jews in the American West in the second half of the nineteenth century were arguably the freest in the world."[16] No place in America was "more secure and open to the Jews."[17]

Even the area's geography arguably contributed to the character of Western Jewry. The West's "spaciousness…awesome beauty, and numerous natural recreational areas encouraged Jews to live a more robust life," writes historians Harriet and Fred Rochlin. The "stunning natural setting," the "great outdoors,"[18] gave room for their spirits to expand and soar, uninhibited.

And soar they did. Some of the most famous "characters" in the early history of San Francisco (and nearby Oakland) were Jewish, starting with Joshua Norton, who in 1859 declared himself "Emperor of the United States and the protector of Mexico."[19] He played the part, too, dressing in royal garments, making proclamations that local newspapers published, and issuing his own currency, which many stores accepted. More sane, but also representative of the same robust San Franciscan free spirit, were people like Hebrew University president Judah Magnes, who "attributed his dissident stance to his western upbringing"; avant-garde author Gertrude Stein, whose relatives "attributed her idiosyncrasies to the fact of her being a westerner"; and "female maggid" Rachel Frank, arguably "the nation's first female rabbi. In short, "Jewish individuality blossomed" out West.[20]

By the time Sol Bloom's family moved to San Francisco, the city's population had increased to approximately 200,000,[21] but the adventurous frontier spirit still filled the air. The city Bloom grew up in offered its citizens the ability to develop freely without inhibition. In his autobiography, Bloom writes extensively of his childhood and teenage years in San Francisco, calling himself "a product of that city" and, in part, "an expansive Westerner."[22] He left the city as a 21-year-old man, but never forgot it, writing to a friend in 1943, "I just love the town and I think of it all the time."[23]

Bloom – who really is the only source for most of what we know about his early life – grew up poor and started working at age six selling newspapers and peddling wares to help his family make ends meet.[24] He only attended school one day in his life. As he tells it, public school students in San Francisco in the 1870s either bought textbooks or received them on loan from the school. The loaned books, however, were marked as such so that everyone in the class knew which classmates couldn't afford to buy a textbook. Young Sol – all of six years old – was too proud to accept charity and quit school as soon as he learned of the arrangement.[25] A year later, at age seven, he began working in a brush factory, where he "swept floors, washed windows, opened boxes and wrapped packages, ran errands, took stock, sandpapered brush blocks, mixed glue, cut bristles, packed crates, and waited on all the other employees." He worked 12-hour days, six days a week.[26]

"Emperor" Joshua Norton (1818-1880), one of San Francisco's unusual Jewish characters.

IN HIS FIRST JOB IN A BRUSH FACTORY AT THE AGE OF 8, MR. BLOOM WAS PAID $1.25 PER WEEK FOR SIX 12-HOUR DAYS.

BLISS 3-5

A comic about Sol Bloom in The Evening Star, March 5, 1946.

From a very early age, though, Bloom's imagination was fired by show business. While passing a theater on the way home from work one day as an eight-year-old boy, he received an offer to play a small non-speaking role in a play that evening for 50 cents. He jumped at the opportunity, and "the effects" of his performance were "permanent," he writes. He "had been bitten by the bug of the theater." Over the next 11 years, he served as an extra, usher, vendor, claque, and hat checker – among other jobs – and, at age 15, he left the brush factory to become assistant treasurer of the Alcazar theater.[27]

During this time period, he also chased numerous opportunities to innovate and make money. For example, as a theater usher, he "noted that there was always likely to be a patron who had forgotten his handkerchief, lost a collar button, or broken a shoelace," and so he "became a walking department store." After all: "[People] in emergency were not only willing to pay two or three times the customary price but usually insisted upon pressing a tip into my reluctant hand." Not all of Bloom's schemes were so straightforward. Some, he readily admits, might "be classified as rackets by the purist." He and his fellow ushers, for example, often pretended to run out of programs so that people would tip them handsomely when they just "happened" to find an extra one. On one occasion, he and several others in the theater coatroom ate two or three cloves of garlic so that patrons wouldn't wait to collect their change when they picked up their coats.[28] Whatever the scheme, he seems to have had a grand time doing it judging from the lively way he relates these episodes in his autobiography. Bloom was also an entrepreneur on the side and by 1888, while still a teenager, was making a staggering $25,000 a year – the equivalent of $769,000 in 2022.[29]

Despite this phenomenal success, he "wanted more action and excitement."[30] And soon he would get it. At age 21 he was hired to head a first-of-its-kind amusement section at the World's Columbian Exposition in Chicago. This exposition – which celebrated 400 years since the discovery of America – opened in 1893 and was the "largest, most spectacular world's fair" ever produced. Its planners aimed for "[e]very square inch…[to] dazzle the senses and stimulate the mind."[31] Indeed, the fair's "White City" was so magnificent that it reputedly served as the inspiration for the magical Emerald City of L. Frank Baum's *Wizard of Oz* books and the lyrics of "America the Beautiful."[32] Among the many features of Bloom's mile-long amusement section were the world's first Ferris Wheel (Bloom's philosophy being "the more novel and startling the better"[33]); an ostrich farm; an Algerian village that introduced belly dancing to America[34]; a Moorish palace; a tethered balloon that carried passengers 1,500 feet in the air; and an ice slide.[35]

Bloom stayed in Chicago after the highly-successful fair and soon

The world's first Ferris Wheel – featured in 1893 at the amusement section of the Columbia International Exposition headed by Sol Bloom.

entered the music industry, opening a music publishing store in 1896. He became well-known as "Sol Bloom, the Music Man"[36] and later expanded to selling musical instruments as well as Victor talking machines. To promote his business, he drew on his creative and enterprising spirit, stationing, for example, one of his employees outside the Copyright Office in Washington, D.C., for several days at the end of December 1899 so that he would secure the very first copyright of the 20th century (for a song) – a move he made sure to advertise for many months thereafter.[37] By circa 1905, Bloom had moved to New York and was operating 80 stores (or music sections of department stores) across the country, including one on 5th Ave. in Manhattan.

In 1910, though, he quit the music industry to work full-time in New York real estate.[38] He bought and improved properties in what is today midtown Manhattan – including a small plot on the corner of 47th St. and Broadway for which he paid $450,000 (the equivalent of $10.3 million in 2022)[39] – and built and renovated numerous Manhattan theaters.[40] He achieved great success to which Bloom credited, among other things, his "sure sense of publicity."[41] However, after 12 successful years in real estate – in December 1922 – Bloom received a phone call from Tammany Hall leader Charlie Murphy that would alter the course of his life. Bloom, the businessman, was about to become Bloom, the congressman. And he would take the brashness and confidence that had served him so well – in his childhood years, at the 1893 world's fair, and in his business and real estate career – with him to Washington.

In any event, it should be evident by now that Bloom *was* brash and confident. Shy and insecure individuals don't become entrepreneurs in their teenage years or get

Sol Bloom advertising his music business in the November 13, 1908 issue of The New York Times.

hired at age 21 to run the amusement section of a world's fair. Nor do they pursue big and bold plans. Some Jews in early 20th century America were timid. Bloom wasn't one of them.

~ CHAPTER 2 ~

RUNNING PUBLIC RELATIONS
FOR GEORGE WASHINGTON

In 1920, New Yorkers elected six Jews to Congress. Not one of them belonged to the Democratic Party. But the party's fortunes improved in the 1922 mid-term elections. With assistance from Tammany Hall – New York's legendary political machine – the Democrats propelled three Jews from Jewish areas in New York into Congress, including Samuel Marx from the 19th congressional district (which included Morningside Heights and portions of Harlem and the Upper West Side).[1] Two weeks after Election Day, however, Marx died suddenly,[2] and shortly thereafter Bloom received a surprise phone call from Charles Murphy of Tammany Hall asking him to run for Congress. In his autobiography, Bloom writes, "Samuel Marx, like myself a Jew, had been able to beat [Republican candidate Walter] Chandler, and Tammany decided that another Jew might be able to repeat the victory in a district having a substantial Jewish population." Bloom was also well-known, apparently well-liked, and financially well-off. "Briefly," he writes, "I had been chosen to run because I was an amiable and solvent Jew."[3]

According to Bloom, he had been looking to pursue something meaningful at the time, so he accepted Murphy's offer.[4] He campaigned aggressively[5] and on January 30, 1923, won the special election by 145 votes out of a total of 35,627 cast.[6] According to a 1944 biographical sketch of Bloom written by Washington Post editor Ira Bennett, Bloom still enjoyed a "wide reputation as a showman" when he arrived in Washington such that "some of his colleagues" would "not have been surprised" had he "attempted to transform the hall of the House into a circus."[7] Indeed, on the day his constituents headed to the polls, Bloom said, "If elected I'll be a hell of a guy or nothing. Billy Sunday won't have anything on me for breaking up the furniture."[8]   Bloom, though, sought to serve his constituents in earnest. (As we will see, he continued to evince a flair for the big and bold, but he did so for higher ends.) The very first week after his election, he pledged to set up an office in his district to help immigrants. "I haven't forgotten," he said, "that my parents came over in the steerage, and I feel I owe it to Almighty God to be of service to those who are arriving that way on Ellis Island every day."[9]   Indeed, helping people became a point of pride for Bloom. In his autobiography, he writes, "I would rather make another person happy than do anything else. The knowledge that I have been able to do something for somebody else is all that I need to bring me contentment at the end of a day's work."[10]

Bloom's first few years in Congress were relatively quiet.[11]   His constituents must have been pleased, though, because he was reelected to office in 1924 by a margin of 9,000 votes and again in 1926 by a margin of 17,000, winning two-thirds of the vote.[12] Indeed, never again would Bloom win an election by anything other than a landslide margin, twice earning more than 70 percent of the vote, including in 1944 when he received 71 percent of the vote.[13]

Bloom made his first splash for a Jewish cause in 1926 when he publicly challenged auto tycoon Henry Ford to prove that the "international Jew" controls the U.S. government's financial divisions as his

Sol Bloom (far right) standing next to President Calvin Coolidge in 1924.

newspaper, The Dearborn Independent, had alleged. Before examining this episode, though – and a subsequent one on a calendar reform proposal that would have greatly impeded Jews' ability to properly observe the Sabbath – it's worthwhile to jump ahead and first review one of the greatest highlights of Bloom's career: directing the government's 200th year birthday celebration of George Washington in 1932, as this saga proves once again that Bloom possessed a bold and confident character, not a diffident and timid one.

In 1925, as a member of the House of Representatives' Committee on Industrial Arts and Expositions, Bloom had suggested holding a world's fair in Brooklyn's Jamaica Bay in honor of the first president.

> With characteristic élan, Bloom sketched out a vision for the largest and grandest exposition ever staged, with pavilions for forty-six nations, landing fields for aircrafts…and a stadium for 200,000 people – larger than anything in the world even today. Above all this would stand a tower twice the height of the Washington Monument, with a searchlight strong enough to project a beam as far away as Detroit or Quebec.[14]

This plan eventually fell through, but Bloom didn't give up trying to celebrate Washington's 200th birthday in grand style, and in 1930 was appointed co-director of the George Washington Bicentennial Commission alongside Ulysses S Grant III (a grandson of the 18th president). When Grant in early 1931 resigned due to competing obligations, Bloom took sole command of the commission's work[15] and aimed, he said, to make the bicentennial celebration nothing less than "the greatest tribute ever paid a human being in the history of the world."[16]

The celebration – which commenced on Washington's birthday on February 22, 1932[17] and lasted until Thanksgiving – was, by virtually all accounts, a resounding success. Nearly 900,000 local bicentennial committees were created, five million news items related to the bicentennial were published in newspapers, 30 million Washington memorial trees were planted,[18] copies of Gilbert Stuart's "Anthenaeum" portrait of George Washington were sent to every classroom in the country,[19] 3.5 million school programs on Washington were held,[20] over 100 bicentennial speeches (including addresses at Washington's tomb and Independence Hall) were delivered by Bloom,[21] numerous academic monographs relating to Washington's life were commissioned, and a definitive 39-volume set of Washington's writings began to be published by the government.[22] Altogether, a total of 4,760,345 bicentennial celebrations of one sort or another took place around the country.[23] In 1932 the government also issued the 25-cent coin bearing Washington's image that we still use today[24] and the prior year, in honor of the upcoming bicentennial, a major bridge linking New York and New Jersey received its current name: the George Washington Bridge.[25]

Bloom continued promoting Washington in the years following the

Inaugurating the George Washington Bicentennial March: Sol Bloom (left), President Herbert Hoover (center), and the U.S. Marine Band.

bicentennial. He often gave speeches on Washington's birthday, and in 1936, made Washington once again the subject of national news when he bet 20:1 that baseball all-star Walter Johnson couldn't throw a coin across the Rappahannock River – a feat George Washington had, according to legend, performed as a youngster. Johnson accepted the challenge and on Washington's birthday, in front of an

JOHNSON THROWS
DOLLAR OVER RIVER

Continued From Page One.

porters climbed into saplings to obtain a better view. Others were scattered back several hundred yards to the road, where automobiles had been parked.

Over on the opposite side conditions were worse, for a greater crowd milled there in the hope of out-scuffling others for the reward.

Distance Hedges Bloom's Bet.

The "stunt" was originally planned as a part of commemoration exercises, in which the chief event was to be the acceptance and planting of cherry trees along the new boulevard from the city to the Ferry Farm.

It gained nation-wide publicity, however, when Representative Sol Bloom of New York, director of the George Washington Bicentennial Commission, came forward with an offer to bet 20 to 1 that Johnson could not match the reputed feat of Washington.

A deposit of $5,000 was promptly made by citizens of this city to "take" $100,000 of Mr. Bloom's money, and the story broke into almost every newspaper in the country.

More space was added each day

The "Big Train" just as he made one of his throws, the spectators watching the dollar sailing to the opposite bank of the river, 268 feet and 6 inches.

Front-page New York Times story on baseball all-star Walter Johnson mimicking a feat allegedly performed by George Washington: throwing a coin across the Rappahannock River.

excited crowd, successfully threw a coin over the river. Over the course of five days, The New York Times ran seven stories on the event, including one on its front page.[26]

Bloom promoted Washington on a large scale one last time in 1939 at the culmination of a celebration of the 150th anniversary of the U.S. Constitution's composition and ratification. President Roosevelt appointed Bloom to head the sesquicentennial celebration, which began on September 17, 1937 with Bloom delivering a speech in the Library of Congress before the Shrine of the Constitution at the very hour it was signed in 1787[27] and ended on April 30, 1939, the 150th anniversary of Washington's inauguration.[28] That same day, the 1939 New York World's Fair opened "follow[ing] an elaborate re-enactment of Washington's journey from Virginia."[29] At the fair, "under the relentless prodding of Bloom and his Commission, Washington was a significant presence" with the fair grounds featuring a 65-foot statue of the first president.[30] The "supersalesman of patriotism"[31] – as Bloom had come to be called by some of his colleagues – had come through again in grand style.

Bloom's activities to promote George Washington indicate once again that the congressman possessed a colorful, confident character. Timidity seems to have been very foreign to him. Nor was his confident métier restricted to patriotic, business, or entertainment activities. It extended to his Jewish identity as well. We've already seen in the Introduction that Bloom was a uniquely proud Jew for a man of his era. In the next chapter, we'll see that Bloom also evidently had no compunctions about drawing public attention to his Jewishness.

Before the George Washington bicentennial celebration in 1932, the quarter featured a battle-ready goddess of liberty instead of the first president.

~ CHAPTER 3 ~

HENRY FORD AND
THE EIGHT-DAY WEEK

The "international Jew is in direct control of all financial centres of government, including the United States Federal Reserve System"; "he pulls so many strings in business that no banker or business man feels safe to oppose him"; "he either owns the press or controls it so that only pro-Jewish facts are ever admitted to print"; and he "is the chief control…in the making of war, of which he also the chief profiteer." So declared an article in the December 25, 1926 issue of The Dearborn Independent.[1] No byline appears above the article, but the paper was published by auto tycoon Henry Ford and was widely understood to enjoy his imprimatur.[2]

When advance proofs of this accusatory article were distributed two weeks prior to its publication, Bloom reacted by employing his characteristic brashness – but this time in defense of a Jewish cause. He publicly challenged Ford to testify before Congress and called for an investigatory body to look into Ford's claim. These moves led to extensive media coverage of an accusation that would otherwise have been quickly forgotten. Bloom obviously knew that publicly challenging Ford would put him and his Jewish identity in the limelight – in fact, five of seven news stories that The New York Times ran on the reaction to Ford's accusation revolved around Bloom – but he evidently didn't care. Not only did he step into the limelight; he actually created it, almost single-handedly making Ford's comments a major news item.[3]

In response to the article, Bloom publicly called on Ford to prove before Congress that "the international Jew," indeed, controlled the United States government's Federal Reserve as the article alleged. He then submitted a resolution before the House of Representatives' Committee on Rules, asking it to appoint a committee with subpoena powers to investigate the charge.[4] Bloom claimed he was offended by Ford's statement as an American, not as a Jew; in a letter to the chairman of the Committee on Rules, Bloom wrote, "A vindication of the Jew is not my resolution's object. My religion and my Americanism are two entirely different matters. Not as a Jew, but as an American, in behalf of constituents, non-Jewish as well as Jewish, I claim the right to know whether or not this Government...is controlled internationally. The issue is of supreme importance."[5] Yet, Bloom's Jewishness almost certainly contributed to his outrage. In his autobiography, he writes, "Ford was guilty of attacking not only a group of people but the integrity of his country's government. As a Jew, I bitterly resented the accusation. As an American citizen, I assumed the responsibility of demanding that Mr. Ford support his charges that there was an 'international' influence in the government."[6] In his resolution, too, Bloom highlights the seriousness of The Dearborn Independent's assertion vis-à-vis Jews specifically, noting that it "presents grave charges concerning the operation of the Government, the activities of the Federal Reserve System *and the Jewish people*" (emphasis added).[7]

The New York Times supported Bloom's resolution – arguing that Ford "unquestionably wrought great harm among many simple-minded citizens" and that requiring Ford to testify before Congress "for such rash and

Henry Ford (left) and Thomas Edison in 1929.

unpatriotic behavior" would "do a lot of good."[8] Bloom's public challenge to Ford, however, didn't sit well with some elements of American Jewry. Both The Jewish Morning Journal and The Jewish Daily News, for example, opposed his resolution, the latter arguing that "Ford's slanders are beneath anything which may be brought before a parliamentary committee for investigation." To "bring the matter to court," it submitted, "is to recognize that there is something in what Ford says that must be reckoned with, that his charges deserve consideration, and that in itself is a victory for Ford." The paper also berated Bloom for acting unilaterally "without consulting anyone."[9] Cyrus Adler, chancellor of the Jewish Theological Seminary and a leader of the American Jewish Committee, also found Bloom's move lamentable, arguing that he was only giving Ford "free advertisement." He advised Bloom that "it would be wisest to let this matter drop."[10]

But Bloom didn't let it drop. On December 23, 1926, he wrote a letter to Ford – and made it public a few days later so that it would receive maximum exposure – asking him to please produce evidence for his claim that "the international Jew" controlled the Federal Reserve. "If it is proved that our financial system is international controlled, I shall resent it as deeply as yourself," he wrote.[11] A month later, he sent Ford another letter – which he also evidently gave to the media – declaring that he won't let the "charge drop until it [was] substantiated or disproved."[12] Bloom also contacted the governor of the Federal Reserve Board, asking if it operated under foreign influence and then publicized the governor's response when he replied in the negative.[13]

Congress ultimately opted not to take up the matter. As one reporter explained, congressional leaders feared that a committee investigating Ford's charges would "become a forum for the airing of religious hatreds, prejudices and animosities."[14] The head of the Rules Committee, Rep. Bert Snell, said "[Ford's] charges are a joke…. Congress should not lower its dignity by even taking the slightest notice of [them]."[15] Bloom himself ultimately decided to back off, arguing in his autobiography that it didn't make sense to pursue the issue after Ford in mid-1927 issued a public apology for The Dearborn Independent's anti-Semitic content in response to an unrelated lawsuit.[16] What's important to note, though, is that Bloom had no problem employing his usual bluster and dramatic flair on behalf of a Jewish cause. An insecure Jew would have shied away from confronting an auto tycoon like Ford over his anti-Semitic views. He would have remained silent, tried backroom diplomacy, or asked a non-Jew to take on the cause. But Bloom did none of the above. He took on the cause himself.

Two years later, Bloom threw himself into another Jewish-related cause, helping defeat a proposal to reform the calendar that would have greatly impeded American Jews' ability to properly observe the Sabbath. Proposals to alter or abandon the Gregorian calendar – under which we currently operate – go back hundreds of years. The French revolutionaries, for instance, famously discarded the Gregorian calendar in 1793 and replaced it with a new one containing 12 months, each month containing three weeks, each week containing 10 days.[17] Motivating many calendar alteration plans was the "irrationality" and "unscientific" nature of the Gregorian calendar, which assigns some months 30 days, others months 31 days, and one month 28 days. Because of February's abbreviated length, the first six months of the year also contain three fewer days than the latter six (181 versus 184). The year's quarters are likewise unequal – containing 90, 91, 92, and 92 days, respectively. Furthermore, because different months start on different days of the week, some months contain four weekends while others contain five. The number of workdays per month thus also varies; workers may have to labor 25 days one month but only 21 the next. Finally, since the Gregorian calendar's 365-day year is not divisible by seven, calendar dates fall on different days of the week each year. Thus, for example, January 1 fell on a Tuesday in 2019 but on a Wednesday in 2020.

Businessmen and statisticians had particular cause to dislike the Gregorian calendar. The dissimilarity between months

The French Revolutionaries revised both the calendar and the clock, making them more "rational." Depicted here is a French clock from the late 18th/early 19th century that divides the day into 10 hours, with 100 minutes per hour.

means that one cannot easily compare monthly sales or productivity. Nor can one easily compare sales or productivity on a given day in different years due to shifting weekends. It would be useless, for example, for a store owner to compare sales on February 3, 2020 with sales on February 3, 2019 because in 2020 that day was a Monday while in 2019 it was a Sunday; Sunday sales are obviously not comparable to Monday sales.

In 1849, a French philosopher, Auguste Comte, designed a calendar (based on the work of philosopher Marco Mastrofini) that eliminates all these irregularities. Comte's calendar contains 13 months of 28 days each; thus, each month has a perfect four weeks. The problem with this scheme, however, is that the solar year is a little over 365 days while 13 months of 28 days only add up to 364. To add a 29th day to December would disturb the calendar's rationality and hinder yearly comparisons since January 1 would then fall on a different day of the week each year. Therefore, Comte proposed tagging a "blank day" to the end of the year that wouldn't be reckoned as one of the days of the week. December 28 would be Sunday, the next day would be "nothing," and January 1 would be Monday. In other words, the last week of each year would effectively contain eight days.[18]

Other calendar reformers followed in Comte's footsteps, and their efforts accelerated in the wake of World War I and the creation of the League of Nations, which offered them an opportune venue to advance their cause. In 1923, in response to lobbying by calendar reformers, the League of Nations created a Special Committee of Enquiry into the Reform of the Calendar, which proceeded to examine 185 proposals for reforming the calendar from 38 different countries. The most popular proposal came from Moses B. Cotsworth, a British statistician, whose calendar was identical to Comte's in every respect except that his months began on Sunday while Comte's began on Monday. In 1926 the League asked 60 countries to form national committees to study the matter further,[19] and 28 countries responded to the call, with the U.S. leading the pack.[20] This alacrity on the part of the U.S. was largely due to the efforts of George Eastman, founder of the Eastman Kodak Company, who became a strong advocate of calendar reform in 1924 and used his personal fortune to promote it.[21] Eastman headed the U.S. committee and was recognized by many as "the international leader of the calendar reformers."[22] As a result, Cotsworth's calendar reform proposal soon became known as the "Eastman plan."

When Jewish leaders learned of the plan, some of them reacted with alarm, noting that the introduction of a blank day in the calendar would undermine the sanctity of the Sabbath and cause economic havoc for Sabbath observers. The Bible instructs Jews to observe the Sabbath on the seventh day of every week to commemorate the seventh day of creation on which the Bible says God rested.[23]   Hence, for Jews, the day after December 28 cannot be "blank." Jews would have to consider this day the first day of a new week ("Sunday") and the next day, January 1, the second day of the week ("Monday") even though the proposed calendar would mark January 1 as a Sunday. In other words, if the Eastman plan were accepted, Jews would find themselves celebrating the Sabbath – their seventh day of the week – on Saturday one year, on Friday the next, on Thursday the next, and on Tuesday the next (due to an extra blank day inserted in leap years). Needless to say, observing the Sabbath under such circumstances would be extremely difficult. Even under the Gregorian calendar, many American Jews in the 1920s found it difficult to observe the Sabbath since their competitors could work six days a week while they could only work five. Under Cotsworth's calendar, observant Jews would only be able to work *four* days a week in many years.

American Jews by and large didn't strictly observe the Sabbath in this era. In 1912, for example, apparently only 25 percent of American Jewry did so.[24] For most Jews, writes historian Henry Feingold, "it was business as usual" on Saturdays.[25] Nonetheless, despite widespread non-observance of the Sabbath laws, many American Jews "remained deeply attached to Orthodox traditions,"[26] and if they violated the Sabbath, they did so largely due to severe economic exigencies. They had to "make an agonizing choice between being observant and earning an adequate livelihood…. [and the] demands of earning a living often won out."[27] The Sabbath itself, though, remained dear to most Jews, and many of them tried to observe it to at least some degree.[28] Hence, when British Chief Rabbi Joseph Hertz publicly objected in 1924 to the introduction of a blank day in the calendar, American rabbinical bodies representing Reform, Conservative, and Orthodox Jews all wrote letters in support of his stance.[29]

Serious American-Jewish objection to the Eastman plan, however, only emerged in late 1928 when Rep. Stephen Porter, chairman of the House of Representatives' Foreign Affairs Committee, introduced a resolution on December 5, asking the president to "propose, on behalf of the United States, to the nations of the world the calling of an international conference for the simplification of the calendar, or to accept an invitation on behalf of the United States to participate in such a conference upon the proposal of some other nation or group of individuals."[30] In response to this resolution, American Jewish leaders quickly organized and attained the crucial assistance of Bloom, who had become a member of the Foreign Affairs Committee earlier that year.

Throughout the hearings held on Rep. Porter's resolution, Bloom offered vigorous and unyielding opposition to the Eastman plan – in sharp contrast to his fellow committee members who seemed to have harbored no strong opinions on the matter one way or another. Indeed, Bloom

Comic in the January 1930 issue of The Jewish Forum
against the Eastman calendar reform proposal.

effectively adopted the cause as his own such that that when a fellow congressman summarized the opposition's view during the hearings, Bloom replied, "That is *our* position entirely" before correcting himself, "I mean the position of the Jewish people" (emphasis added).[31] During the 10 days of testimony before the committee, no one interrupted witnesses more often and more antagonistically than Bloom. Repeatedly, Bloom asked questions like: "Do you…know what would happen if this 13-month calendar were to be adopted…the effect on the Lord's Day and the Sabbath?" and "What do you think is more important – for a change in the calendar to allow the Sabbath and the Lord's Day to remain the same as it has been for hundreds and thousands of years, or do you think it is more important to change it for commercial benefits?"

Bloom held nothing back, sometimes posing rather caustic questions. Take the following exchange between Bloom and W.S. Clithero of Armour & Co., for example:

> MR. BLOOM: For thousands of years we have had a Sabbath and the Bible tells us certain things. I suppose you read the Bible once in a while?
>
> MR. CLITHERO: Occasionally.
>
> MR. BLOOM: Don't you think it rather serious for the Congress of the United States to absolutely destroy the Lord's Day and the Sabbath?

Just moments later, Clithero states, "That particular detail of moving away from the Sunday as we now have it in the sequence that you mention it, strikes me as being a detail." "Certainly it is a detail," Bloom responded. "I mean a rather immaterial detail," Clithero replied. When another witness mentioned in a light aside that one of the founders of his company still possessed all his teeth at age 99, visited the office often, and attended a vaudeville show every week, Bloom immediately asked in feigned wonderment, "That is all under the Gregorian calendar?"[32]

Bloom was likely responsible for Porter's resolution dying in committee and thus never making it to the House floor for a vote. He opposed it throughout the hearings and arguably also helped secure the testimony of the several Jewish[33] and Christian clergy who testified against it at the hearings. "[I]f it had not been for Sol Bloom," The Jewish Tribune argued, "the Porter resolution would have passed on the first day of its scheduled hearing. Uncle Sam would now be practically committed to a 'thirteen month, twenty-eight days a month calendar.'"[34] Three years later, Rabbi Hertz echoed this verdict, writing, "But for the fact that Congressman Solomon Bloom, of New York, was a member of that Committee [on Foreign Affairs], the resolution would have slipped through unopposed."[35]

Bloom's involvement in efforts to defeat the Eastman plan didn't stop after the hearings. In March, he addressed calendar reform at the convention of the Union of Orthodox Jewish Congregations of America,[36] and shortly thereafter Bloom joined the newly-formed League for Safeguarding the Fixity of the Sabbath, remaining a vice president of that organization until at least 1941.[37] Bloom continued battling the Eastman plan in Congress as well. He writes in his autobiography, "Ordinarily I would have been completely satisfied with the quiet demise of a bill I had opposed, but in this case I wanted a state funeral — so that a permanent monument would be erected to warn future calendar reformers."[38] On June 11, 1929, Bloom inserted an 18-page long speech in the Congressional Record[39] in which he advances numerous arguments against the Eastman plan. For example, he asks: Why cause such mass confusion, why deprive millions of their birthdays and render many contracts non-sensible, when no popular support for reforming the calendar exists? Bloom quotes a newspaper editor who noted, "We hear complaints about practically everything else — the weather, taxes, the high cost of living, inefficient government, the local baseball team, street paving, and the low quality of peanuts being sold, but when do you ever hear the enraged taxpayer stand up on his hind legs and complain because April has not as many days as July?"[40]

The new calendar, Bloom argued, would also harm American workers since they would have to pay 13 monthly bills instead of 12. Additionally, annual rent prices would likely quickly increase while salaries would not (at least initially).[41] As one rabbi said in his testimony before the Foreign Affairs Committee. "[T]he big people will gain. The working

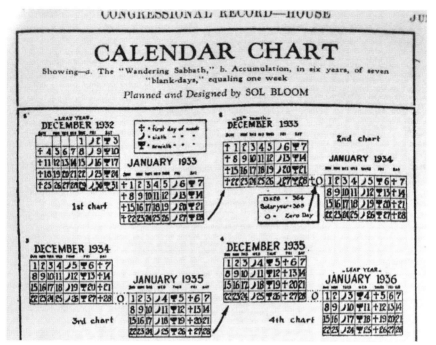

Partial view of chart inserted into the Congressional Record by Sol Bloom depicting what would happen to the Jewish Sabbath (represented here by a menorah) if the calendar reform plan favored by George Eastman were adopted in 1933.

classes…will suffer."[42]

Finally, Bloom stressed the religious problems that introducing a "blank day" into the calendar would create. It would cause a wandering Sabbath for Jews, a wandering Lord's Day for Christians, and a wandering Jumu'ah for Muslims. Never in the history has a day of the week ever been "skipped," Bloom said. "The Jewish race which has been strict in its observance of the seventh day Sabbath as long as history can recall, has never altered its observance of the Sabbath day on the seventh day of the week." Indeed, he noted to his colleagues in Congress that the Hebrew word for "week" (sans vowels) also means "seven."[43] Bloom maintained not only that Congress had no constitutional authority to change the calendar or interfere with Americans' right to freely practice their religion, but that doing so would be unwise, arguing that genuine "religious observances must not only be tolerated but respected."[44] Congress ought not to permit "the trampeling under foot for commercial purposes of that which is considered sacred by so many citizens of our country," he said.[45]

Ultimately, the various arguments Bloom and American Jewish leaders[46] raised against the Eastman plan had a cumulative effect, and at a major international calendar reform conference in Geneva in October 1931, the "United States assumed no official position" on the matter.[47] Subsequently, the plan suffered a fatal blow at the conference when the 42 represented countries voted that "[t]he present is not a favorable time, taking into account the state of opinion, for proceeding with a modification of the Gregorian Calendar."[48] Efforts to reform the calendar continued after 1931, but reformers never came as close to their goal and never enjoyed as much prestige as they did in the 1920s and early '30s.[49]

As with his response to Ford, Bloom clearly had no problem placing himself in the public limelight on behalf of a cause that was likely seen by many as at least partially Jewish in nature. It's true that Bloom and other American Jewish opponents of the Eastman plan constantly stressed that it would adversely affect every American: Jewish and otherwise. But no Christian group other than Seventh Day Adventists and Seventh Day Baptists testified against the plan in Congress.[50] Bloom and others claimed that most Christians were simply unaware of its implications. "[W]hen all of the details of this calendar reform are understood by leaders in every denomination, there will be a hue and outcry from sources unexpected," Bloom said.[51] Nonetheless, the fact is that the religious opposition to the Eastman plan was largely Jewish. Of the eight witnesses testifying against the plan before the Foreign Affairs Committee on religious grounds, *five* were rabbis. Only three were Christian leaders (representing Seventh Day Adventists and Seventh Day Baptists). In other words, 63 percent of the religious opposition (and there was hardly opposition of any another kind) to the Eastman plan was Jewish even though Jews only constituted three percent of the U.S. population at this time.

The fight against the Eastman plan thus may not have been strictly Jewish in nature, but Jews spearheaded it and Bloom became their congressional mouthpiece. Had Bloom been uncomfortable with his Jewishness, he would have taken a much smaller role (if any) in opposing the Eastman plan. He certainly wouldn't have opposed it as aggressively as he did or given mini Hebrew lessons to his colleagues on the connection between the Hebrew words for "week" and "seven." But Bloom – the evidence suggests – wasn't uncomfortable. He was a proud and confident Jew who had the gumption to publicly challenge Henry Ford for making anti-Semitic charges and later to vigorously oppose the Eastman plan.

Bloom's pro-Jewish advocacy, however, receded into the background once the Nazis threat surfaced in the late 1930s and he became chairman of the Foreign Affairs Committee. Starting in mid-1939, Bloom had a single overriding priority: helping Roosevelt ensure that the West prevail over Nazi Germany. And this priority shaped how he responded to calls for the U.S. government to save European Jews from the Nazis.

Part II – Bound by Duty

~ CHAPTER 4 ~

SHOULD WE LET THE
NAZIS CONQUER EUROPE?

I t was my privilege to have the confidence of [President Roosevelt] and to be consulted frequently by him. ...I believe I am justified in saying that I comprehended his impelling purpose during the years that preceded Pearl Harbor.

That purpose was to prepare the American people for war.

...The technique of preparation resembled somewhat the "technique" of an individual in increasing his tolerance for strong drink. Just as an inexperienced drinker literally cannot stomach a substantial dose, so the American people could not have stomached strong [interventionist] legislation before they had learned to accustom their system to it.

— *Sol Bloom*[1]

Until 1939, Bloom was generally free to act as he pleased. His interests and passions – whether Jewish or not – didn't clash with his obligations as a U.S. congressman. That was no longer the case once he assumed the chairmanship of the Foreign Affairs Committee in the House of Representatives in mid-July 1939, just six weeks before Hitler invaded Poland.[2] A strong sense of duty now rested on his shoulders which affected how he responded to calls to help his religious brethren both during and after the Holocaust. He was now the congressman most responsible for the national security of the United States in the House of Representatives, and he took this responsibility very seriously.

When World War II broke out on September 1, 1939, opposition to joining the war was extremely high in America. Approximately 95 percent of U.S. citizens told pollsters in 1940 that they opposed declaring war on Germany or sending American troops to Europe.[3] The prevailing viewpoint was that the "United States needed to concentrate on its own problems and keep the various European nations at arm's length."[4] Anything "that hinted of international involvement was politically toxic."[5] Many Americans didn't even regard Hitler as a threat, believing that the Atlantic Ocean amply protected them. Thirty years after the war, prominent isolationist Rep. Hamilton Fish (R-N.Y.) recalled a sentiment held by many Americans at the time, writing, "If the armed might of the German army could not cross the 20-mile English Channel, crossing 3,000 miles of Atlantic Ocean to the United States would be utterly impossible."[6]

Roosevelt saw the geopolitical situation differently.[7] He warned that if Hitler conquered Europe, the U.S. wouldn't be able to "survive as a happy and fertile oasis of liberty surrounded by a cruel desert of dictatorship."[8] Due to modern technological advances, the vast Atlantic Ocean no longer guaranteed America's safety, Roosevelt argued.[9] Thus, according to Secretary Treasury Henry Morgenthau, Roosevelt regarded "the Maginot line [in France as the U.S.'s] first line of defense."[10] This assessment, in turn, led Roosevelt to support arming Germany's enemies despite the isolationist mood in the country. Hence, shortly after World War II broke out, he suggested to Congress that it permit all nations to buy weapons from the U.S. on a "cash and carry" basis – i.e., that they pay in cash and carry the weapons home themselves. (Practically speaking, this proposal would only help England and its allies since the British navy controlled the seas.) "I am almost literally walking on eggs," Roosevelt wrote to a foreign official shortly after proposing the idea, alluding to the opposition he faced.[11] But he succeeded in getting it through Congress, and Cash-and-Carry became law as part of the Neutrality Act of 1939.

Almost a year later, in September 1940, Congress approved the first peacetime draft in U.S. history; six months after that, in March 1941, Congress approved "Lend-Lease" legislation, which permitted Roosevelt to lend or lease to England any war materials it needed (since England had run out of cash to pay for these items by that time); five months after that, in August 1941, Congress voted to extend the period a draftee had to serve an additional 18 months (without this vote, all the men who had been drafted in 1940 would have returned home); and three months after that, the House of Representatives narrowly voted to permit the arming of American merchant ships. Each one of these bills only passed after a bitter political battle[12] with Bloom at the center of it. Historian Arthur Schlesinger Jr. recalled the isolationist-interventionist political debate of this time period as "the most savage" of his lifetime – even worse than the debates over McCarthyism or Vietnam, he said. "[N]one so tore apart families and friendships as this fight," he told an interviewer.[13] Even "lifelong friendships broke under the strain," remembered Bloom's daughter.[14]

Like Roosevelt, Bloom had to navigate hostile waters during these years. In fact, his position may have even been more difficult than that of the president as opposition to American involvement in the war was arguably greater in Congress than among the general population.[15] Furthermore, Bloom had to contend with a Congress that no longer rubber-stamped Roosevelt's every proposal as it had in the mid-1930s. In fact, 1938 "was the lowest point of Franklin Roosevelt's presidency." The country was suffering from an economic recession, "Roosevelt's exceedingly bitter campaign to purge his

Sol Bloom standing to the right of Queen Elizabeth and King George VI on their visit to Washington, DC, in June 1939.

congressional opponents [had] resulted in disaster," and Congress had voted down his Court-packing scheme the previous year, thus breaking his aura of invincibility.[16]

In addition to isolationism and the anti-Roosevelt backlash, Bloom also had to grapple with a rise in anti-Semitism in the United States. Anti-Semitism was never stronger in the U.S. than during the mid-1930s to mid-1940s. Much of this anti-Semitism was rooted in social, economic, ideological, racial, or religious factors.[17] From 1938-1941, however, anti-Semitism also stemmed from a very specific political claim – that Jews were trying to push the United States into war.[18] This claim was advanced by a number of isolationists. Aviation hero Charles Lindbergh, for example, infamously leveled this accusation in a speech in Des Moines, Iowa, on September 11, 1941 when he included Jews among the "three most important groups who have been pressing this country toward war" (the other two were the British and the Roosevelt administration). He also spoke of American Jews' alleged "large ownership and influence in our motion pictures, our press, our radio, and our government."[19]

Other isolationist leaders also "blamed Jewish influences for pushing America toward war."[20] As early as 1933, Rep. Louis T. MacFadden (R-Penn.) warned that Jewish bankers sought to push the U.S. into hostilities with Germany "so that they may…reap rich profits of everything an army needs."[21] Representatives John C. Schafer (R-Wisc.), Jacob Thorkelson (R-Mont.), John E. Rankin (D-Miss.), and William P. Lambertson (R-Kan.) also accused Jews of driving the U.S. to war.[22] Senators Burton K. Wheeler (D-Mon.) and Gerald Nye (R-N.D.) were particularly concerned about the influence of Hollywood – most of whose major executives were Jewish[23] – on the public's attitude to war. Nye said the movies "have become the most gigantic engines of propaganda in existence to rouse the war fever in America and plunge this nation to her destruction."[24] The two, with the help of several colleagues, even established a congressional sub-committee to investigate Hollywood's role in pushing for America's involvement in the war.[25]

Many of these isolationist leaders were arguably not anti-Semitic. Lindbergh's wife – who was mortified by her husband's Des Moines speech – wrote to a friend at the time that she wouldn't stay with her husband if he were the anti-Semite the media portrayed him to be, adding that she never heard him "tell a Jewish joke" or "say anything derogatory about a Jew as such."[26] One of Lindbergh's daughters wrote years later – after listening in horror to a recording of her father's speech – that her father taught her that anti-Semitic sentiments were "repellent and unspeakable" and "never to say, never even to *think*, such things."[27] Isolationist politicians weren't necessarily anti-Semitic either. According to historian Edward Shapiro, "Most of the members of Congress who made anti-Semitic statements were not intrinsically anti-Semitic. Rather, they were motivated by a genuine fear that Jews were pushing the United States into war with Germany."[28] And the fact is that "a far larger percentage of Jews than non-Jews supported an interventionist foreign policy for Europe" in the 1930s, judging from polls and statements made by Jewish leaders at the time.[29]

Some isolationist leaders even openly stated that they didn't blame American Jews for wanting the U.S. to enter the war. Lindbergh, for example, said, "I am not attacking either the Jewish or the British people. Both races, I admire. But I am saying that the leaders of both the British and the Jewish races, for reasons which are as understandable from their viewpoint as they are inadvisable from ours, for reasons which are not American, wish to involve us in the war."[30] Harvard historian William Langer, in expressing his views on Jewish newspaper publishers and editors in 1939, said, "I suppose if I were a Jew, I would feel about Nazi Germany as most Jews feel, and it would be most inevitable that the coloring of the news takes on that tinge."[31]

Ultimately, however, whether Lindbergh and various politicians were personally anti-Semitic is irrelevant. What's relevant is that they created an environment in America in which many Jews feared publicly supporting greater American involvement in the war lest they be accused of trying to send gentile American boys to die in battle to save their Jewish brethren in Europe.[32] New York Times publisher Arthur Sulzberger, a Jew, said in September 1941 that he expressly did not promote the interventionist case more strenuously for this reason.[33] Writing to his parents in July 1941, philosopher Isaiah Berlin – then working for the British Diplomatic Service – observed that American Jews are "above all things, terrified of being thought warmongers and to be acting in their own, rather than general, American interests."[34]

Even the Roosevelt administration feared accusations that it was acting in "Jewish" interests by advancing legislation to help England. Thus, although Bloom – as chairman of the Foreign Affairs Committee – should have been the one to introduce Lend-Lease legislation in the House of Representatives, Roosevelt wanted someone else to do it "to get away from [it being called] the Bloom bill." In an interview in 1977, Rep. John McCormack explained: "[W]henever any legislation came out of his committee, [many congressman would call it] the *Bloom* bill. And out to the country would go the Jew bill, don't you see?" Thus, McCormack ultimately introduced the bill instead of Bloom.[35]

Bloom felt the same pressure experienced by other American Jews during this time of isolationist fervor, but as a prominent Jew in public office, he arguably felt it much more keenly. A group of women protested outside his Manhattan residence on Riverside Drive on June 18, 1939 because he supported Cash-and-Carry legislation.[36] In an effort to discredit this legislation as "Jewish" in nature, a congressional colleague later that year called it the "Bloom-Baruch bill."[37] During Congress's consideration of Lend-Lease, 250 women heckled senators in the Capitol building, asking them, "Why do you let Sol Bloom and his henchmen send our boys to war?"[38] The group's headquarters were reportedly in D.C.'s Plaza Hotel, which was "a distribution point for much anti-Semitic literature," often dwelling "on the theme of "international Jewry's responsibility for the war."[39] Nine days later, on February 22, women of the New York Council of the American Peace Mobilization picketed outside Bloom's Manhattan residence,[40] and a day after that, a group of women from a group called Mothers Crusade to Kill Bill 1776 (i.e., the Lend-Lease bill) tried to hang an effigy of journalist Dorothy Thompson on the gate of the White House's east entrance with a placard stating, "Eleanor R and Dottie T, too, / With the greedy Sol Bloom-Hillman crew, / Are shouting to spend for war again / A million boys' lives in blood and pain."[41]

The protests continued after Lend-Lease passed. On May 10, 1941, 150 women from the American Peace Mobilization marched near Bloom's Manhattan office.[42] At one point during the neutrality debates, a group of veiled women picketed outside Bloom's home for several days. On the first night of the picket, anonymous protesters called Bloom's phone every five minutes with messages like "The Mothers of America warn you that you are first on Hitler's list!" The calls continued the following day.[43] In his autobiography, Bloom writes:

> This was the…most agonizing period of my life. I was the
> special target of all the emotional outbursts. I was assailed
> by enemies, both in and out of Congress, as the "Jewish
> warmonger." I was the ogre who wanted to prepare young
> men to die in battle. My house was picketed for days, at
> the very time when [my daughter] and I were mourning my
> dear wife, her beloved mother…. Threatening telephone
> calls came by the hundreds, day and night.[44]

Despite the pressure and vitriolic atmosphere, however, Bloom
helped advance the Roosevelt administration's pro-British legislation
through Congress. After failing – by two votes – to pass Cash-and-Carry
legislation in the summer of 1939, in what Bloom called a "bitter defeat,"[45]
Congress approved the measure in November, shortly after World War II
broke out. Bloom's work in getting the bill through the House of
Representatives was "masterly," in the eyes of Felix Morley, editor at The
Washington Post, who sent a letter to Bloom congratulating him following
its passage. "To have secured a turnover from over forty adverse votes to

Veiled women picketing outside Bloom's home in 1941.

over sixty favorable votes on the embargo repeal issue," he wrote, "is indeed an outstanding triumph, the more so because of the strength and intensity of the propaganda to which you and your colleagues were subjected."[46] Bloom also received special congratulatory messages for his efforts from Secretary of State Cordell Hull ("You never failed to exert yourself to the utmost") and Speaker of the House William Bankhead.[47]

Bloom also worked "day and night"[48] to push Lend-Lease through Congress in what he later regarded as "the greatest battle of [his] whole career." He acknowledges that he essentially acted as "the party wheel horse" but writes that he performed the job gladly: "I would not have yielded that work for any reward the republic could have given me."[49] Later that year, Bloom also worked to arm American merchant ships and to extend the service of Americans who had been drafted a year earlier following Congress's authorization of the first peace-time draft in U.S. history. Both these pieces of legislation came after Bloom lost his wife of 44 years on June 24, 1941. The two had "always [been] sweethearts,"[50] in Bloom's words, and contending with strenuous isolationist opposition and anti-Semitic sentiment in the months following her passing couldn't have been easy for him. "[T]he cheer went out [of my home] when my dear wife died," he wrote several years later.[51] But he forged ahead nonetheless.

Congress passed the draft-extension bill less than two months after his wife died. Had it

Sol Bloom conferring with State Department officials on proposed amendments to the country's neutrality laws. (L-R) Seated: W. Walton Moore, State Department counselor; Rep. Sol Bloom; and Green H. Hackworth, State Department legal advisor. Standing: Carlton Savage, assistant to Moore; and Rep. Charles A. Eaton.

failed, "the Army stood to lose about two-thirds of its strength and three-fourths of the officer corps."[52] But it passed – by one vote, 203-202 – and, if Bloom is to be believed, he physically barred the path of a congressman who after voting for the extension wished to alter his vote (which is permitted while voting is still ongoing). "[Y]ou'll have to knock me through the doorway if you want to return to the [House] floor," Bloom allegedly said to him. A few months later, Bloom was again called on "to be the House wheel horse" to "line up the necessary votes to revoke, in effect, the prohibition against armed merchant vessels in the 1939 neutrality law."[53] Bloom succeeded – barely – and the measure passed 212-194.

The vigorousness with which Bloom worked to see all these pieces of legislation through Congress despite strenuous isolationist animosity and anti-Semitic hostility marked the beginning of a new phase for Bloom – one bound by duty to his country – which coincided with his rise to the chairmanship of the House of Representatives' Foreign Affairs Committee. He now saw it as his job to help Roosevelt protect the United States from possibly the greatest threat the world has ever faced: Adolf Hitler. This mission, however, affected how much he was willing to do for Europe's endangered Jews.

One last point before turning to Bloom's activities in relation to these Jews: The legislation that Bloom helped push through Congress aided England in staving off a Nazi invasion[54] and buttressed the United States' military capability in advance of its entry in World War II.[55] Had the Nazis successfully invaded England, 300,000 British Jews likely would have died in the Holocaust. Had the Nazis "only" succeeded in pressuring England to sue for peace – which was apparently Hitler's preference[56] – Palestine's 400,000 Jews likely would have been slaughtered (for it was British forces, aided by American supplies, that stopped German troops from conquering Palestine in 1942)[57] and the Soviet Union and all its Jews may very well have come under Nazi control too, considering that Hitler would have been free to concentrate all his forces on the eastern front.[58] In short, without England in the fight, the total Holocaust death toll may have been double, since, as Roosevelt defender Robert Rosen reminds us, Hitler's "goal in Europe was to murder eleven million Jews, not six million."[59] A primary reason England didn't surrender to Hitler was American support in 1939-1941, and Sol Bloom was at the center of the effort to give England this support.   Thus, Bloom arguably helped save the lives of hundreds of thousands – if not millions – of Jews in England, Palestine, and elsewhere who would have been targeted had London fallen.

~ CHAPTER 5 ~

SORRY, THE DOORS ARE CLOSED

In advancing war legislation backed by Roosevelt, Bloom may have indirectly benefited millions of Jews overseas, but numerous others died, unable to escape to America due to the Roosevelt administration's restrictive immigration policy, which went unchallenged by Bloom. In other words, in regards to immigration policy, the Roosevelt-Bloom partnership arguably harmed Jews rather than helped them as Bloom chose to remain silent rather than advocate for his co-religionists.

During the 12 years of the Nazis' reign, Bloom almost never tried to soften U.S. immigration law. Indeed, he even helped make it more *restrictive* in 1941 by introducing the Bloom-Van Nuys bill.[1] Bloom did propose legislation in May 1933 – shortly after Hitler assumed total power in Germany – to permit German visitors in the U.S. to remain in the country for an additional two years and also supported a bill in 1940 permitting American ships to bring refugee children from Great Britain to the United States.[2] Neither of these bills, however, made any headway in Congress,[3] and Bloom doesn't appear to have introduced any other piece of legislation from 1933-1945 that would have made it easier for Jews wishing to leave Europe for the U.S. to do so.

Bloom, however, was hardly alone in not fighting to liberalize U.S. immigration law. Indeed, even leading American Jewish organizations refrained from publicly taking on the cause.[4] When Rep. Samuel Dickstein, for example, introduced a bill in March 1933 to make it easier for German Jews to immigrate to the United States, the American Jewish Committee, the American Jewish Congress, and B'nai B'rith all refused to back it.[5] America was suffering through the Great Depression, and they seconded the argument of restrictionists who maintained that the economic security of American workers should come before the interests of persecuted German Jews. "I do not favor opening the doors to people who are laborers to come here and be in competition with our citizens here," said Max J. Kohler in testimony before Congress on behalf of B'nai B'rith and the American Jewish Committee.[6] Similarly, in 1937, Celia Davidson, representing the American Jewish Committee and the National Council of Jewish Women, testified before Congress, "I think there are very few of us who want to open the doors to new immigrants at this time."[7]

Several Jewish leaders feared that pushing for looser immigration laws during such harsh economic times – the unemployment rate was 25 percent in 1933 and still an alarming 19 percent as late as 1938[8] – would exacerbate anti-Semitism in the U.S.,[9] which was already at an all-time high.[10] Thus, in the late 1930s, for example, Rabbi Stephen Wise, perhaps the most powerful rabbi in America, wrote to a senator who wished to introduce a bill permitting people fleeing Nazi persecution to seek asylum in the United States, "I have every reason to believe, unfortunately, that any effort that is made at this time to waive the immigration laws will result in a serious accentuation of what we know to be a rising wave of anti-Semitic feeling in this country."[11]

Even if Wise was wrong, fighting for a more generous immigration policy would arguably have been an exercise in futility since congressional opposition to it was fierce. In March 1938, Vice President John Nance Garner told Roosevelt that if Congress could vote secretly, it would eliminate *all* immigration to the U.S.[12] According to historian Henry Feingold, "opening the gates wider for the Jewish refugees [during this time period] was politically virtually impossible."[13] Even after Kristallnacht in November 1938, a poll found that 83 percent of Americans opposed amending American law to permit more European refugees to enter the U.S.[14] Keenly sensitive to public opinion, President Roosevelt therefore refused to support a bill two months after Kristallnacht that called for admitting 20,000 refugee children from Germany outside the immigration quotas.[15] Historians surmise that Roosevelt didn't wish to lose political capital that he desperately needed to nudge Congress and the country toward fighting the Nazis (directly, or indirectly through aid to England) – a matter on which he believed many more than 20,000 lives were at stake.[16]

Cognizant of the same public opinion that influenced Roosevelt's actions, American Jewish organizations also failed to lobby for the bill, and it died in committee.[17]

It of course should be borne in mind that hardly anyone in the 1930s thought Hitler would conquer Europe and aim to murder every last Jew.[18] In fact, as historian David Wyman notes, "[u]ntil 1941 the main purpose of Nazi persecution of Jews was to force them to leave Germany, not to exterminate them."[19] Life was unpleasant in Germany, not impossible, and many German Jews hoped that matters would soon blow over and everything would return to normal. Thus, when America refused to open its doors wide to Jewish refugees in the 1930s, it thought it was denying them a *better* life – not life itself. The same is true of the Roosevelt administration's notorious refusal to allow the *S.S. St. Louis* to dock on its shores in early June 1939. The administration had no idea it was condemning some of the ship's passengers to death in making this decision.[20] Indeed, in returning to Europe, the *St. Louis* passengers themselves thought they had been saved, heading as they were to what seemed to be the safety of England, France, Belgium, and Holland (and 73 percent of them did in fact ultimately escape Hitler's clutches). "Our gratitude is as immense as the ocean on which we are now floating," they wrote to a Jewish official on their return journey.[21]

Once war broke out, it of course became increasingly[22] clear that permitting Jews to come to the U.S. could be a matter of life and death, but at that point Americans feared, not only the prospect that European Jews would take America jobs, but also the possibility that German spies would slip into the U.S. with the refugees and undermine the country from within.[23] A "fear about spies and saboteurs" – which was reinforced by the media and Hollywood[24] – was "sweeping the country"[25] at this time. Only one spy during the entire war was discovered to have posed as a Jewish refugee,[26] but hindsight is always 20/20; at the time, people were frightened, and they had good reason to be. As one historian has written, "To many Americans, the speed with which Denmark, Norway, France, Belgium, and the Netherlands were conquered in early 1940 seemed inexplicable without the involvement of a traitorous fifth column boring from within the targeted countries."[27] President Roosevelt himself echoed this fear, noting during a June 5, 1940, press conference that "it is rather a horrible story but in some of the...countries that refugees out of Germany have gone to, especially Jewish refugees, they found a number of definitely proven spies."[28]

Bloom – who continued to be largely silent on liberalizing immigration law once war broke out – clearly shared this fear of German infiltration, writing to a friend in mid-1940 about helping a certain woman: "I will be glad to help in every way possible, but you will agree with me that in these days, with the fifth, sixth and seventh columns working overtime, your Congressman must and will be damn careful that he doesn't recommend in any way, any person unless he knows that they are strictly all right in every way."[29] A week earlier, he wrote to someone else, "[A]t the present time and under the present war conditions, you can readily understand that it will be impossible for us to give letters of recommendation or introduction to people whom we do not know. I have no doubt that everything is alright but still you will agree with me that we have to be very careful."[30] And on November 25, 1941, Bloom wrote to his secretary about a 15-year-old boy who begged him to save his parents and grandmother in Germany: "if you are satisfied after talking to this boy that he is alright *and there is no Nazi plot in it, which I am always afraid of*, if there is anything we can do to help, let us do it" (emphasis added).[31] This fear helps explain why in 1941 Bloom was "prevailed upon"[32] by the Roosevelt administration to introduce legislation – the Bloom-Van Nuys bill – that allowed American consulates to deny refugees a visa if they had a close relative in Nazi Europe. The administration feared that the Nazis would force a refugee to spy on their behalf by holding his or her relative hostage.[33]

It perhaps should come as no surprise, then, that during World War II "*hundreds* of bills were introduced in Congress to *decrease* immigration" (emphasis added).[34] Equally unsurprising is the restraint Jewish organizations showed in these years vis-à-vis several bills that would have eased immigration restrictions.[35] They didn't advocate for them, at least in part, because they simply didn't feel comfortable challenging anti-immigration sentiment that was "couched in terms of national security." They feared doing so would "impl[y] a lack of Jewish patriotism" or "a greater concern for [European] Jews than for the welfare of America"[36] which they evidently believed would be both morally wrong and dangerous considering the intensity of anti-Semitism in America at this time, which sociologist David Riesman characterized as "slightly below the boiling point."[37] Just maintaining the status quo was difficult enough for pro-immigrant advocates.

Could Bloom have tried introducing legislation to relax U.S. immigration policy as did his colleagues Samuel Dickstein and Emanuel Celler?[38] Yes. But perhaps he didn't think it wise to do so when such legislation had no possibility of passing and would likely fuel anti-Semitism. Furthermore, after he became the chairman of the Foreign Affairs Committee, he likely regarded helping the Roosevelt administration pass

July 20, 1940

Mr. Louis Bernstein,
Shapiro, Bernstein & Co., Inc.,
1270 Sixth Avenue,
New York, N. Y.

My dear Louis:

Acknowledging and answering your of the 18th with reference to Mrs. Yenta Berman, permit me to state that she was not introduced to me by a United States Senator; she was introduced to me by Hardie Meakin, who is the manager of Keith's Theater here in Washington, and a very lovely fellow.

But, he did not know anything about Mrs. Berman. Someone introduced her to him. Of course, Louis, I will be glad to help in every way possible, but you will agree with me that in these days, with the fifth, sixth and seventh columns working overtime, your Congressman must and will be damn careful that he doesn't recommend in any way, any person unless he knows that they are strictly all right in every way.

Regards and best wishes.

Sincerely yours,

Bloom expressing concern about the Nazis using
immigrants to infiltrate and undermine the United States.

legislation like Cash-and-Carry and Lend-Lease as his first duty.

Politics is in many ways a team sport, and Bloom was firmly on Roosevelt's team.[39] Upon becoming committee chairman, Bloom wrote to Roosevelt, "I…want to assure you that it will always be uppermost in my mind and thoughts to cooperate to the fullest possible extent in following the views of your administration on foreign affairs."[40] In a 1939 correspondence, he wrote, "I support the President 100%."[41] Bloom, like so many other Jews in America at this time, held Roosevelt in great esteem.[42] Indeed, so strong was the "Jewish 'love affair' with Roosevelt"[43] that Jews were said to believe in three "*velts*" (Yiddish for "worlds"): this *velt*, the next *velt*, and Roose*velt*.[44] Their admiration for him was due to several factors. First, they saw him, as did many other Americans, as "the champion of the common man."[45] Second, they saw him, more specifically, as a friend of the Jews amidst rising anti-Semitism. In 1932, Roosevelt actually "became the first presidential candidate in history to criticize anti-Semitism,"[46] and, after he became president, "appointed more Jews to high places [in government] than any prior executive" – people such as Ben Cohen, Henry Morgenthau, Jr., Felix Frankfurter, and Herbert Lehman. Jews actually comprised 15 percent of his appointees.[47] As far as American Jews were concerned, Roosevelt was also hated by all the right people (e.g., open anti-Semites like Father Charles Coughlin).[48]

Third, American Jews saw Roosevelt as the man calmly leading America out of the Great Depression, which threatened to destroy democracy in America – a country that had given refuge and opportunity to millions of Jews. In the early 1930s, writes historian William Leuchtenberg, "farm strikes [and other] spectacular incidents…led men to speculate [that] the country faced imminent revolution."[49] One financier in 1932 remarked that "the mention of revolution is becoming quite common." A writer that same year observed that "the word revolution is heard at every hand."[50] As William Green, president of the American Federation of Labor, warned in 1931, "Revolutions grow out of the depths of hunger."[51] This revolution never came, in part because Roosevelt was elected and gave Americans hope. As Bloom writes about the beginning of Roosevelt's administration, "There was no financial panic because one man drove it from the minds of the people. One man gave them courage. One man showed them how to go ahead. Millions believed, as I did, that this man could lead them out of

Millions of American Jews and non-Jews virtually worshipped President Franklin D. Roosevelt. On April 13, 1945, The New York Times quoted a congressman's remarkable reaction to the death of Roosevelt.

SHOCK, DISBELIEF ECHO IN CONGRESS

Said Representative Clarence Cannon, Democrat, of Missouri, chairman of the House Appropriations Committee:

"My God, how terrible! The greatest man in the world." Representative Robert R. Ramspeck of Georgia, Democratic House Whip, made almost identical comment.

depressions, and because so many conquered their despair we did come out of the depression."[52]

Fourth, American Jews saw Roosevelt as a visionary who understood the threat Nazi Germany posed to the world long before others did and prepared the country to confront it. They would have agreed with The New York Times editorial on Roosevelt's death, which boldly proclaimed:

> Men will thank God on their knees, a hundred years from now, that Franklin D. Roosevelt was in the White House, in a position to give leadership to the thought of the American people and direction to the activities of their Government, in that dark hour when a powerful and ruthless barbarism threatened to overrun the civilization of the Western World and to destroy the work of centuries of progress. And when, in that dark hour, Britain stood alone, it is to Mr. Roosevelt's everlasting credit that he was among the first to see that we could not permit her to go under without losing for ourselves every liberty and every value we hold dear.[53]

In light of all of the above, Bloom – like many other Jews at the time – gave Roosevelt "the benefit of the doubt."[54] So if Roosevelt didn't wish to lose political capital by fighting for immigration reform, Bloom likely believed it was his duty as a team player to support him. Besides, the Roosevelt administration was already trying to help Jewish refugees in various ways, so why should Bloom push it to help in the one way it preferred not to? In other words, as far as Bloom (and other Jews) could tell, the Roosevelt administration was a friend of the Jewish cause, not a foe. For example, approximately 40,000 European Jews immigrated to Latin American between 1938-1941 thanks to help from Washington. Paraguay alone apparently agreed to take in 5,000 Jewish refugees due to Roosevelt's personal intervention.[55] During this time period, Roosevelt often discussed settlement projects for endangered European Jews and even initiated a secret "M" project in 1940 to consider various settlement options for them.[56] Additionally, thanks to him, 32 countries sent representatives to a conference in July 1938 to explore possible relocation destinations for German Jews. This conference – the Evian Conference – was largely an embarrassing failure as no country outside the Dominican Republic agreed to change its immigration policy to help these Jews. Nevertheless, the fact that Roosevelt called for such a conference in the first place is significant as it indicates concern on his part.[57] After all, in pushing for this conference "he had little to gain and much to lose politically from potentially antagonizing anti-Semites and restrictionists."[58] The evidence suggests that he pushed for it anyway because he was a humanitarian who understood the dire straits German Jews faced and wished to help them.

In retrospect, we know that Roosevelt's grand resettlement projects never came to fruition, that the Evian Conference was a failure, and that six million Jews died in the Holocaust. But at the time, to people like Bloom, it seemed like Roosevelt was trying to help European Jewry. As a team player, therefore – and as someone who, starting in mid-1939, was fighting Roosevelt's opponents tooth and nail to amend U.S. neutrality laws so the president could help England stand up to Hitler – he was not going to abandon or berate Roosevelt for not challenging Congress to amend the country's immigration quotas. If Roosevelt believed the fight was either futile or not worth expending political capital, Bloom likely felt it was his duty to stand by his commander in chief.

~ CHAPTER 6 ~

SAVING LIVES BEHIND THE SCENES

Working closely with President Roosevelt kept Bloom from challenging U.S. immigration policy, but it also enabled him to rescue Jews behind the scenes. Bloom's papers in the New York Public Library reveal that from the late 1930s until the end of World War II, Bloom sent many thousands of letters to government officials on behalf of European Jews seeking to flee the Nazis. And since Bloom was a powerful, well-liked politician, these letters were almost certainly read with greater attention and eagerness to help than had Bloom been disfavored by the Roosevelt administration.

The most famous person whose life Bloom helped save was the Gerrer Rebbe (also known as the Imrei Emes) – Rabbi Avraham Mordechai Alter (1866-1948) – who led possibly the largest chassidic group in Poland.[1] Bloom first learned of the Rebbe's dire predicament in late September from Rabbi Herbert S. Goldstein, head of the West Side Institutional Synagogue, where Bloom was a member.[2] Goldstein and Bloom shared a relationship going back many years,[3] and Bloom told him on several occasions that he should always feel free to ask him for assistance. "I want to help you. So remember, don't be bashful," Bloom wrote to him in 1933, for example.[4] Bloom forwarded Goldstein's letter about the Gerrer Rebbe to Assistant Secretary of State George Messersmith, adding, "I would appreciate your advising me as to what can be done to assist Rabbi Alter."[5] Messersmith evidently couldn't help,[6] but on September 30, Bloom received a letter from A. M. Warren, chief of the State Department's Visa Division, which seems to have come in response to a separate letter Bloom had written about both the Gerrer Rebbe and Rabbi Chaim Ozer Grodzinski (a highly prominent

Lithuanian rabbi) at the behest, apparently, of the Agudas Harabonim (the Union of Orthodox Rabbis of the United States and Canada). Warren wrote to Bloom, "As you know, before the aliens may effect their entry in the United States they must be in possession of appropriate immigration visas issued by an American consular officer abroad. In view of the existing situation in Poland all functions of the American Consulate General at Warsaw have been temporarily suspended." Warren assured Bloom that if the rabbis were able to escape to a country with a functioning American Consulate, "every consideration will be accorded their application for appropriate visas for admission into the United States." He also suggested that the Agudas Harabonim "prepare a statement in affidavit form regarding the proposed affiliation of the aliens in this country" if they are to receive "nonquota visas [as] ministers of religion."[7] Bloom sent a copy of this letter to the Agudas Harabonim with the comment, "I trust the enclosed report is self explanatory and if there is anything further that I can do to assist in this matter, please do not hesitate to call on me."[8]

Bloom's papers at the New York Pubic Library contain only one letter to or from Bloom about the Gerrer Rebbe over the next six weeks. One historian claims Bloom didn't immediately appreciate the importance

The Gerrer Rebbe, Rav Avraham Mordechai Alter (center),
flanked by an entourage in Poland.

of rescuing the Rebbe and only agreed "to undertake sustained diplomatic initiatives" after Rabbi Menachem Kasher, a noted author and prominent Ger devotee, "camp[ed] out in Bloom's office on the Sabbath," which convinced Bloom "of the seriousness of the situation.[9] Perhaps this lobbying by Kasher came during these six weeks. In any event, on November 14, Bloom responded to a letter by Goldstein about the Gerrer Rebbe, informing him that he could "count on [his] very best efforts in the matter."[10] By December 28, plans to bring the Rebbe to America had apparently been scrapped and Bloom wrote to Goldstein again, informing him that he had contacted the Romanian Legation in Washington and was told that the Romanian Minister in D.C. would ask his counterpart in Budapest "to extend to Rabbi Alter [i.e., the Gerrer Rebbe] every consideration possible and that a transit visa will be given to him to go to Palestine" as soon as the minister learns the Rebbe is on his way to Budapest. Bloom adds, "I am trying to do everything I possibly can, but I don't seem to be able to get the proper information or connection to understand what the situation is with Rabbi Alter in Warsaw. I can act very fast from this end, when this information is furnished to me. Please remember that I am more than pleased to do everything I possibly can to assist in this matter."[11]

That same day, Bloom spoke to Assistant Secretary of State Messersmith and sent him a follow-up letter the next day, noting – with perhaps some hyperbole – that the Gerrer Rebbe "has the reputation of being the chief and the highest of all Rabbis throughout the world." He asks for Messersmith's help in getting the Rebbe out of Poland so he could head to Budapest to "obtain a transit visa to travel through Rumania" to Palestine. Bloom promises to pay for any government cables sent or received in relation to the Gerrer Rebbe and concludes with – again some hyperbole – "Please help me in this matter if you can, because the Jews of the entire country are interested, as you will note by the enclosed telegrams."[12]

A few days later, though, Bloom was pursuing a different avenue of escape for the Rebbe – through Italy[13] – and on January 12, 1940, Bloom sent telegrams to Goldstein and others, stating that the Italian embassy in Washington had that day received the following cable from Rome: "Request of Congressman Bloom has been benevolently examined and has been already wired to Warsaw for the documents."[14]   Bloom then received word from Messersmith that the American Embassy in Berlin would inform the Gerrer Rebbe in Warsaw (who was in hiding) that Italy had agreed to help him leave the country and was requesting, as Bloom wrote to Kasher, "that a report concerning the Rabbi's plans for leaving Poland be expedited and furnished by cable."[15]

The next significant communication from Bloom on this matter comes a month later. The Italian representative in Warsaw was apparently ready to grant the Gerrer Rebbe and his immediate family transit visas, but someone claiming to be the Rebbe's spokesman insisted that an entourage of 30 – which was later reduced to 10 – travel with him. The Italian representative contacted Rome for further instructions, but Bloom wanted to know: "who is the Rabbi's spokesman and by what right should anyone change my request to the Italian government, which request was complied with, and ask that thirty persons be included as an entourage."[16] This interference "may disturb the entire case and defeat our whole purpose," he warned a few days later.[17] A subsequent cable from Rome confirmed to Bloom that the request for visas for an entourage of 30 "just destroyed all of the work that we had already done." Bloom assured Rabbi Kasher, however, in a letter on February 28, "I have requested the Italian government to reopen the matter and also done everything I possibly could with the authorities at the Department of State."[18]

Ultimately, the Rebbe successfully escaped Nazi-occupied Poland. On March 25, 1940 – six months after Rabbi Goldstein first contacted Bloom about the Gerrer Rebbe – the Italian Embassy's Eugenio Bonardelli wrote to Bloom, "I am very pleased to inform you that the Ministry of Foreign Affairs has authorized the Italian Authorities in Warsaw to issue transit visas to Chief Rabby [sic] Alter and to the members of his household." Among the household members – 12 in total – were the Rebbe's son-in-law Yitzchak Meir Levin, who would sign Israel's Declaration of Independence eight years later, and three sons who succeeded their father as Rebbe and led the rebuilt Ger dynasty in Israel until 1996.[19] On April 14, Rabbi Kasher sent Bloom a telegram informing him that the Rebbe had arrived safely in Trieste, Italy and thanked him for the "splendid fruition of [his] efforts."[20] When Bloom passed away in 1949, the Gerrer yeshiva in Israel placed a death notice in The New York Times, thanking him for his efforts. "It was through the personal intervention of

Congressman Bloom that the life of the founder of the Yeshiva [Sfath Emeth], the Gerer Rabbi, as well as those of his family were saved during the Hitler invasion," it stated.[21]

This saga is important, not only because of the Gerrer's Rebbe prominence, but because it illustrates Bloom's ability to use his government contacts to save people. To rescue the Rebbe, Bloom corresponded with

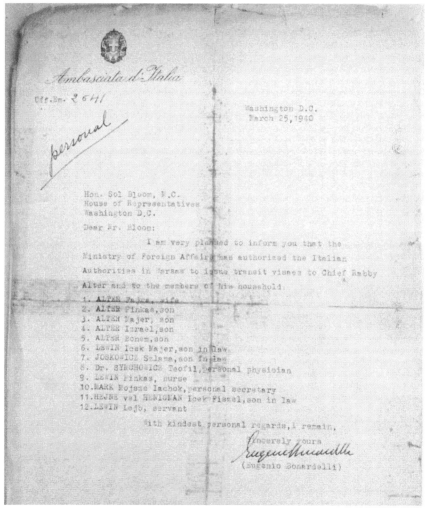

Letter to Sol Bloom from Eugenio Bonardelli of the Italian Embassy in Washington informing him that Italy will be giving the Gerrer Rebbe and his family transit visas to leave Warsaw, Poland, where he was hiding from the Nazis. The Rebbe and his family successfully escaped to Palestine where they rebuilt the Ger movement.

Assistant Secretary of State Messersmith; Avra M. Warren, chief of the State Department's Visa Division; the Romanian Legation in Washington; and the Italian Embassy in Washington. None of these parties had to help him. And government officials would, in all likelihood, have been less inclined to do so had Bloom denounced U.S. immigration policy and antagonized people like President Roosevelt and Secretary of State Cordell Hull. But Bloom was in the good graces of the administration.[22]

Indeed, Bloom was generally in *everyone's* good graces. He had "genial personality and friendly spirit," in the words of his secretary,[23] and two months before he died in 1949, he wrote, "[F]riends to me in life mean everything," adding, "I never lost a friend."[24] Bloom also loved hosting and attending diplomatic parties. According to an article in The New York Times in 1935 on the political impact of these parties, Bloom was "a close friend of many diplomats," was "invited everywhere," and "entertain[ed] frequently and elegantly."[25] In just one two-week period in 1931, for

Sol Bloom enjoying a light moment with
Rep. Edith Rogers and U.S. Ambassador Claude Bowers.

example, Bloom held four dinners at which he hosted, respectively, the German ambassador, the Japanese ambassador, the Minister of the Irish Free State, and Assistant Secretary of State Wilbur Carr; the Brazilian ambassador; the Polish ambassador, the Minister of the Netherlands, and the chief of the Eastern European Division of the State Department; and then again the Polish ambassador the following night.[26] Washington Post columnist Hope Ridings Miller noted that Bloom and his daughter (following his wife's death) were "popular centers of attention at every diplomatic reception."[27] Bloom's contemporaries sometimes poked fun at him for socializing *too* much,[28] but Bloom's social habits helped cement friendships that almost certainly enabled him to help people he otherwise could not have helped. In 1943, Lord Halifax, ambassador to the U.S. from Great Britain, wrote to Bloom, "I did so much enjoy our luncheon with you last week, and I think these opportunities for discussion have a value which it is not possible to estimate."[29] The topic of their conversation is unknown, but Lord Halifax's comment on the intangible benefit of personal conversations and relationships is well put.

In addition to saving the Gerrer Rebbe, Bloom also played a small role in saving the life of Rabbi Joseph Isaac Schneersohn, the sixth rebbe of Lubavitch,[30] and may have played a role in saving the life of Rav Aharon Kotler, the founder of Beth Medrash Govoha in Lakewood, NJ.[31] Bloom also tried, unsuccessfully, to save the lives of such prominent rabbinic leaders as Rabbi Chaim Ozer Grodzinski (mentioned earlier); Rabbi Avraham Dov Ber Kahana Shapiro, the chief rabbi of Kovno, Lithuania;[32] and Rabbi Elchonon Wasserman.[33] After the war, Agudath Israel Youth Council of America thanked Bloom for helping it "obtain four hundred emergency visas for rabbis and scholars from war-torn Europe to enter the United States."[34] Holocaust historian Esther Farbstein writes that an old tradition calls on Jews to "[p]reserve the spiritual leadership so that the nation can go on, especially when danger of annihilation lurks."[35] Rabbis – as teachers and guides – are, in many respects, the heart of the Jewish nation, which is perhaps why the Nazis went out of their way to harass and torture them. As Farbstein writes, "abusing the rabbis was a way of breaking the spirit of the entire nation."[36] Saving them thus arguably had the opposite effect.

In trying to help these rabbinic leaders, Bloom often worked at the behest of the rabbis associated with the Vaad Hahatzala Emergency Committee, which put a premium on saving the lives of Torah scholars and yeshiva students.[37] Thanks in large part to the humanitarian impulse of a Japanese official, Chiune Sugihara, many of these yeshiva students found refuge in Japan and later Shanghai, China. The Vaad Hahatzala, though, was apparently convinced their lives were in danger even there (perhaps due to a severe food shortage[38]) and worked throughout the war to bring them to the United States.[39] Rabbi Goldstein remembers "frequently" visiting Bloom in Washington along with Rabbi Avraham Kalmanowitz of the Vaad Hahatzala. "Our visits," he writes, "generally consisted of helping the students of the 'Mir' Yeshiva" in Shanghai who had fled Lithuania.[40]

In helping the Vaad Hahatzala, Bloom once again took advantage of his government connections. In late 1943, for example, it seemed possible for some rabbis and students to leave Shanghai with British help, so Bloom wrote to Lord Halifax and secured a meeting with him for Rabbis Goldstein and Kalmanowitz along with Jacob Rosenheim and Mike Tress of Agudath Israel.[41] Bloom also helped set up meetings for rabbis from the Vaad Hahatzala or Agudas Harabonim with Under Secretary of State Sumner Welles,[42] Assistant Secretary of State Berle,[43] the Minister of Switzerland,[44] War Refugee Board Director John Pehle,[45] and possibly Secretary of State Cordell Hull.[46] In May 1943, Bloom even got an American official to personally approach Soviet Premier Joseph Stalin and his foreign minister, Vyacheslav Molotov, about helping a group of Jews – presumably the above-mentioned rabbis and yeshiva students.[47]

Bloom may have felt particularly comfortable helping the rabbis of Vaad Hahatzala since he shared a similar religious background with them. He grew up in an Orthodox Jewish family and as a boy prayed at Beth Israel, the most Orthodox synagogue in San Francisco.[48] As an adult, Bloom was not ritually observant,[49] but he identified as an Orthodox Jew and belonged to an Orthodox synagogue.[50] In 1944, he told a reporter, "I am an Orthodox Jew; I have never prayed without a hat; I follow Judaism in the footsteps of my father and mother, and they were Orthodox Jews."[51] An even more fundamental reason that Bloom helped the Vaad Hahatzala, however, was that he could do so within the confines of his loyalties and duties as chairman of the House Foreign Affairs Committee working in concert with Roosevelt to prosecute a world war.

In any event, requests from the Vaad Hahatzala for Bloom often went through Rabbi Goldstein – probably because of the longstanding relationship between the two of them. Several hundred documents from, or to, Goldstein appear in Sol Bloom's Papers at the New York Pubic

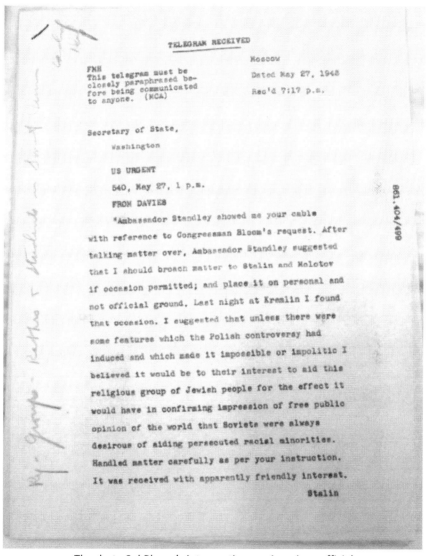

Thanks to Sol Bloom's intervention, an American official (presumably former ambassador to the USSR, Joseph E. Davies) personally asked Joseph Stalin to facilitate the emigration of a group of (several hundred?) rabbis and yeshiva students fleeing the Nazis.

Library.   In mid-1939, Goldstein wrote to Bloom's secretary Beth
Flegelman. "I am happy that I have a Congressman Bloom whom I know
so that I can keep him busy with my immigration matters"[52] – or "many
'mitzvohs' [i.e., good deeds]," as he put it in another letter.[53] Goldstein
recommended at least several dozen immigration cases to Bloom during the
war and the years leading up to it.

For example, on October 31, 1940, Goldstein wrote to Bloom's office
about a Rabbi Stam of the Upper West Side who wished to bring his
daughter's family to America from the USSR. His daughter's husband,
Rabbi Aaron Shapiro, was hired to teach at the Mir Yeshiva in Brooklyn,
but his visa expired and Goldstein wanted to know if it could somehow be
renewed.[54] A year later, on August 8, 1941, Goldstein asked Bloom to
intercede on behalf of the family of Rabbi Max Fisch in Hyeregyhara,
Hungary. The family had visas to come to America, but they had expired.
Rabbi Fisch applied for new visas and asked Bloom to use his influence
with the State Department to expedite consideration of the applications as

Sol Bloom – seated back right, wearing a yarmulke –
at a traditional Jewish meal, possibly a Pesach Seder.

well as ask the Department to cable the American Consulate in Budapest, Hungary once it approves them.[55]

In an unpublished autobiography, Goldstein recalls an exchange he had with Bloom about some of the cases he brought to his attention:

> Congressman Bloom said to me one day, "Rabbi, tell me, do you like that trip from New York to Washington that you take so often to ask favors?" I knew what he meant since I had gone there always to seek assistance for many of our Jewish people. Congressman Bloom never refused to grant me these favors, which I always appreciated. I then replied, "No, Congressman, if you think I am a pest, I won't come anymore." His response was, "Oh, no, Rabbi, excuse me. I know when lawyers come to get favors from me they receive a fee, but when you come for a favor you do it for a Mitzva [i.e., to do a good deed]. You can come as often as you find necessary.[56]

Rabbi Leo Jung of the Jewish Center on the Upper West Side, which was in Bloom's district, also referred cases to Bloom. For example, on December 10, 1939, Jung asked Bloom if he could use his influence to expedite consideration of the visa applications for a father and son in Germany. Their wife and mother, Mrs. Irma Fuchs, was an American citizen and she feared that "delay in the granting of the visa might jeopardize and

Letter from Rabbi Herbert S. Goldstein to Beth Flegelman, one of Bloom's secretaries. He writes, "To whom shall I turn for help next to G-d, Sol Bloom of course."

endanger the lives" of her loved ones.[57] A year later, he wrote to Bloom about a Rabbi Felix Singerman in Berlin who wished to immigrate to the U.S. but who had not yet been granted a visa because the salary he was promised in America was considered insufficient to support his family.[58] In mid-1941, Jung wrote to Bloom about five of his own relatives in Switzerland, whom he wished to bring to the United States.[59]

Bloom also received countless letters from ordinary constituents about relatives in Europe whom they desperately wished to bring to the safety of American shores. In some cases, Bloom would write a letter on the constituent's behalf to a government official and then, upon receiving the official's response, be forced to reply that he regretfully couldn't help. This June 30, 1941 letter to someone who had asked for Bloom's assistance in bringing his mother-in-law to America is typical:

> My Dear Lieutenant Jaffe:
>
> For your information, I am enclosing herewith a copy of a self-explanatory report which I have just received from the Department of State concerning the visa application of [your mother-in-law].
>
> Regretting that I could not have had more favorable news for you at this time....[60]

In other cases, Bloom (and his office staff[61]) sent multiple letters, seeking help for a constituent. For example, in late 1940, Mrs. Sofie Laufer of West 100th St. evidently wrote to Bloom asking for help in getting her mother – Mrs. Mina Mirl Greif – out of Europe. On December 14, 1940, Harry E. Carlson of the American Consul in "Vienna, Germany" wrote to Bloom (in response to a letter he wrote on her behalf) informing him that Greif's application for a visa under the quota for Romania (where she was born) would "not be reached for consideration before the lapse of a protracted period." Bloom passed along this response to Laufer, but Laufer wouldn't give up. On April 7, she wrote a letter to Bloom begging him to save her mother, noting that the Nazis had already killed her father in a concentration camp. "I lost my father in such a tragic way, please, help me to save my mother." Laufer writes that her mother had a ticket to board a ship leaving Lisbon, Portugal on May 9. "Everything is arranged; this may be her last chance; if she loses it she may be sent to Poland, as so many people of Vienna." Additionally, she writes, "Every day counts now, for [my mother] cannot obtain transit visas and exit permits before the US visa is issued."

On April 9, Bloom sent Laufer's letter to A. M. Warren, chief of the State Department's visa division, along with an attached letter reviewing the details of the case and concluded, "In view of the circumstances of this case, I would appreciate your rendering every possible assistance to Mrs. Greif in obtaining an immigration visa promptly. I shall be very pleased to reimburse the Department of State for any cable expense which may be incurred in connection with this matter and trust that you will give the same your prompt attention." Warren responded on April 16 stating that Greif will have to wait her turn for a visa: "there is nothing the Department may do to expedite the issuance of a visa to Mrs. Greif." He did offer, however, to send a "cablegram to [the U.S.] Consul at Vienna at the expense of an interested person asking for a brief cabled report as to when it is expected her case will be reached for final consideration." On May 5, Warren followed up stating that he received a cablegram from Vienna informing him that Greif still has "to wait a considerable time before her turn is reached."

What happened in the immediate aftermath of Warren's letters is unclear, but by April 16 of the following year – 1942 – Greif had made it to Havana, Cuba, and Bloom wrote to Secretary of State Cordell Hull on that day asking him for "prompt attention and consideration" of her case. Eliot B. Coulter, acting chief of the visa division, responded on Hull's behalf a week later promising him that "examination of Mrs. Greif's case will be completed as soon as possible" and that he will be notified "when a decision is reached." Finally, on October 29, 1942, Bloom was able to wire Sophie Laufer, informing her "that advisory approval [was] telegraphed to American Embassy at Havana for issuance of immigration visa to Mrs. Mina Mirl Greif."[62]

Bloom's papers contain files on thousands of similar cases. Some ended well, some didn't. Some were easy to tackle, some weren't. Bloom could more easily help people when the law permitted government officials to use their discretion.   If an ordinary Jew from Poland, for example, applied for a visa to come to the U.S. in 1940, the chances of him or her getting it were essentially nil considering the strict immigration quota for Poles (which was 6,524 that year).   Even if the person met all the many requirements and filled all the necessary forms, the quota was already filled and officials would simply place him or her on a long waiting list.   In a February 19, 1940 letter regarding someone seeking to escape Poland, Bloom wrote that the State Department informed him that no fewer than 113,804 people were already on this waiting list and the person "cannot expect to receive his visa for many years."   Bloom concludes, "I…regret that there is nothing which can be done" to help him get his visa faster.[63]

If the applicant were a famous rabbi, however, he could possibly gain a "non-quota" visa if he met certain requirements.   Thus, in 1938, for example, Bloom was able to help a visiting Lithuanian rabbi by writing apparently just a single letter.   Rabbi Lebia Perskis, vice president of the Slabodka yeshiva in Lithuania, came to America in 1937 evidently to lecture and fundraise for the institution and decided the following year to apply for a permanent visa to continue his work on behalf of the institution.   Asked to help the rabbi, Bloom wrote to Marshall M. Vance on March 28 at the American Consul in Windsor, Ontario in Canada: "One of my constituents is interested in the visa case of Rabbi Lebia Perskis…. I will appreciate any consideration extended to this applicant and would thank you to favor me with report regarding the status of his visa application."   Just 10 days later, on April 8, Vance wrote back stating that Perskis had been awarded a non-quota visa.[64]

Judging from the 60 boxes of Bloom's papers in the New York Public Library, Bloom never refused to take on a case.   He did seem to cajole more, however, when a case was brought to his attention by a friend or when several independent people or groups petitioned him to help.   For example, on December 13, 1939, Bloom wrote to Edward J. Shaughnessy, the deputy commissioner of immigration and naturalization at the U.S. Labor Department, about the Belgian wife of an American medical student (studying abroad) who wished to receive a visa.   Rather than ask for assistance, Bloom peremptorily and uncharacteristically writes, "I trust that favorable and prompt action will be taken on this petition and would appreciate your advising me when the same has been acted upon."[65]   Bloom seemed to have used stronger language than usual because the case came from a friend.

Files in Bloom's papers are often incomplete – meaning we know that he interceded on a person's behalf, but it's not known if the person ever actually made it out of Europe or not. For example, on February 21, 1941, Bloom wrote to the American Consul in "Vienna, Germany," about a woman, Auguste Graf, whose brother, Fred Abeles, desired to bring her to America. "He has been highly recommended to me," writes Bloom, "and I shall appreciate your advising me concerning the present status of her application." On that same date, Bloom wrote to Secretary of State Cordell Hull asking him to forward his letter to the American Consul "through the diplomatic pouch." Three months later, on May 12, Bloom received a reply from the Consul informing him, as Bloom wrote to Abeles, that "the documents of support which have been submitted in her behalf have been approved upon preliminary examination and she has been informed that she will be invited to file a formal visa application…upon submission of satisfactory proof of the arrangements which have been made for her transportation to the United States." Two days later, Abeles sent Bloom a thank-you note, and Bloom responded that helping him was a pleasure, ending, "I do hope that she will soon be able to join you in the United States."[66] Did his sister, in fact, join him in the U.S.? Bloom's papers are silent on this question.

In other cases, we know that a case concluded happily, but it's not clear how Bloom facilitated the happy ending. For example, on February 9, 1943, a man named Lazar Margulies wrote to Bloom, "I need not tell you how grateful my brother and I are for your intervention on his behalf; without it, we are both certain, he would still be in France."[67] A few months later, on June 7, another man, Reynold W. Herz, thanks Bloom for saving his parents' lives due to his "untiring assistance in procuring visas for them which finally enabled [him] to rescue them from Europe and bring them over to this country."[68] How Bloom did so is unclear. Earlier in the war, in 1940, Bloom apparently intervened to help some of the hapless Jews of the *S.S. Quanza* who initially weren't allowed to disembark in the U.S. and were in danger of being sent back to Europe. One passenger, Leopold Steinreich, thanked Bloom heartily for personally vouching for him and his wife and for "work[ing] for days in behalf of all refugee passengers to make the officials realize what they were doing in refusing to allow us to land."[69]   Other than Steinreich's letters, however, no other documents in Bloom's papers mention the *S.S. Quanza*.   Most likely, Bloom's lobbying efforts in this instance primarily took place in phone calls or face-to-face conversations in Washington, D.C.   Few records of Bloom's in-person conversations or phone calls exist, however, which means the details of some of Bloom's rescue activities will forever remain unknown.

In helping people during the war, Bloom sometimes pressured but never went beyond what was legally permitted.   On October 13, 1940, he wrote to someone seeking to bring his brother-in-law and niece (natives of Poland) from England to the United States: "even though we wish it were possible to bring them all out of the danger zone, the law will not permit it."[70]   In an August 27, 1941 letter, he wrote to someone: "tell your friends in the future not to ask me to do anything that is against the law."[71]   In one instance, he acknowledged regarding the American Consul in Warsaw that it requires "a great deal of pressure" to get it "to merely assist in what legally should be done," adding, "There is no attempt [on its part] to do anything beyond the law."[72]   Nevertheless, Bloom was not willing to do anything illegal to compensate for the Consul's stubbornness.

Bloom took great pride in helping people.   To one person who approached him with a certain case, he responded:

> if it can be done, it will be done. And, please, my dear Sir,
> do not ever think that you bother me by sending to me any
> cases that you feel are worthy cases, of people who desire
> help of some kind. You know I just feel that the good
> Lord has given me this position to try and assist the
> unfortunate people who are in difficulty, and as long as I
> am in this position and am able to do these things, I can
> assure you that it will be my pleasure to do so.[73]

One can find similar sentiments in many places in Bloom's papers and works. For example, he wrote to a friend in 1943: "that is all that we can expect to get out of this life, that is, the good we do to help those who are less fortunate than ourselves."[74] In 1940, he wrote to radio personality Harry Hershfield that should someone need help in DC, he should come directly to him: "if I can't help them in Washington I don't know anyone who can, and that isn't conceit either."[75] To his physician, Dr. Benjamin Salzer, Bloom wrote in 1937, "Please don't think for one moment that you ever bother me at any time or under any circumstances. I would get really angry if I thought that I could be of service to you in any way and you did not ask me to do something for you."[76]

Estimating how many individuals Bloom saved by writing to government officials on their behalf is very difficult. As mentioned above, from his papers, it's often hard to tell which cases concluded happily and which didn't. He helped many, though. Three years after the war, apparently in reaction to some murmuring against him, Bloom wrote, "I have no hesitancy in saying that I have received more 'God bless you' letters and have saved the lives of more Jews than any other individual in this country today." This sentence follows several angry comments in

Madame Chiang Kai-shek, the First Lady of the Republic of China, addressing a joint session of Congress on February 18, 1943. The photo is autographed by her and dedicated to Bloom (sitting, bottom left).

which Bloom notes his preference for working behind the scenes to help people:

> If the Jews want to defeat me in the next election, I won't suffer by it, but they will. If they want an agitator and want someone who just talks through the newspapers and tries to have people believe that he is doing something that he is not doing, of course then they don't want Sol Bloom. But if they want a real Jew and one who believes in the protection of the Jews...and who does not brag every day about what he is doing, I feel I have acted that part ever since I can remember.[77]

One thing is clear. Although it's true that Bloom never publicly criticized or challenged the Roosevelt administration's immigration or rescue policies, he did try to help as many individuals as he could who wrote to him appealing for assistance by leveraging his position as chairman of the House Foreign Affairs Committee and taking advantage of his political connections.

~ CHAPTER 7 ~

BLOOM IN BERMUDA

S ol Bloom was just one of three U.S. representatives sent to Bermuda in April 1943 to confer with British officials on how their respective governments could save Jews and others from Nazi-occupied Europe. A half year earlier, the U.S. government had confirmed a report that the Nazis planned to exterminate European Jewry, and the "Bermuda Conference" marked the climax of public reaction to this revelation.[1] Many hoped that Bloom and the other delegates at Bermuda would develop concrete plans to save Europe's remaining endangered Jews. Little, however, came of the conference, and Holocaust historians roundly condemn both it and Bloom's participation in it. Indeed, they regard it as having been essentially a sham, a "façade for inaction."[2]

This assessment, however, is far too simplistic. Government documents indicate that the delegates at Bermuda genuinely wished to help Jews but were hampered by the narrow instructions they had been given by their respective governments. These documents also indicate that they agreed on plans that would have saved numerous Jews had their governments properly pursued them. Their governments opted not to, but blame for this inaction should not be laid at the feet of the Bermuda delegates.

The conference convened in April 1943 because by that point the American government had received compelling evidence that European Jewry faced possible extermination by the Nazis. Eight months earlier, on August 8, 1942, the State Department received what became known as the "Riegner cable." It read in part:

Received alarming report stating that, in the Fuehrer's headquarters, a plan has been discussed, and is under consideration, according to which all Jews in countries occupied or controlled by Germany number 3½ to 4 million should, after deportation and concentration in the East, be at one blow exterminated, in order to resolve once and for all the Jewish question in Europe.... Our informant is reported to have close connexions [sic] with the highest German authorities, and his reports are generally reliable.[3]

Three and a half months later, the State Department confirmed to Rabbi Stephen Wise that the gist of the telegram was true, prompting Wise to publicize the news.

Previously, the Nazis' plan to annihilate the Jewish people had not been widely known or confirmed. During the first three years following the Nazis' invasion of Poland in 1939, informed Americans knew that Jews were being killed in Europe, but Jews were hardly the only ones affected by the outbreak of hostilities. Between 1939-1941, "Poles were even more exposed than Jews to arrest, deportation, and death,"[4] according to historian Richard Lukas, and as "of the spring of 1942, the Germans had murdered more Soviet prisoners of war than Jews."[5] An additional half-million people died of starvation and cold in the first winter of the Nazi siege of Leningrad, in 1941-1942.[6] Because of such atrocities, stories of Jewish suffering in the years 1939-1942 didn't stand out. They "blended into the background of Nazi terror against civilians all across Europe."[7] Many Americans were also unsure whether to fully believe reports of atrocities since two decades earlier, during World War I, British

Rabbi Stephen S. Wise (1874-1949), arguably the most powerful American rabbi of his era.

propagandists had publicized similar reports, which subsequently proved to be false. Thus, horrific tales about German behavior in World War II were initially "met with much skepticism."[8] Even later in the war, such stories were viewed as "at least partly exaggerated." After all, as one Jewish editor explained years later, "[s]uch things did not happen in the twentieth century"[9] – certainly not at the hands of Germany, arguably the most cultured nation on earth.

But by late 1942, it had become evident that the Nazis had a particularly diabolical plan – one of extermination – for the Jewish people. The Riegner report plus a steady stream of news accounts of Jews being massacred in Europe, prompted England, the U.S., the Soviet Union, and eight governments-in-exile to issue a statement on December 17, 1942 condemning "in the strongest terms [the Nazis'] bestial policy of cold-blooded extermination" of the Jews. It also declared "that those responsible for these crimes shall not escape retribution."[10] The British and American governments, however, were under public pressure to do more,[11] so in early 1943, Great Britain's Foreign Office suggested to the American State Department that delegations from the two governments meet to discuss the matter further. The State Department eventually agreed, and three-member delegations from both countries were appointed to meet on the island of Bermuda from April 19-29.[12] Representing England would be Richard K. Law, parliamentary undersecretary of state for foreign affairs; Osbert Peake, parliamentary undersecretary of state for the Home Department; and G.H. Hall, parliamentary and financial secretary to the Admiralty. Representing the United States would be Harold Dodds, president of Princeton University; Senator Scott Lucas from Illinois[13]; and Sol Bloom.

Bloom was on good terms with the State Department and may have been chosen in large part for that reason. Some Jewish leaders, including Stephen Wise, objected to Bloom's selection – perhaps considering him *too* friendly with the State Department and thus unlikely to sufficiently advocate for Europe's Jews – but their objections went unheeded.[14] Little, indeed, would come of the conference, but the problem wasn't Bloom's close ties with the State Department; it was the conference's circumscribed agenda as set by the American and British governments. To start with, both governments agreed that the conference shouldn't exclusively concern

Jews.[15]   The official "Agenda for Bermuda Conference" states, "The refugee problem should not be considered as being confined to persons of any particular race or faith.   Nazi measures against minorities have caused the flight of persons of various races and faiths, as well as of other persons because of their political beliefs."[16]   A U.S. government memorandum on this agenda explains, "False charges have been made by the Nazi-Fascist propagandists who have attempted to distort the humanitarian interest of the [Allies] into a sole interest of certain minorities."   Hence, the "conference in their findings should endeavor to avoid any possible implication which might be of assistance to the Nazi-Fascist propagandists."[17]

This last comment reflected a longstanding government concern that World War II not be seen as a "Jewish" war.[18]   Assistant Secretary of State Breckinridge Long, for one, feared that a perception that the Allies were "fighting this war on account and at the instigation and direction of [America's] Jewish citizens" would alienate neutral countries like Spain and Turkey and turn the Arab world against them.[19]   Additionally, while ordinary Americans could be inspired to fight for their country – or perhaps even Christendom or Western civilization writ large – they wouldn't be inspired (or feel the same obligation) to fight for European Jews.   Indeed, for that very reason, the Nazis repeatedly tried to convince Americans that the war *was* being fought for the Jews' sake.   One of the Nazis' chief propagandists, for example, called Churchill a "darling of Jewish finance" and argued that World War II was in essence, "a Jewish war with good honest-to-God American Gentile blood being shed for it."[20]   The Roosevelt administration feared that this kind of propaganda – which its own critics echoed to some degree in the years leading up to the war[21] – could be effective, and therefore endeavored to avoid doing anything that would lend it credibility.   Whatever the wisdom of this strategy for the larger war effort, it certainly didn't help the delegates at the Bermuda Conference rescue Jews.[22]

The conference was hampered in other ways too.   First, the British had already ruled out opening up Palestine to Jewish refugees, the most natural place for them to find shelter.[23]   Second, both governments agreed that the conference should concern only refugees who had already escaped to neutral countries such as Spain.   Nothing should be done for those trapped in Nazi Europe (i.e., Germany, Poland, etc.) except win the war as quickly as possible.[24]   Third, "both governments announced" in advance "that the discussions would be 'primarily exploratory' in nature."[25]   The American delegation was tasked, not with making decisions, but with making recommendations to the Intergovernmental Committee on Refugees (ICR), which had been set up in wake of the Evian Conference in 1938. This committee hadn't accomplished much during the previous five years and was largely moribund by this time, but the two governments sought to revitalize it. In the letter asking Bloom to represent the U.S. at the Bermuda Conference, President Roosevelt is quite explicit about the conference's purpose:

> The American Government has had an exchange of communications with the British Government in which it has been decided to ask the Executive Committee of the Intergovernmental Committee on Refugees to take appropriate steps.   Preliminary to that meeting, the American and British governments have agreed to discuss certain matters which might be presented to the Intergovernmental Committee for its attention and action.[26]

Thus, the delegates were empowered to do relatively little. And to ensure that public pressure wouldn't unduly influence the delegates, the U.S. and U.K. governments permitted only select media outlets to send reporters to the conference, which was otherwise inaccessible as it was held on the island of Bermuda, territory that only military aircraft could approach during the war.[27]

Also plaguing some of the delegates was a lack of basic information on the refugee problem. According to a post-conference U.K. government report, the American delegation was "led by men who had no knowledge of and no public responsibility for the problem under discussion." It states candidly, "Dr. Dodds, the chief United States delegate, cheerfully admitted that he had had such little warning of his appointment that he knew nothing about refugees until after he had arrived" in Bermuda.[28] For his part, Bloom clearly knew very little about the ICR before the Bermuda

Conference, with the official minutes recording, "Mr. Bloom asked how the Committee came into being and how it had functioned up to this time."[29]

The day before the first formal discussions between the two delegations at Bermuda, Richard Law telegraphed the Secretary of State for the Colonies already anticipating that European Jewry would benefit little from the conference: "The results...are likely to be so meager at the best," he writes, "that I think it essential that we should keep on as good terms as possible with the press. Otherwise they will murder us."[30] American and British Jews hoped that the conference would yield a plan to somehow stop the slaughter of millions of European Jews. Law saw matters differently. He believed the conference would be a success if, among other things, 1) it defined "the problem in terms of practical possibilities (i.e. in thousands rather than in hundreds of thousands [of Jews saved])"; 2) it attained "some formal agreement [from the American delegation] about what is impossible, i.e. that we *cannot* ask Hitler to send us his Jews, that we *cannot* exchange dangerous Nazis or prisoners of war for German Jews, that we *cannot* send food in through the blockade to feed the Jews" (emphasis added); and 3) it enabled the American delegation "to state unpalatable facts to their own pubic opinion."[31]

American Jewish organizations were not naïve. In a memorandum to Under Secretary of State Sumner Welles on April 14, the Joint Emergency Committee for European Jewish Affairs – which represented virtually all of organized American Jewry – expressed grave doubts about the potential of a "primarily exploratory" conference to do much good. "When millions of human beings have already been done to death, and the fact of their murder has been authenticated by the [Allies], the time for exploration has long since passed, and the time for action is long past due." It warned, "Unless action is undertaken immediately, there may soon be no Jews left alive in Europe."[32] The Committee asked for permission to attend the Bermuda Conference and submitted a 12-point rescue plan to the American delegation that included calls to negotiate with Hitler to release the Jews in his jurisdiction; ease administrative hurdles preventing legal immigration to the U.S.; open Palestine, Latin America, several British territories, and other areas to Jewish refugees; send food to the starving Jews of Europe; and create an intergovernmental agency to rescue Jews.[33]

A more radical outfit – the "Bergson group," operating under the name of The Committee for a Jewish Army of Stateless and Palestinian Jews – called for "the immediate creation of...[an] Agency, of military and diplomatic experts, with *full authority to determine and effectuate a realistic and stern policy of action*, to save the remaining millions of Jewish people who are marked for cold-blooded slaughter by Hitler" (emphasis in original). In other words, it too called for an intergovernmental agency, although it envisioned a more aggressive role for it. It wanted this agency to transfer Jews "from German-dominated countries to Palestine or to any temporary refuge" and sought the "immediate creation of a Jewish Army of *Stateless and Palestinian Jews*, including 'Suicide' Commando Squads which will raid deep into Germany, and Air Squadrons for retaliatory bombing" (emphasis in original).[34]

Before the conference began, several Jewish leaders wrote to Bloom, including Joseph Proskauer, president of the American Jewish Committee, who urged him not to preclude negotiating with the Nazis to save Jews in places like Germany and Poland.[35] Perhaps appealing to Bloom's affinity for grandiose plans, Proskauer wrote:

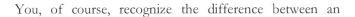

You, of course, recognize the difference between an

At Bermuda (L-R): G.H. Hall, Harold Dodds,
Richard K. Law, Sol Bloom, and Osbert Peake.

> attempt to save hundreds and an attempt to save hundreds
> of thousands – and that difference is enormous. ... [T]he
> big problem should be tackled in a big way, and there will
> be a sense of complete let-down if this Conference tackles
> the smaller things and lets the bigger ones go.... [T]his is a
> crisis which calls for imagination and daring on the part of
> the diplomats concerned.[36]

A delegation from the Joint Emergency Committee for European Jewish Affairs met with Bloom before he left to Bermuda and reported that he "had a very encouraging attitude." They were skeptical, however, and, considering the restrictions under which the conference would operate, they had reason to be.[37]

Indeed, on the very first day of formal discussions at Bermuda, Richard Law dismissed the proposal to negotiate with Hitler to release the Jews in Axis territory as one of several "exaggerated ideas" and "impossible" solutions that shouldn't even be entertained.[38] But Dodds, who headed the American delegation, wished to discuss it, so they proceeded to do so. Law argued that negotiating with Hitler could prove to be highly embarrassing: "if Hitler accepted a proposal to release perhaps millions of unwanted persons, we might find ourselves in a very difficult position," he said, since the Allies would have no way of transferring them out of Europe due to "the shipping problem."[39] Bloom, however – perhaps having taken Proskauer's appeal for grand action to heart – said "we should at least negotiate and see what could be done." Dodds disagreed, and at that point, according to the official American minutes of the discussions, "a rather extended argument developed."

The minutes record that Bloom then "offered the suggestion that we propose that Hitler release each month the number of refugees that we find it possible to handle." A member of the British delegation said Hitler would never agree to release Jews without getting something in return and reiterated that the Allies had no available ships to transport Jews to safety. Bloom, however, "argued that it was more preferable to negotiate so that we could determine what the Germans were willing to do." He also "suggested that we be not too explicit as to what we could do and that it was better to leave the matter entirely open and conclude with a recommendation that we would try to do it if the opportunity arises." It was only after "an extended conversation" between Dodds and Bloom – during which Dodds noted that "Bloom's proposal was completely against the policy of our Government" – that Bloom "began to recede from his former rather uncompromising position." At that point, a member of the British delegation reiterated Law's point about Hitler possibly embarrassing the Allies by agreeing to let the Jews go: "To open up negotiations and to have Hitler agree that we can take all we want and have us then to have to say that we cannot take them would place us in an impossible situation." Ignoring Dodds's earlier admonition, Bloom countered that he wanted "to somehow not close the door" and "insisted that we should leave the possibility open of negotiating with Germany whether or not we actually make the recommendation that this be done."[40]

Both the American and British governments noted Bloom's protestations. A post-conference report by the British delegation to Anthony Eden, the U.K.'s secretary of state for foreign affairs, states: "Mr. Sol Bloom, doubtless with a view to quieting his Jewish conscience, was inclined to make difficulties [regarding the ban on negotiating with the Nazis], but he was firmly overruled by Dr. Dodds and the State Department officials, who were even more emphatic than ourselves in

-4-

then returned to his first point and argued that it was
much more preferable to negotiate so that we could determine
what the Germans were willing to do. He suggested that we
be not too explicit as to what we could do and that it was
better to leave the matter entirely open and conclude with
a recommendation that we would try to do it if the opportunity
arises. There then occurred an extended conversation between
Dr. Dodds and Mr. Bloom, Dodds pointing out that Mr. Bloom's
proposal was completely against the policy of our Government
and that we were on record against negotiating on any terms
with Nazi Germany. Bloom then began to recede from his former
rather uncompromising position.

Top half of page 4 of the American minutes
of the discussions at the Bermuda Conference.

rejecting these particular extreme suggestions from the 'pressure groups.'"[41] In addition, an undated American government memorandum states, "Congressman Bloom argued at considerable length on this question" and "persisted in his position" until "Dodds finally silenced him by calling his attention to the definite statement of this Government's policy which was supposed to govern the American delegates."[42] The evidence, thus, clearly indicates that Bloom made an honest effort during this opening salvo of the conference to save as many European Jews as possible.

After concluding the discussion on negotiating with Hitler, the delegates proceeded to the next solution that Law regarded as "impossible": exchanging German prisoners of war for Jews. No one argued in favor of this proposal – probably because the released German prisoners were likely to return to the battlefield and kill Allied soldiers – so the delegates moved on to the last of Law's impossible solutions: sending food to European Jews so they wouldn't starve to death. Bloom apparently opposed the idea, and Dodds believed the entire question beyond the purview of the conference as it would require violating the military blockade of Nazi Europe,[43] which was thought to be a key element in defeating Germany.[44]

Having dismissed the proposal to send food to Europe, the delegates then moved to what became one of the central topics of the conference: finding temporary places of asylum for refugees who had escaped the Nazis. Tens of thousands of Jews and other refugees had fled to, and were stuck in, neutral countries like Spain and Turkey. The 5,000 Jewish refugees in Spain – whom Law called "the hard core of the problem"[45] – were relatively safe, but their prolonged presence in the country meant other Jews were in danger of being turned away from Spain's border since Spain didn't want to be flooded with refugees.[46] "It is of supreme importance," the British delegation wrote, "that this channel [out of Spain] not become blocked as the consequences would be…that the admission of further refugees would be prevented by the Spanish Government."[47] From a more activist perspective, clearing Spain of its Jewish refugees would give hope to Jews in the rest of Europe as it would signal that an avenue of escape existed. "We want the word to get into Europe as much as possible," said Dodds, "that if you get to Spain you can be taken care of."[48] He explained, "If we can remove from Spain those who are there now, Spain evidently is prepared to receive new ones and if we can keep that flow and can arrange a device for keeping that going, we will have accomplished something."[49]

All the delegates, including Bloom,[50] agreed with this assessment, and they discussed at some length how these Jews could be transported out of Spain and where they could be taken. The first question revolved around available shipping: Which boats could transport Jews out of Europe? The delegates consulted, and trusted, Julian Foster, a shipping expert at the U.S. State Department, who told them no American ships could be used for anything other than military purposes for at least 12-18 months. Only ships belonging to neutral countries like Portugal, Spain, Turkey, and Sweden could be used, and only a limited number of these could possibly be secured to transfer refugees.[51] Loading refugees onto empty ships that had just dropped off Allied soldiers was ruled out. The conference's final report states, "The assembly of refugees at ports where troops were landed would interfere with military movements and presented insurmountable security difficulties: to divert the transports to other ports would cause delay in the movements of the armed forces of the [Allies] and of essential war supplies."[52] Foster also claimed that refugees in Belgium and France during the invasion in those countries had gotten in the way, interfered with communications, and caused numerous other difficulties."[53] In questioning Foster, the delegates learned of many logistical hurdles involved in securing ships to transport refugees to the point that Dodds remarked that "it does seem to be a fairly gloomy picture" and Bloom commented "that if the people knew all of the difficulties connected with shipping it would be better."[54]

The next question, tied to the first, was: To where could these refugees be taken? The U.S. was initially ruled out as a possibility. The American government couldn't guarantee shipping or safe conduct, and it preferred that refugees be kept close to home so they could be easily repatriated after the war. A refugee brought to America might wish to stay there, and shipping him or her back over the Atlantic Ocean after the war – especially against his or her will – would be a "task which definitely should be avoided," the U.S. delegates were told before leaving to Bermuda.[55] Bringing them to America permanently was also initially thought not possible because of the country's strict immigration quotas. As a U.S. government memorandum on the Bermuda agenda explained, there "is no indication that the Congress would be likely to act favorably upon any proposal that the immigration laws be relaxed or suspended in behalf of the refugees."[56] Indeed, both Bloom and Senator Lucas argued that "any effort to tamper with the quotas in Congress would be likely to result in a *reduction* of the quotas" (emphasis added).[57]

Robert Clark Alexander, a State Department immigration expert, noted that no new legislation was necessary for the U.S. to admit some of these refugees since its annual quotas were actually not being filled.[58] They remained unfilled in part because some American consulates acted in the spirit of an internal memo Long had written in 1940 (in response to a solicitation of his views on emergency tactics the United States could theoretically take[59]): "We can delay and effectively stop for a temporary period of indefinite length the number of immigrants into the United States.... by simply advising our consuls to put every obstacle in the way and to require additional evidence and to resort to various administrative devices which would postpone and postpone and postpone the granting of the visas."[60] Item number three on the Joint Emergency Committee for European Jewish Affair's 12-point rescue program called for simplifying the immigration process so that Jews who were eligible for visas could, in fact, receive them. In a pre-conference meeting with President Roosevelt, a group of Jewish congressmen (which included Bloom) had "especially asked the President to decide on a simplification of the procedure for admission into this country." Nothing significant, though, seems to have resulted from this request. Roosevelt told them to meet with Long and said "perhaps visitor's visas would again be issued" to Jews escaping Europe.[61]

Bloom didn't advance this suggestion at Bermuda – perhaps it had already been nixed by the State Department – and he concurred when Dodds argued that loosening immigration restrictions could backfire. "[I]f one or two saboteurs should get through the ports of entry the repercussion would be likely to result in a drastic curtailment of immigration," he said.[62] In an April 25 meeting with the American delegation, George Backer, a member of the Executive Committee of the Refugee Economic Corporation, argued that security rules could be eased somewhat, saying he knew of only a single case of a saboteur entering the U.S. Bloom, however, countered that security must be paramount. Robert Borden Reams, secretary of the American delegation, argued: "You have one or two cases of enemy action or sabotage by those whom you let into the states; let it be made public knowledge and how many more refugees are ever going to come into the states?"[63]

On the last day of formal discussions, the U.S. delegation said it could possibly take in 1,000-1,500 refugees from Spain under its quota system, but another destination was clearly necessary for the vast majority of Spain's refugee population – especially if the evacuated refugees were to be the vanguard of a continuous flow of people leaving the country with thousands constantly replacing the ones just evacuated. Several places were discussed, including Angola, Madagascar, and Jamaica, but the most practical suggestion – considering the limited availability of ships and the distances involved – was North Africa.[64] Bloom argued strenuously against sending refugees to North Africa, believing it would interfere with the war effort.[65] In objecting to a temporary asylum in North Africa for Jewish refugees, Bloom and Dodds were apparently following instructions from their superiors. In a telegram to the Secretary of State for the Colonies on April 22, Law writes, "The U.S. Delegation was rigid and uncompromising about North Africa, maintaining that this was a military problem with which they were not concerned. Dodds afterwards told me that resistance to any proposal regarding North Africa was the most categorical part of their instructions."[66] The minutes record, "Mr. Bloom then interjected to say that after all we have a war on and that he was thinking about the people at home but that he was thinking more of the military authorities who all say that this situation in North Africa is a military situation and we cannot do anything about it just now."[67] Dodds, too, objected to North Africa as a destination for the refugees, calling the prospect "impossible… because of military necessities."[68]

Law insisted, however, that the idea be considered seriously and suggested setting up a refugee camp under British control. Law told the U.S. delegates "that they were under very great pressure on the part of the public opinion in Great Britain to do something immediately and renewed his plea for something to be done here and now."[69] In a telegram to the Secretary of State for the Colonies, Law writes, "The British Delegation feels strongly that world opinion will be bitterly disappointed by the results of the Conference, if all future action is relegated to Inter-Governmental Committee" to which the delegations were asked to make their recommendations.[70] It thus submitted a formal proposal to their American counterparts "that a temporary rest camp under British administration should be formed at some point in North Africa to be elected by the

American authorities, as far as possible from the scene of military operations, and removed from the lines of communication." The occupants of this camp would be "several thousand refugees, mainly of German origin and Jewish race," and the cost of running the camp would be borne jointly by the U.S. and England.[71] The American delegation agreed to submit the proposal to Washington, and it appears in the delegations' final report as one of several suggestions to solve the Spanish refugee problem.[72]

Another significant recommendation in the final report was issuing a formal declaration assuring neutral countries that they wouldn't be stuck after the war with refugees they allowed into their countries. Such an announcement, it was thought, would encourage neutral countries to permit more refugees to cross their borders. The Swiss, for example, indicated to the British that "what really worries them is whether there is any limit to the number of refugees they are expected to take and what is going to happen to these refugees after the war." Will these refugees "be taken home or will they be left permanently in Switzerland?"[73] For countries to welcome persecuted Jews and others across their borders, they needed a guarantee that they wouldn't remain after the war. The delegates recommended that their governments – along with nine others – issue a joint declaration on this matter. The delegates also recommended that the ICR be immediately revived and reinvigorated and that it consider, among other things, paying for the food and maintenance of refugees in neutral countries.[74]

The report records that "at the end of the conference it was agreed that none of the delegates, and neither of their Governments would disclose any of the proceedings of the Conference or its recommendations except by mutual agreement sought through the diplomatic channel." The reason for this agreement is not entirely clear. In the communiqué issued to the press, the delegates explain, "Since the recommendations necessarily concern Governments other than those represented at the Bermuda Conference and involve military considerations, they must remain confidential."[75] This explanation is arguably plausible, but the desire for secrecy may have been motivated more by fear of public opinion.[76] During the April 25 meeting of the American delegation, Backer warned that "at least 125,000 people have got to be taken out of eastern Europe if this Conference is to yield a result" that would satisfy American Jewish groups.[77] Nowhere near that number were being saved at the conference. So claiming that strict silence on what occurred at Bermuda was necessary for reasons of "security" may have been tempting. Law hints to this ulterior motive in a telegram to the Secretary of State for the Colonies:

> The American representatives explained that they were prepared to take the line in the House and Senate, where they will be subjected to much pressure, that they cannot add anything to publish communique without playing Hitler's game.[78] We have agreed therefore that nothing shall be disclosed of discussions or recommendations in Parliament or in Congress without the previous agreement between our two governments."[79]

But if the American delegation's purpose in staying silent was to forestall public criticism, it didn't work. Jewish officials denounced the conference. Rabbi Israel Goldstein, president of the Synagogue Council of America, said the "job of the Bermuda Conference apparently was not to rescue victims of the Nazi terror but to rescue our State Department and the British foreign Office from possible embarrassment."[80] For its part, the Bergson group called the conference "a mockery and a cruel jest."[81] Yet, it's hard to read the minutes of the Bermuda proceedings and come to that conclusion. The delegates honestly seemed desirous to help within the restrictions placed upon them. And they were especially anxious to do something lest they face the public's wrath.[82]

A case can be made that people like Dodds and Bloom had no business attending a conference on a topic on which they lacked so much knowledge. A case can also be made that they should have refused, on principle, to attend a rescue conference when the most natural rescue solutions – negotiating with Hitler and opening up Palestine, the U.S., and the U.K. to refugees – were essentially taken off the table before the conference even began.[83] But it can also be argued that a person should try to help even when his or her hands are tied, and if that's true, then considering the parameters within which they were working, the delegates seem to have done a relatively decent job. First, they went beyond their instructions to merely come up with recommendations for the ICR and made several recommendations to their own governments. Second, their main recommendations were promising and could have saved many Jews had they been followed up by their respective governments. The plan to create an escape valve in Spain through which a continuous flow of refugees could flee to safety was, in fact, taken up (in expanded form) a year later by the much-praised War Refugee Board.[84] The scheme to create temporary shelters in North Africa, though, barely got off the ground. Prime Minister Churchill and President Roosevelt discussed the idea, and the latter approved it in both May[85] and June. England and the U.S. both committed to contribute $500,000 towards the project. Ultimately, however, due to various bureaucratic objections[86] and delays, only one camp was built to which a total of 600 Jews were brought.[87] Yet, this ultimate failure cannot be placed on the shoulders of Bloom or any of the other delegates. Their task was to make recommendations, not implement them.

The failure of the ICR to do much also cannot be pinned on the delegates. Both the Joint Emergency Committee and the Bergson group recommended creating an inter-governmental agency to save Jews. The Bermuda Conference recommended reviving an already existing agency to do just that. There doesn't seem to be any meaningful distinction between creating a new body and reviving an old one.[88] In other words, the Bermuda Conference delegates arguably set up the kind of organization Jewish groups were seeking. It took approximately half a year to revive the

The upper part of a full-page ad the Bergson group placed in
The New York Times after the conclusion of the Bermuda Conference.

ICR, which ultimately "demonstrated a consummate inability to accomplish much of anything."[89] But that wasn't the fault of the Bermuda Conference attendees. They envisioned a revamped ICR with someone new and highly qualified at the helm. Dodds wanted its heads to be "men of outstanding reputation and position whose prestige would contribute to [the ICR's] new set-up." He said, "We want to start off the reorganized administration [of the ICR] with all the prestige possible."[90] In its official recommendations, the delegates stated, "The future welfare of these refugees will be largely dependent upon the successful prosecution of the duties which may be entrusted to the Committee. Special care therefore must be taken to define accurately the scope of these duties and to expand wherever necessary the powers and responsibilities of the Committee."[91]

In a speech on May 23 at a HIAS luncheon – three weeks after the conference – Bloom said, "No one can criticize what we did in Bermuda without knowing what we did. But I as a Jew am perfectly satisfied with the results."[92] Three weeks earlier, The New York Times reported that Senator Lucas and Bloom "said that they believed the conference had been successful and that the plans made would prove their value."[93] Bloom, however, didn't merely defend the Bermuda Conference publicly. He did so – repeatedly – in private, which seems to indicate that he truly believed it had, in fact, been a success. On May 3, a day after he returned to New York, he wrote to his doctor, "[T]he deliberations of the conference were a complete success notwithstanding the criticisms in the newspapers and also the criticism of the pressure groups." The criticism, he argued, stemmed from ignorance. "[W]hatever we did we could not make public because by making our decisions public, we would have been giving aid and information to our enemies and it would have prevented us from accomplishing anything at all."[94] A day later, in a letter to a friend, Bloom called the conference "an outstanding success," adding, "There were things, of course, which were utterly impossible to do, but we succeeded in taking care of the refugee problem in Spain and many other things which cannot be made public because they would help the enemy."[95] In a letter to a different friend that same day, Bloom wrote, "We accomplished everything that we started out to do." As for his own role, Bloom wrote, "I did everything that I possibly could do and I don't know anyone who could have done half as much."[96]

Ten days later, Bloom hadn't changed his mind, writing to a friend that "the Bermuda conference did everything that it possibly could do," and he and his fellow delegates at the conference "did a very good job."[97] A month later, Bloom was still defending himself, writing in a letter, "The Jews have been attacking me because they seem to be dissatisfied with what we did at the Bermuda Conference, but they do not know what we did and for military reasons, we cannot tell them they have no reason to criticize. I personally believe we did everything we possibly could do and some day when the facts are known, they may think differently."[98] A week later, Bloom was still at it, telling Zionist leader Louis Lipsky "that the statements which have been made about [him] are cruel and untrue." His critics, he writes, "do not understand the situation at all."[99] Five days later, Bloom "complained bitterly" to World Zionist Congress president Nahum Goldmann "about the attacks made on him after the Bermuda Conference," according to the minutes of a meeting between the two of them. He reportedly told Goldmann that "nothing affected him more than doubts cast on his devotion to the Jewish people" and said he was "disappointed at the delay in implementing the decisions of the Bermuda conference" and planned to approach the State Department about the matter."[100] Apparently in response to all the criticism, a meeting was arranged between Bloom and several Jewish journalists at the home of businessman Max Manischewitz. Bloom evidently made a good impression, with Dr. Samuel Margoshes, a columnist and former editor for The Day, writing to Bloom in its wake, "I only wish your efforts in behalf of our Jews before, during, and after Bermuda were better known than they are. They most decidedly deserve a better reporting than they have received hitherto."[101]

Despite some criticism from public officials and Jewish leaders, Bloom did not suffer electorally the following year, winning 71 percent of the vote, the highest total in his entire congressional career. In the aftermath of the conference, he also received friendly coverage from the Yiddish press. The Forward reported on Bloom's May 23 HIAS speech in defense of the Bermuda Conference on its front page but carried no editorial criticizing it. Neither did The Day (which covered the story on page two) or The Morning Journal.[102]

In any event, all the available evidence suggests that Bloom sought to help Jews at Bermuda but was restrained by factors beyond his control. Thirty years later, Rep. Emanuel Celler testified that Bloom told him, "I was helpless [at Bermuda]."[103] Historian Laurel Leff writes, "Even before the conference began, all involved, including the press, understood the talks were likely to be a failure."[104] By failure, she means that the overwhelming majority of European Jews would derive no benefit from it. Yet, to borrow words from two other historians, "little could be expected" of a conference whose "final decisions [were essentially] arrived at even before the conference opened."[105] The American and British governments had made clear even before the conference began that it would be extremely limited in scope. Unfortunately, "many illusions had been fostered regarding the scope and possibilities" of the conference.[106]

A deeper, more fundamental reason, however, lies at the heart of why the conference yielded only minimal results. In its post-conference report, the British delegation admitted candidly that efforts to rescue Jews won't be very successful "so long as…the present combination, in so many countries, of pity for Jews under German control and extreme reluctance to admit further Jews into their borders persists."[107] This comment calls to mind the observation of Zionist leader Chaim Weizmann regarding European Jews in 1936: "[T]he world is divided into places where they cannot live and places where they cannot enter."[108] Saving Jews was simply not a top priority for the Allies and thus their borders (as well as those of Palestine) remained largely closed. As historian Michael Neufeld argues, "For the supreme Allied leadership in the West (not to mention the East), there were many more urgent priorities, such as doing everything militarily possible to win the war as soon as possible; rescuing refugees, Jewish or otherwise, just got in the way."[109] The April 25 meeting of the American team at Bermuda contains a revealing exchange after several members argued repeatedly that negotiating with Hitler was ill-advised since the Allies would have no way of evacuating the Jews from Europe should Hitler agree to free them:

> MR. BACKER: If 100,000 Germans would offer to surrender we would find some way to get them out.
>
> DR. DODDS: From the standpoint of war, there is a difference between 100,000 German prisoners and 100,000 refugees.[110]

In other words, we would figure something out if we had to, but only solutions to help win the war – not any other purpose – can be explored. Backer accepted this point, and later said point-blank that "there is no moment when it can be justified that the removal of a single child from wherever he may be can cause an hour's loss in the war or the death of one American soldier."[111]   Sen. Lucas made this point even more poignantly:

> I am not only thinking about persecuted peoples in Europe but I am thinking about the millions of boys in this country who are fighting on every front of this war. I am thinking of the mothers of those boys whose hearts are aching just as much as others throughout the world. I am thinking about casualty lists and the thousands and thousands that are going to return to be charges of this Government after the war is over. Every day you postpone bringing this war to a conclusion you just take upon your hands the blood of American boys.[112] That is the thing in the back of my mind all the time. The sooner we can defeat Hitler the better it will be for the whole civilized world, including the Jews.[113]

In his autobiography, Bloom writes:

> The humanitarian motive to aid individuals…had to be subordinated to the greater humanitarian motive of rescuing whole peoples. Any plan that might interfere with winning the war had to be rejected. We could divert no force, not a single ship, in direct use against the enemy to succor any of his victims. At this time – not until a month later did the German forces in Africa surrender; not for another five months were Allied soldiers to set foot in southern Italy; not for more than a year would General Eisenhower's forces land in France – no one could guess how long the war might last and every effort must be spent

that could shorten it by even as little as a day.[114]

In an interview decades later, Dodds said that Bloom – "as loyal [a] Jew as I've ever met" – pledged not to put anything above the war effort, including rescue efforts, "with tears on his face."[115] Historian Monty Penkower criticizes the Bermuda Conference, saying it was bound to fail as long as the Allies refused "to match Hitler's fanatic determination to murder all of European Jewry with an equally determined effort to rescue them."[116] He may be right, but surely the U.S. cannot be blamed for putting its own interests above all else – especially during wartime when the lives of its soldiers are at stake. The Allies probably could have found a way to save more Jews, but winning the war was their priority, and Bloom, operating under strict guidelines, was at the conference to promote America's interests, not those of European Jewry.

~ CHAPTER 8 ~

WHY WASN'T HE MORE HELPFUL?

A mong major Jewish organizations, none denounced the Bermuda
Conference more vehemently than the Bergson group. Headed by
Hillel Kook – who adopted the name Peter Bergson in America[1] –
the organization took out a full-page ad in The New York Times on May 4,
1943 blasting the conference as a "cruel mockery" to "5,000,000 Jews in the
Nazi death-trap."[2]   Earlier that year, the group had concluded that
mainstream American Jewish groups weren't responding to the Nazi
slaughter of European Jewry with sufficient urgency, so they decided to
step into the breach. Operating on chutzpah, charisma, and feverish
energy,[3] Bergson and his associates persuaded many prominent non-Jews to
lend their names to a campaign to save European Jewry, and in November
1943, their hard work led to the introduction in Congress of two identical
rescue resolutions, H. Res. 350 and H. Res. 352.[4] They read in part:

> Whereas the Congress of the United States, by concurrent
> resolution adopted on March 15 of this year, expressed its
> condemnation of Nazi Germany's "mass murder of Jewish
> men, women, and children," a mass crime which has
> already exterminated close to two million human
> beings…and which is growing in intensity as Germany
> approaches defeat…. Therefore be it
>
> *Resolved*, That the House of Representatives recommends
> and urges the creation by the President of a commission of
> diplomatic, economic, and military experts to formulate

and effectuate a plan of immediate action designed to save the surviving Jewish people of Europe from extinction at the hands of Nazi Germany.[5]

As head of the Foreign Affairs Committee, Sol Bloom called for hearings on the resolutions, which took place over the course of five days in November and December. They were never reported out of committee, but the publicity surrounding them helped Treasury Secretary Henry Morgenthau, Jr. convince Roosevelt a month later to issue an executive order creating the War Refugee Board (WRB),[6] which saved numerous Jews[7] from the Nazi death machine and constitutes America's most significant response to the Holocaust. Bloom handled these resolutions as he did the Bermuda Conference, from the perspective of a leading U.S. congressman advancing his country's interests in the middle of a world war. And that meant he had to oppose them at least to some degree since these resolutions implicitly criticized President Roosevelt and other leading members of the administration for not doing enough to save European Jewry.

In responding to the resolutions, Bloom enjoyed much more leeway than he did in Bermuda where he was only one member of a larger delegation and hampered by instructions from Roosevelt and the State Department. In the House Foreign Affairs Committee, in contrast, Bloom reigned supreme and was theoretically free to do as he desired. Thus, if he had agreed with Bergson's cause, Bloom could have taken the highly

unusual step of ignoring the wishes of Roosevelt and other leading members of government who were heading the Allied effort in World War II. Bloom, however, didn't agree with Bergson – indeed, felt personally attacked by him – and knew that mainstream American Jewish leaders were ambivalent, at best, about the resolutions. Thus, like at Bermuda, Bloom tried to please Jews who wanted greater government action in

Peter Bergson (1915-2001)

rescuing European Jewry but ultimately fulfilled his patriotic duty as he understood it and hindered speedy passage of the resolutions.

During the hearings on resolutions 350 and 352 (hereafter just called "the resolution"), Bloom repeatedly said that he favored helping Europe's endangered Jews,[8] yet he derailed the hearings from the very beginning by focusing on tangential matters relating to his personal honor and that of the committee rather than the resolution itself. For example, the Bergson group had sent out a telegram to supporters in advance of the hearings asking for funds so that it could continue its activities abroad and "force" passage of the rescue resolution in Congress; Bloom took offense at the word "force" and grilled Bergson and a fellow witness at great length about who was responsible for the telegram's language, to whom the telegram was sent, how much money was raised through it, etc.[9] He was somewhat upset on the first day of the hearings but downright hostile on the second day, unexpectedly calling on Bergson to testify under oath and interrogating him about the telegram, his organization, and even his personal finances.[10] Bloom spent so much time on these subjects that one of his colleagues asked, "Is this an investigation or a hearing on the resolution?"[11]

Bloom also derailed the hearings by focusing at great length on a radio broadcast that accused him of opposing the resolution. He demanded a retraction and wanted to know who authorized the broadcast and on what sources it was based.[12] Bloom claimed that both the telegram and broadcast were inaccurate[13] and said he felt compelled to hold hearings immediately lest his inaction be misinterpreted. The telegram "places the chairman and the committee in a very embarrassing situation," he said. "[W]e feel that we are on trial."[14] Bloom was also upset because some of the testimony that had been given in executive (i.e., secret) session on the first day of the hearings was apparently leaked.[15]

When Bloom wasn't grilling Bergson and others about the telegram and broadcast, he seemed at least somewhat open to the resolution.[16] His primary reservations were two. First, he wondered why the formation of another rescue entity was necessary when the Bermuda Conference had already decided to revive the Intergovernmental Committee on Refugees a half year earlier.[17] Second, he feared that passage of the resolution might be read as a backhand critique of the Roosevelt administration, which was on record as stating that it was doing everything possible to save Jews in

Europe. By passing the resolution, Bloom and several of his colleagues argued, they would essentially be saying to the administration, "No, you aren't."[18] At one point, Bloom said, "I think we can all take the word of [Secretary of State] Cordell Hull and his messages and his promises that everything that possibly can be done is being done and will be done."[19] Bloom actually published a booklet, which he distributed to his fellow committee members, that contained pronouncements by Roosevelt and Hull condemning Nazi atrocities against Jews and asserting their commitment to help.[20] Hull, for example, had issued a statement on July 26, 1943 declaring, "The rescue of the Jewish people...is under constant examination by the State Department, and any suggestion calculated to that end will be gladly considered." Roosevelt, for his part, said in a message on September 9, 1943, "I wish to emphasize that all feasible measures are being adopted to lessen the sufferings of the persecuted Jews of Europe."[21]

In response to the Bloom's first concern – that the resolution constituted a repudiation of the work done at Bermuda – Bergson argued that the delegations at Bermuda actually did a fine job, but they only tackled the question of what to do with Jews who had *escaped* Nazi Europe while he was concerned with those who hadn't.[22] Bergson said, "Criticism was directed, to my mind, against the Bermuda Conference unjustifiably, because this was a conference on the refugee problem, and it did a very good job on the refugee problem." Bloom must have been surprised by this statement because he responded, "Will you repeat that? This is the first time anyone ever gave me a pat on the back."[23] In explaining his position, Bergson said, "I am interested in the people in Warsaw, not [the refugees] in Spain." The Jews trapped in Nazi Europe cannot be lumped in with a general refugee problem, he said, because they are neither refugees nor potential refugees; "they are potential corpses." He declared, "All we want, instead of making them potential corpses, is to make them refugees."[24]

As for the second objection – that the resolution would be interpreted as an attack on the administration – Bergson said, perhaps semi-disingenuously, that the resolution would actually help the administration do what it already desired to do. Asked in late 1943 about government efforts to save Europe's endangered Jews, President Roosevelt replied that "the heart's all right – it's a question of ways and means."[25] Bergson said, "I most sincerely hope that this resolution before you is the first and the best proposal as yet as to solving the ways and means difficulty."[26] Another witness on behalf of the resolutions, publisher Howard Ziff,[27] said rescuing Jews "requires the intervention of a [government] group that has nothing else to do." Without such a group, he said, nothing will be accomplished – and not for lack of sympathy:

> There are other things which occupy [the government's] attention which are even more important and more pressing. After all, when you come down to a situation where you allow a forced comparison between values, you are then creating a comparison between the immediate needs of the war effort and the needs of people who are facing extinction, or many other needs which are of vital importance. So long as you leave this thing, divided and subdivided between a great many departments…it is not anyone's particular business. Everyone has sympathy; everyone has the best of intentions. But this requires coordinated effort. Of that I am certain.[28]

Bergson also argued that the creation of a government rescue entity would free busy administration officials from having to constantly meet people like him. "I know that on many occasions I personally had to express regret to high officials when I had to take up 1 or 2 hours of time discussing this problem," he testified. A government body devoted to rescue would, for example, "save the Secretary of State a great deal of valuable time," he said.[29]

On the last day of the hearings, December 2, 1943, Rabbi Stephen Wise testified and effectively undermined the resolution by arguing that the people behind it were "unauthorized, irresponsible, quasi-spokesmen" of a "small group of American Jews" who pay for "rashly written and rashly published advertisements."[30] He also cast aspersions on the Bergson group's financial integrity[31] while puffing up his own group – the American Jewish Conference – as the "responsible, authorized, organized Jews of America" and "the most widely and democratically organized, the most widely representative Jewish organization in this country."[32] Wise said he supported the resolution but insisted that it include a provision demanding that Palestine be open to unrestricted Jewish immigration.[33] Bergson, a staunch Zionist, also wanted Palestine's borders opened to Jews. Indeed, he declared that one of the first steps he would take after the creation of a government rescue entity would be to lobby it to pressure England to revise its Palestine immigration policy.[34] Yet, Bergson specifically didn't want Palestine mentioned in the resolution because he knew some congressmen would be loath to vote for a bill that implicitly criticized its closest ally in the middle of a world war (as it was England that was keeping Palestine's borders largely closed).[35] But when Rep. Will Rogers, Jr., one of the bill's co-sponsors, suggested that "it would be unwise to inject" the "acrimonious Palestine question" in the bill, Wise didn't even deign to respond to his argument. "I don't care to answer it," he said.[36]

Much more damaging to the resolution, however, was Assistant Secretary of State Breckinridge Long's secret testimony on the fourth day of the hearings, November 26.[37] Before voting on the resolution, members of the Foreign Affairs Committee wished to know the State Department's view on it and the government's record on rescuing Jews up to that point. Long was deemed the right man to provide this information. During his testimony, Long refused to say if he favored passage of the resolution despite being asked multiple times.[38] He did, however, spend a great deal of time touting what he regarded as the government's many efforts to help Jews. Among other things, he said the government had admitted 580,000 refugees since Hitler began persecuting Jews in 1933,[39] and, to the relatively uninformed members of the Foreign Affairs Committee, his testimony

sounded impressive.[40] In fact, so impressive did they regard it that they insisted that at least part of it be made public so the American people could better appreciate everything its government had done, and was doing, for Europe's endangered Jews.[41] Bloom told Nahum Goldmann of the World Jewish Congress that Long's testimony "indicates that every conceivable effort"

Breckinridge Long (1881-1958) testifying in front of a congressional committee in 1939.

to save Jews is already being "made and, therefore, there is really no necessity" for the creation of an American government rescue entity.[42] Bloom said he didn't think his committee would "report the resolution out, and that [would] be the end of it."[43] Publication of Long's testimony, however, did not serve its intended purpose and angered rather than pacified activist Jews. In a statement, the Bergson group said that America's record of admitting refugees was "irrelevant" and a "smokescreen"; the main issue was saving the "four million innocent [Jews] upon whom Hitler is now venting his fiendish savagery."[44] Furthermore, only a third – or 190,000 – of the 580,000 refugees that the U.S. had taken in were, in fact, Jewish according to the World Jewish Congress.[45]

The argument against creating a government rescue commission thus suffered a blow, and in mid-December, the Jewish Telegraphic Agency (JTA) reported that New York Rep. Andrew Somers accused Bloom of causing "unnecessary delay" in reporting the bill out of committee.[46] Three weeks after that, on January 7, 1944, the JTA reported that "Bloom said he would support the bill, in committee and on the floor, despite his belief that it could accomplish little." Bloom noted that the American Jewish Conference believed the sponsors of the resolution had made "rash and exaggerated claims as to what [it would] accomplish," but said further discussion, or a vote, on the resolution would come up the following week.[47]

It never did, however. The Senate Foreign Relations Committee had approved an identical resolution two and a half weeks earlier on December 20, but Bloom was apparently stalling for time.[48] It probably didn't help matters that Harry Shulman, a representative of the American Jewish Conference, told Bloom on January 12 that his group opposed the creation of an American government rescue body (as opposed to a joint American-British body) that would work outside the framework of the ICR.[49] Another factor that probably kept Bloom from moving ahead was a suggestion by government official Oscar Cox to Bloom in late December that Roosevelt create a rescue body by executive order rather than congressional legislation. (Cox actually sent Bloom a draft of the executive order he had in mind, complete with an accompanying press release.[50]) In fact, at his January 12 meeting with Shulman, Bloom said, according to a record of the meeting, that "he had an executive order in his pocket" – probably the one Cox sent him – that would create a government rescue body that would meet the approval of the American Jewish Conference.[51]

Indeed, on January 22, Roosevelt rendered moot the debate over the congressional resolution when he signed an executive order establishing the War Refugee Board (thanks to the intervention of Treasury Secretary Henry Morgenthau, Jr., who convinced the president that the State Department was hindering rescue efforts). In his autobiography, Bloom praises the creation of this rescue agency,[52] but he certainly did little to help bring it to life. If anything, he tried killing it in utero. Nor was this the first time that Bloom tried obstructing the Bergson group's efforts. In 1942, Bloom seems to have hindered passage of a bill initiated by the group that called on Roosevelt to pressure England to allow Jewish units to form in Palestine that would fight alongside the Allies,[53] and in the fall of 1943, Bloom reportedly opposed the Bergson-led Rabbis' March in Washington urging greater government action to save European Jewry. According to Eri Jabotinsky (a member of the Bergson group), Bloom told one of the rabbis before the march plans had been finalized that "it would be very undignified for a group of such un-American looking people to appear in Washington."[54] (If Bloom opposed the march, though, he later changed his mind. He met the rabbis at the steps of the Capitol along with every other Jewish congressman and wrote to a friend shortly thereafter, "I know you will be pleased to know that the meeting the other day in front of the Capitol by the Rabbis was, to my way of thinking, a very successful affair. It was conducted in a most dignified manner and I am so happy to say that no one, no matter how critical he may be, could find anything to criticize at that meeting."[55])

Considering his love of the theatrical, Bloom should have appreciated – one would think – Bergson's dramatic flair in publicizing the plight of European Jewry, but as a U.S. congressman and close ally of the Roosevelt administration, Bloom held very different priorities than those of Bergson. One Bergson group member said years later that Bloom was "in a position to push the [Roosevelt] administration, but [was] afraid to do so."[56] The evidence suggests, however, not that Bloom was *afraid* to do so, but thought it *inappropriate* to do so – inappropriate to push for action that the men in charge of conducting the war weren't interesting in taking (especially if they said it would interfere with the war effort, which they frequently did). Bloom, after all, regarded himself as an American congressman above all else, which meant putting America's interests first.

He said as much in a 1939 letter: "My duty as I see it comes first as an American. All else whatever it may be is secondary."[57] He sounded a similar note during the hearings on the resolution: "I am 100 percent Jewish, but I am sitting here as an American. I am not occupying this chair as a Jew."[58] Other prominent Jews in America shared Bloom's sense of duty. For example, American Jewish Committee president Joseph Proskauer opposed vociferous Jewish protests against Nazi Germany in 1933 because it would harm the American economy. "We are Americans first and must be loyal above all else, to America," he said.[59] Wise testified in his autobiography that he "never voted as a Jew" in U.S. elections; he did so "always as an American."[60] These American Jewish leaders have been accused of fearing to pressure the American administration to rescue Jews lest they be seen as "less than loyal citizens of the United States."[61] It's more likely, though, that they thought it *wrong* to push for sectarian interests during wartime.

The Bergson group was not restricted by such considerations. The six founding members of the group were not American, but Palestinian. They had no allegiance to America and were not primarily concerned with America's interests in the war. They were concerned with the fate of European Jewry. Their *only* loyalty was to the Jewish people. Historian Judith Tydor Baumel writes, "As Palestinian Jewish nationals in a foreign land, [the Bergson group] did not feel themselves bound by the social, diplomatic, and emotional constraints governing patterns of interaction between local Jewish organizations and the American administration." That's why "they had no inhibitions about employing any and all means, even those seen as being exhibitionist, in order to forward what was for them a burning issue."[62]

Indeed, Bergson didn't even see himself as a Jew. He regarded himself as a member of the Hebrew nation and thus an unambiguous foreign national on American shores. Indeed, he explicitly distinguished Western Jews from people like himself. In a 1944 public statement, Bergson declared: "The Jews today who live in the European hell together with the Jews in the Land of Israel constitute the Hebrew nation.... We must state it clearly: the Jews in the United States do not belong to the Hebrew nation. These Jews are Americans of Hebrew descent."[63] Thus, advocating for the rescue of European Jewry was relatively simple for Bergson. It was not so simple for American Jews like Bloom who owed loyalty to the country whose pledge of allegiance they recited.[64]

Compounding the difficulty was the dominant cultural mood of the time. Whereas multiculturalism – and to some extent identity politics – is celebrated in 21st century America, for much of American history, it wasn't. "[I]ntegration was [thought to be] key to the realization of a pluralistic, democratic society,"[65] and American Jews felt "strong pressures of conformity."[66] In the 1940s, placing sectarian interests above those of the country – even thinking in terms of sectarian interests when it came to matters of national importance – was considered improper. Thus, lobbying for the American government to rescue Jews overseas while hundreds of thousands of American "boys" were in harm's way fighting Hitler struck many American Jews as unpatriotic and wrong.

Likely increasing Bloom's reluctance to push for efforts to rescue European Jewry was America's long tradition of non-interventionism in foreign affairs – a tradition that was often invoked in the leadup to America's entry in World War II. This tradition had its roots in George Washington's famous 1796 Farewell Address and was articulated most starkly by the country's sixth president, John Quincy Adams, who said: "[The United States] goes not abroad in search of monsters to destroy. She is the well-wisher to the freedom and independence of all. She is the champion and vindicator only of her own."[67] Over its history, the U.S. had on occasion interfered abroad for humanitarian reasons on a relatively small scale[68] and interfered abroad more fundamentally toward the end of the 19th century and beginning of the 20th century – especially by entering World War I and trying to reshape the world in its aftermath.[69] To a large extent, however, the U.S. re-embraced its traditional foreign policy after the war and "reverted to familiar and soothing isolationism," in the words of historian Arthur Schlesinger Jr.[70] It rejected calls to become a member of the League of Nations, it refused to join the World Court, it ignored the unprecedented crimes of Lenin and Stalin in the USSR in the 1920s and '30s, it said little when Japan bombed Shanghai in 1932, it didn't get involved in the Spanish Civil War of 1936-1939, and it didn't interfere to stop Japan's Rape of Nanking in 1937, during which anywhere from 100,000 to 300,000-plus Chinese were killed and tens of thousands raped.[71] Indeed, the 1930s arguably was the most isolationist decade in American history,[72] and the era's tenor likely influenced Bloom's behavior. Bloom was an interventionist, but even interventionists in this period based their position on what was best for America rather than humanitarian concerns. (They believed America needed to help Britain because "if Britain fell America would be the next to feel the power of Hitler's might," historian Wayne Cole notes.[73]) Saving European Jewry, however, was a purely humanitarian endeavor.[74]

Bloom's close ties with top officials in the Roosevelt administration like the president,[75] Hull,[76] and Long[77] also made it unlikely that he would take action that could be interpreted as a backhanded slap of the president. Bloom had fought in the political trenches with the administration in 1939 and 1941, and, by 1943, had only grown closer to it. That year, Isaiah Berlin referred to Bloom's "blind loyalty to the President's policies" in a report he wrote for the British Foreign Office.[78] Bloom's position as "one of the inner circle of House leaders close to the White House"[79] likely only solidified his loyalty. The New York Times reported that Bloom was one of just 11 congressmen with whom Roosevelt shared the Allies' war plans for 1943 "under a pledge of secrecy."[80] Thus, acting against the administration on the Bergson-backed resolution was not something Bloom

Chinese victims of the Rape of Nanking (1937-1938), one of several major interwar incidents in which the United States declined to involve itself.

could easily do. Indeed, Treasury Department official Ansel Luxford surmised that Bloom didn't want to report the resolution out of committee because "he probably feels that it will be a blow to the Administration to have this thing thrown out on to the Floor of the House and debated on the basis that it will be debated."[81] Cox shared this view, commenting that Bloom believed that it "would be a direct attack on the Administration, including the President, for having failed to act" to rescue Jews.[82]

Had Bloom been convinced of the importance of passing the resolution, he may have sought a way of supporting it without violating his sense of patriotic obligation. But he wasn't convinced – for several reasons. For one, he may not have appreciated the magnitude of the Holocaust – which would explain why Bloom tended to trivial affairs even while millions of Jews were being slaughtered in Europe. In July 1943, for example, he wrote to a colleague about helping get a young man admitted into Yale University.[83] Two months earlier, shortly before he left to the Bermuda Conference, Bloom sought the advice of Columbia University President Nicholas Murray Butler on whether he should write his autobiography.[84] In June 1944, he took the time to write to the War Production Board asking it to grant the Manischewitz food company permission to buy another car.[85] M.J. Nurenberger – a Yiddish journalist who considered Bloom a "personal friend" in "certain respects" – wrote about him 40 years later: "[H]e remained the little man who liked to help people, do favors for constituents and obtain visas for would-be immigrants…. Bloom could not visualize the full extent of the slaughter overseas. His limited vision of history did not allow him to perceive the macabre picture of the millions locked in Hitler's Fortress Europe."[86]

But Bloom was hardly alone in this respect. Decades after the war, William Casey, chief of the OSS intelligence in Europe, wrote: "We knew in a general way that the Jews were being persecuted…and that brutality and murder took place in these camps. But few if any comprehended the appalling magnitude of it."[87] Thus, for example, an organization like the Vaad Hahatzala did not initially change its focus when it learned that Hitler was exterminating all of European Jewry; it continued to concentrate on saving a small group of yeshiva students and their teachers.[88] Many synagogue newsletters also didn't reflect the horrors of the Holocaust. In the middle of the Warsaw Ghetto Uprising, for example, Manhattan's West

Side Institutional Synagogue announced a "fascinating guest speaker" at the synagogue's next Women's League meeting. The topic? The "Personal and Social Life of the Chinese People."[89] A later installment of the newsletter – its December 8, 1944 issue – announced "a very fine program" for its "Metropolitan Opera Concert Sunday evening."[90] Another Manhattan synagogue, meanwhile, Kehilath Jeshurun, held a theater party as well as an "Annual Smoker" for men in January 1944.[91] Indeed, while millions of Jews were being exterminated in Europe, Bloom received requests from several prominent rabbinic families to help them with personal favors. He was asked, for example, to help the daughter of Rabbi Chaim Heller secure a job as a censor in the Post Office[92]; to help get a commission in the army (and later a job at the Board of Economic Warfare) for Dr. Samuel Soloveichik, brother of Rabbi Joseph B. Soloveitchik[93]; to help the son of Dr. Bernard Revel, president of Yeshiva College, become Chief of the Semitic Division at the Library of Congress[94]; and to help the son-in-law of Rabbi Wolf Gold, head of Mizrachi, get a commission in the army in the field of camouflage, poster illustration, or propaganda.[95]

So it's possible Bloom didn't appreciate the extent or the seriousness of the Holocaust,[96] but, if so, he's in the company of many other good people who arguably should have known better.[97] Perhaps, as historian Jeffrey Gurock and others suggest, "the unbelievable details and extent of the atrocities" were simply too much for

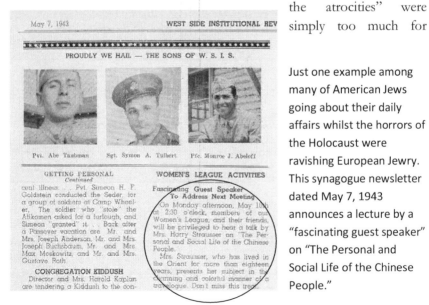

Just one example among many of American Jews going about their daily affairs whilst the horrors of the Holocaust were ravishing European Jewry. This synagogue newsletter dated May 7, 1943 announces a lecture by a "fascinating guest speaker" on "The Personal and Social Life of the Chinese People."

them to grasp.[98]   It's also possible that Bloom and many others truly believed the quickest way to save the greatest number of Jews was to win the war as quickly as possible.   Much of the Jewish press apparently held this belief, as did most American Jewish leaders.[99]   Some Holocaust historians dismiss this assumption as self-evidently ridiculous.   It's not clear why, though. Historian Gerhard L. Weinberg notes that thousands of Jews died every day of the war, arguing that even a delay of one "week or ten days" in the war's conclusion would have resulted in more deaths than "the total number of Jews saved by the various rescue efforts in 1943-1945."[100]

Also likely influencing Bloom's attitude toward the Bergson-backed resolution was the stance of America's mainstream Jewish leaders, to which Bloom – both as a U.S. congressman and as a Jew – undoubtedly gave considerable weight.   At the hearings on the resolution, Wise – who represented mainstream American Jewish organizational life – claimed to support it, but he also didn't want it passed as written.   Others actively lobbied against it.   On the day the Senate Foreign Relations Committee voted on the same resolution that Bloom's committee was considering in the House, one senator remarked, "I wish these damned Jews would make up their minds what they want. I could not get inside the committee room without being buttonholed out here in the corridor by representatives who said that the Jewish people of America did not want the passage of this resolution."[101]

Bloom knew Wise since at least 1924. That year, Bloom sought his endorsement for his reelection bid – which Wise granted[102] – and also asked him after his victory "for the benefit of [his] advice during the coming session of the House." In the same letter, Bloom wrote, "If at any time you should think of something that would be of interest to our Country and to our people, I would consider it a great personal favor if you would advise me so that I can present same for the consideration of the House. I also want you to feel that you can always call upon me to serve you in any way possible."[103] Wise did call on Bloom for favors over the years, and Bloom obliged him.[104] In 1936, he also sent Wise an extremely warm letter, in which he wrote, among other things, "[Y]ou are just as good a Jew as I have ever met in my life."[105]   Considering their longstanding relationship and Wise's leadership position in American Jewish life, Bloom was likely inclined to listen to Wise when it came to Jewish matters, and he treated him very cordially when he testified before the Foreign Affairs Committee about the resolution.[106]

Bloom was a people pleaser and may have been more partial to the resolution had American Jewry stood united behind it, but it was divided. Indeed, historian Henry Feingold writes that American "Jews did not find agreement on a single issue during the Holocaust."[107] Bloom himself complained about this disunity. In mid-1943, he wrote to a friend, "I do wish that something could be done so as not to have so many different factions among the Jewish people fighting between themselves."[108] And after the war, in response evidently to a query about uniting different Jewish organizations in America, Bloom wrote, "I have been trying to do this for years, but that is impossible; every person wants to be a General…nobody wants to be a Private."[109]

Finally, Bloom may have been less than helpful to the Bergson group because of a flaw in his character: pettiness. In May, the Bergson group had publicly slammed the Bermuda Conference as a "cruel mockery," and Bloom almost certainly had not forgotten this attack.[110] Bloom was generally, as noted earlier, a jovial man who loved doing people favors.[111] In his autobiography, Bloom boasts: "for more than a quarter of a century, at an average rate of fifty a day, people have been coming to my offices in Washington and New York with problems of every conceivable nature. These people are white and colored, Democrats and Republicans, Jews and Protestants and Catholics. All of them are treated alike." Helping these people was a "privilege," he writes. "And my reward – the opportunity to go on helping people in this way – has been very great indeed."[112] In his memoir, congressional doorkeeper William "Fishbait" Miller relates this anecdote about Bloom:

> Back in the early 1930s, a penny was a coin that bought a big chunk of candy, like a licorice whip. Sol would walk up the steps of the Capitol every morning, strewing pennies, nickels and dimes along his path like Hansel and Gretel had done with crumbs in the fairy tale. He tried to be inconspicuous, but I caught him at it and asked him what he was doing. He said, "Shhhh. Let the little children find them when they come to see the Capitol. In

this Depression, someone has to show them that good things can happen."[113]

In his profile of Bloom in *Tales of San Francisco*, author Samuel Dickson calls Bloom "the man who had infinite compassion for the suffering of underdog humanity."[114] Isidore Grossman, president of the Tomche Torah society, wrote to Bloom, "From personal knowledge we know you have dried the tears of thousands of families who came to you for help in their need."[115] Every year on his birthday, Bloom organized parties in several orphanages and homes for the elderly.[116] Bloom took great pride in helping people. "To me it is a trust," he wrote in 1948, "to be in a position where I might be able to help even a little bit."[117]

Yet, Bloom could also be petty.[118] For example, Charles Burton Marshall, a staff consultant on the Foreign Affairs Committee, related that when the Democrats regained control of the House of the Representatives in November 1948, Bloom fired all professional staff who had been hired during the previous two years when Republicans controlled the Foreign Affairs Committee. But the committee wouldn't let Bloom fire Marshall. As a result, "Bloom never spoke to [him] again," Marshall recalled. "I'd meet him in the elevator and he would not say, 'Good morning.' He'd look the other way."[119] Rep. Will Rogers, Jr. had a similar experience with Bloom after he started associating with the Bergson group.[120] An anecdote by Durward Sandifer captures well both elements of Bloom's character – his impulse to help people (his emotional largesse, if you will) and his pettiness. Sandifer was secretary general of the U.S. delegation to the 1945 San Francisco Conference – which included Bloom – at which

A cheerful Sol Bloom.

the Charter of the United Nations was drafted. He relates the following:

> I didn't really take hold of the distribution of tickets to the American delegation for the opening session of the conference. What resulted was a lot of dissatisfaction on the part of people like Bloom. He was a key person who had a lot of clients that he wanted to take care of and, being chairman of the Foreign Affairs Committee of the House, he had a very considerable sense of pride and prestige. ... I made up my mind that when it came to the *closing* session that this was not going to happen. One of my assistants and I spent hours and hours getting hold of a sufficient number of tickets.... I sent the tickets down to Bloom's office about 10 or 11 o'clock at night and within 15 minutes I got a telephone call. Bloom on the line himself. He said, "Mr. Sandifer, I want you to know how much I appreciate the way you treated us in these tickets." He said, "This is wonderful. If there is ever anything you want from the Foreign Affairs Committee, or Sol Bloom, you just let me know, and you'll get it." And I did. I didn't try to cash in on that too often, but he was very receptive and helpful from then on.[121]

The Bergson group had criticized the Bermuda Conference, and the resolution itself was an implicit criticism of the conference – and by extension Bloom. After all, if a new rescue body was needed, that meant the recommendation at the Bermuda Conference to revive the ICR had been insufficient. Bloom may not have had it in him to swallow his pride and ignore this attack on his record. Thus, he followed the lode star that appears to have governed all major steps he took since 1939 – patriotism – and approached the Bergson-backed resolution with the overarching aim of protecting his commander in chief who was leading a world war against the greatest enemy Western democracy has ever faced.[122]

* * * * *

Bloom never embraced the Bergson group. In mid-1944, for

example, he warned John Pehle, director of the War Refugee Board, not to align his operation too closely with it. Pehle recalls Bloom being "hot under the collar" and said Bloom "was worried about the [Bergson group] because they have attacked him very heavily" in the past.[123]   Bloom apparently even wished to deport Bergson from the U.S. "on the grounds that [his] militant activities 'would eventually provoke sufficient antagonism among the citizens of the United States to cause anti-Semitic pogroms.'"[124] Bloom, however, modified his attitude toward rescue efforts shortly before D-Day when victory for the Allies was clearly in sight.   At that point, rescuing Jews had also become official U.S. policy and the Bergson group was no longer involved in it. (After the WRB's creation, the Bergson group shifted focus, pursuing Zionist activism.)   Bloom could thus in good conscience as a leading American congressman call for rescuing Jews. On June 21, 1944, in what the Associated Press termed "a highly unusual action," the Foreign affairs Committee – after hearing testimony from WRB director John Pehle – issued a statement calling on Hungary to "stem the tide of inhumanity toward the helpless [Jews] within her borders."[125] Two days later, the committee passed a resolution – submitted by Bloom – expressing "its deep concern over the plight of the threatened millions in Nazi-occupied and Nazi-dominated territories" and its "approval of the activities of the War Refugee Board."   It declared, "[T]he House of Representatives is not content merely to join with those who have expressed their horror at the barbarism of the governments involved" in exterminating Jews and others in Europe. Rather, it:

> expresses its determination that the criminals who are guilty of this inhuman conduct shall be brought to justice, and hereby requests the Secretary of State to convey, through such means as he may find appropriate, this concern and determination of the House of Representatives…. [which] is particularly directed to Hungary, where the lives of a million Jews hang in the balance.

That same day,[126] Bloom introduced another resolution calling on

Secretary of State Cordell Hull to urge "the Government of Turkey in the interests of humanity [to] facilitate the entry into Turkey of refugees who can escape from the Nazis, and establish in Turkey a refugee camp in which such persons can be temporarily sheltered." The resolution noted that "there are great opportunities for the evacuation of refugees from the Balkan countries through Turkey of which full advantage has not been taken." In a letter to Treasury Secretary Henry Morgenthau, Pehle argued that "[b]oth of these resolutions, whether or not approved by the House, will be very useful in the work which we are doing with OWI [Office of War Information]."[127] Hull sent the text of the first resolution to American officials in England, Turkey, Spain, Portugal, Sweden, and Switzerland with the instruction: "You are requested to convey the contents of this resolution to the appropriate authorities and to use all possible means to give the resolution the widest possible publicity, particularly in Europe.... In addition, through such channels as may be available to you, this action of the House of Representatives should be brought to the attention of the Hungarian Government."[128] He sent the text of the second resolution to the U.S. ambassador in Turkey, Laurence Steinhardt, with the direction that it "should be given local publicity and may be used by you in bringing further pressure on the Turkish government."[129]

According to the American Legation in Bern, Switzerland, the "Swiss press published the [Hungary] resolution widely," and a "copy for possible transmission to Hungary was furnished to a leading Hungarian." The Turkey resolution ultimately died in committee after Ambassador Steinhardt argued that it contained inaccuracies and opened the U.S. to criticism for not taking more action itself to rescue Jews.[130] Based on Steinhardt's arguments, Pehle sent a letter to Bloom asking him to take no "further action" on the resolution since it "is no longer necessary in the interests of refugees and might perhaps have detrimental effects."[131] Bloom acceded to this request.[132] A week later, though, Bloom wrote to Pehle about another rescue proposal, asking him what he thought of a resolution introduced in his committee that called on Roosevelt and Hull to set up "mass emergency rescue shelters" for Jews in Palestine.[133] Pehle responded that he couldn't really comment until the facts on the ground in Europe become clearer and also noted that the proposed camps' location in Palestine "involves complicated political considerations."[134]

Thus, while Bloom had not helped Bergson create a government agency, he did work with it in trying to rescue Jews – not just quietly via diplomatic connections, but through public legislative action – once the outcome of the war was certain, the Bergson group was out of the way, and rescue had officially become part of the administration's agenda. At that point, to promote rescue resolutions was to further the administration's aims rather than frustrate them and Bloom could therefore do so as a patriotic American congressman.

~ CHAPTER 9 ~

THE ZIONISTS COME TO CONGRESS

Rescue activists were not the only ones pushing Bloom to take legislative action he felt inappropriate during a world war. American Zionists acted similarly in seeking to advance a congressional resolution calling for unrestricted Jewish immigration to Palestine and a Jewish state. Bloom responded to them as he had the rescue activists – by attempting to please while ultimately doing what he thought best for his country. Two key differences, however, distinguish the Zionist effort from that of the Bergson group: 1) it was backed by almost all of organized American Jewry; 2) it came later in the war when Allied victory was more assured. Yet, despite these facts, and despite Bloom's desire to satisfy American Jewish leaders, he only helped them fully in late 1944 when U.S. victory over the Nazis was nigh at hand and the administration had softened its opposition to the Zionist agenda. Before that point, Bloom once again put the wishes of the administration first.

In lobbying Congress in late 1943, the Bergson group had aimed to rescue Jews in Nazi-occupied Europe. Mainstream American Zionist leaders, however, had a much larger goal in mind: the "absolute end to the persecution which had plagued the Jewish people for two thousand years." And to achieve that end, they believed the establishment of a Jewish state necessary.[1] "Fundamentally, the root of [anti-Semitism is] that the Jewish people [are] a national homeless people in the world and the only solution for national homelessness is a national home," said Rabbi Abba Hillel Silver, chairman of the executive committee of the American Zionist Emergency Council, in testimony before Congress.[2]

At New York's Biltmore Hotel in May 1942, Zionist leaders "resolved to [put] a permanent end to anti-Semitism by initiating a well organized campaign in support of a Jewish commonwealth."[3] They knew that doing so might mean "that mass meetings protesting the Nazi massacres would have to stop."[4] They also knew rescue proposals might suffer as a result,[5] but their "fight was not only against Hitler but against a world order that had for two thousand years condemned the Jewish people to murder and hatred."[6] Creating a Jewish state was, in effect, their long-term rescue proposal.[7] And so they pushed for it, sometimes without regard to shorter-term rescue proposals.

On January 27, 1944 – thanks to activism by the American Zionist Emergency Council – two identical resolutions (numbers 418 and 419) were introduced in the House of Representatives calling on the United States to "use its good offices and take appropriate measures to the end that the doors of Palestine shall be opened for free entry of Jews into that country, and that there shall be full opportunity for colonization, so that the Jewish people may ultimately reconstitute Palestine as a free and democratic Jewish commonwealth."[8] The immediate impetus for the resolutions' introduction was an impending deadline: March 31, 1944. On the eve of World War II, England had issued a policy paper – known as the White Paper of 1939 – that capped Jewish immigration to Palestine at 75,000 over the ensuing five years.[9] By early 1944, however, only 45,000 Jews had made it to Palestine, so England decided to allow an additional 30,000 Jews to enter Palestine after March 31.[10] No additional Jews, however, would be permitted to immigrate to Palestine after that

Attendees at a seminal Zionist conference at the Biltmore Hotel in New York City in 1942. Participants included prominent Zionist leaders like David Ben-Gurion, Chaim Weizmann, and Nahum Goldmann.

date without Arab approval.

When resolutions 418 and 419 (hereafter "the resolution) were sent to the Foreign Affairs Committee, Bloom's initial inclination was not to hold hearings on them. He told a State Department official that he would gather his committee, "merely read Prime Minister Churchill's statement [in 1939] objecting to the White Paper; and then report the resolution out favorably and let it go at that."[11]   Bloom, however, ultimately held hearings on the resolution over the course of four days in February.[12] Perhaps as a result of his antagonistic behavior less than three months earlier when the committee had considered the creation of a government rescue commission, members of the press had heard "many rumors prior to the hearings that [Bloom] was opposed to the resolution."[13]   But Bloom turned out to be "a very pleasant surprise," wrote one reporter. He not "only supported the resolution, but on numerous occasions he was able to use his prerogative as chairman in ironing out an embarrassing situation, or in reminding a [pro-Zionist] witness of a particularly helpful document."[14]   Bloom even compiled a 100-page booklet for the hearings, which one government observer called "extremely pro-Jewish in its treatment of the Palestine question."[15]   Indeed, fully three-quarters of it featured criticism of the White Paper (while the other quarter contained relevant primary documents).

Twice during the hearings, Bloom pointed out that he was giving equal time to both supporters and opponents of the resolution. "I do not want the thought to go out that we are not fair in dividing the time for the witnesses," he said on day three of the hearings.[16] But while Bloom may have allocated time fairly during the last two days of the hearings, he did not do so during the first two days. Moreover, he was hardly a neutral conductor of the hearings; as historian Richard Stevens notes, there was "no doubt as to the cause Bloom supported, and, indeed, eagerly wished to appear as supporting."[17]   Several times during the hearings, he actually directly challenged people testifying against the resolution.   On three separate occasions, he brought up a U.S.-U.K. agreement signed by President Calvin Coolidge, which many Zionists believed prohibited the U.K. from altering the conditions of its mandate over Palestine without first receiving U.S. approval. "Would you not say that that [agreement]…in its entirety should be lived up to by the signatories of that convention?" he asked one anti-Zionist rabbi during the hearings.[18] Another anti-Zionist witness, Faris S. Malouf, president of the Syrian and Lebanese American Federation of the Eastern States, said Zionist leaders were "shrewd" for eliciting the Balfour Declaration from England while it "was fighting with its back against the wall." Bloom protested, "[T]here are so many things in your statement as to the Jews I object to.... You called them shrewd Zionist leaders. I think Dr. [Chaim] Weizmann and all of those people did not do anything improper, and they were working for something the Jews have been praying for for thousands of years, and I think it is wrong to put in the record that these people were shrewd."[19]

To another anti-Zionist witness who accused the Jews of seeking to transfer the Arabs out of Palestine, Bloom interjected to make sure the committee knew that the official Zionist movement had never tendered this proposal. That same witness accused the Zionists of dispossessing Arabs by buying their lands. "They sold it of their own free will," Bloom interjected. At another juncture, he asked Emanuel Neumann to make clear for the record that Jews had not bombed a mosque in 1929:

> Dr. NEUMANN: ...For example, the riots of 1929 in Palestine were started by spreading a wild rumor that the Jews had bombed a mosque in Jerusalem.
>
> Chairman BLOOM: Have they done it?
>
> Dr. NEUMANN: They have other things to do.
>
> Chairman BLOOM: I know the answer.
>
> Dr. NEUMANN: I am sure you all know it.
>
> Chairman BLOOM: But you had better have the record show.
>
> Dr. NEUMANN: The Jews never bombed any mosque. Of course, it's absurd.[20]

On another occasion, Bloom evidently wished to suggest that no violence would erupt in the Middle East should the resolution pass, so when one Zionist witness pointed out that 260 members of Congress signed a pro-Zionist statement in 1942, Bloom asked sarcastically, "There were no riots after that statement?"[21] In responding to another witness, an agricultural expert, Bloom seemingly wished to highlight the impressive nature of the Zionist project, so he asked, "Have you found any other part of the world in all of your travels inspecting farms and so forth in which there is anything comparable to what the Jews have done in Palestine so far as the cultivation of the soil is concerned?"[22] At another juncture, Bloom apparently forgot his position as chairman of the committee and refers to the Zionist cause as his own: "Now *we* are only saying this, *we* would like to have the things we have already agreed upon carried out" (emphasis added). Perhaps Bloom's most biased statement, though, came during the opening minutes of the hearings when a colleague asked him who authored the resolution. Bloom responded, "The author of the idea goes back 2,000 years, if I remember."[23]

Bloom earned much praise from Zionist quarters for his handling of the hearings. Rabbi Abba Hillel Silver, for example, wrote to him on February 19, three days after the hearings concluded, "I have just returned home and I regard it as my first pleasant duty to write to you and to tell you how grateful I am and my friends are to you for the superb manner in which you conducted the historic hearings on the Palestine Resolution. No one who attended those hearings could fail to be impressed by your unfailing fairness, courtesy and good humor."[24] Another Zionist leader, Louis Lipsky, wrote to him, "I need not say how deeply all of us appreciate – and especially myself – the admirably fair and genial way you conducted the hearings during the entire proceedings. You have created a tremendous amount of good will toward you which you earned during these trying days."[25]

Bloom's conduct during the hearings was not entirely surprising. He had, in fact, been a longtime supporter of Zionism.

Rabbi Abba Hillel Silver (1893-1963)

"From the time of the Balfour Declaration, in November, 1917, which promised a home for the Jewish people in Palestine, I have been an earnest and public advocate of that promise's fulfillment," he writes in his autobiography.[26] In a statement he inserted in the Congressional Record, Bloom recalls, "Palestine and the love of Zion were…a part of the life and thinking of my family. … From my earliest childhood, which goes back more than 70 years, I recall having repeated with [my parents] the age-old prayer 'L'shono Habo B'Yerusholayim' (next year in Jerusalem)." He took pride in the fact that his family had contributed to the United Charity Institutions in Jerusalem since 1894 and noted that he was a board member of several institutions in the holy land.[27] It's not clear if he ever visited Palestine,[28] but in the 1920s and '30s, Bloom was associated with various Palestine organizations and projects such as the United Palestine Appeal,[29] the United Galil Aid Society of New York,[30] the Maccabean Festival,[31] and the Jewish National Fund.[32] He was also one of just four Jewish signatories on, and presenters of, a 1930 memorandum to the British colonial secretary that expressed "regret that recent events have seriously shaken the confidence of the Jews of [their] countries in Great Britain." The memorandum – submitted by Jewish members of the legislatures of Poland, Latvia, South Africa, and the U.S. – called on England to fulfill its promise to secure a national home in Palestine for the Jewish people.[33] Eight years later, Bloom signed a petition asking Roosevelt to urge England to keep the doors of Palestine open to Jewish immigration,[34] and in 1939, Bloom protested the White Paper.[35]

But although Bloom was a Zionist, he was first and foremost a high-ranking member of a government at war with Nazi Germany. Therefore, in deciding whether to help American Zionists during World War II, Bloom had to consider the same question that arose in relation to rescuing European Jews: Would it hamper the war effort? And if the answer to this question was yes, did the benefit of ignoring this fact outweigh the grave cost? In his autobiography, Bloom writes:

> When I am certain that my course is right, I am ready to proceed without thinking in terms of losing friends and making enemies. But there are so many things in life,

especially in public life, that cannot be decided on simple terms of "right" and "wrong." Most of the time I find that the "right" thing is looked upon also as "wrong" in other quarters. I know of no touchstone. To paraphrase Oscar Wilde's epigram on truth, Right is seldom pure and never simple.[36]

For American Zionist leaders like Abba Hillel Silver, Zionism was an urgent existential cause; it was the permanent solution to anti-Semitism. Bloom likely saw it, however, as did the average American Zionist in his era, "primarily as a philanthropic ideal."[37] Indeed, a May 11, 1943 letter by Bloom makes clear that his vision of the Jewish future differed greatly from Silver's. In response to a suggestion that a Jewish settlement be created in Brazil, Bloom writes:

> Why should not the Jews be permitted to live in the countries that they have been living in for centuries and in the countries in which they are accustomed to live?
>
> Why should not the [Allies] in their peace conference guarantee equal rights to all nationals of all countries? If that guarantee could be brought about by the [Allies] would not that solve the problem of the Jews in Poland, in Czechoslovakia, in Italy, in Holland, in Belgium and in all other countries throughout the world?
>
> Why not ask for that which we are entitled to instead of seeking places to live in that we do not want to live in. The Jews have their rights the same as other people of all countries. Why not try and see that those rights are guaranteed to us? This is my idea. That is what I have been working for and I honestly believe that I am right.[38]

Considering Bloom's beliefs about the Jewish future, it's no wonder that he thought Zionists were inappropriately pushing their agenda while Hitler threatened to destroy Western civilization.[39] Thus, in May 1939, he objected – according to a State Department memo – to "high-pressure publicity tactics" that he believed Wise and other Zionists were employing to push the State Department to "take action of dubious propriety with the British Government."[40]   In early 1943, Vice President Henry Wallace complained to Bloom about an unpleasant conversation he had with Rabbi Meir Berlin, a leader of the Mizrachi movement, during which Rabbi Berlin pressed him for a message of Zionist support he could convey to the Jews of Palestine.   Bloom responded, according to Wallace's diary, "that the Zionists were troublemakers; if I had any more trouble with fellows like Rabbi Berlin to send them over to him."[41]   Bloom tried to protect the administration from Zionist activity in late 1943 as well.   On October 5, two sons of the Saudi Arabian king were scheduled to visit the U.S., and the State Department told Bloom it wished to avoid Zionist attacks against them during their visit.   Bloom conveyed this message to his fellow Jewish congressmen and asked Nahum Goldmann of the World Zionist Congress to speak to the Jewish press and to Rep. Emanuel Celler who refused to accede to the State Department's wishes.[42]

For its part, the administration objected to vigorous Zionist activity during the war for relatively straightforward reasons.   It didn't want to upset England while the two countries were fighting together to defeat the Nazis. Furthermore, the U.K. had stressed to the U.S. that advancing the Zionist cause during the war could undercut the fight against Hitler.   During a congressional hearing in November 1943, one witness dismissed a query on whether Arabs in Palestine desired more Jewish immigration as a "question of politics."   Charles Eaton, the highest-ranking Republican on the committee, responded, "The question of politics in that country immediately assumes the form of a bayonet, so we have to face the realities of the situation."[43] As Eaton explained to another witness:

> Great Britain is involved in a life and death struggle, as we
> are too.   And you understand, of course, the Moslem
> situation.   I imagine in the background of their thinking
> and acting is the fear that letting in a lot of Jews into
> Palestine might result in a Moslem uprising, which might
> penetrate into the unsettled conditions in India, where
> there is a Moslem-Hindu conflict, and lead to one of the

supreme world tragedies.... [They would probably like] to
defer a conflagration of that kind until the present world
conflagration is settled.[44]

Indeed, the American and British governments had actually
contemplated issuing a joint statement the previous year (on July 27, 1943)
declaring that they had "taken note of public discussions and activities of a
political nature relating to Palestine and consider that it would be helpful to
the war effort if these were to cease." They argued it is not "essential that a
settlement of the Palestine question be achieved prior to the conclusion of
the war."[45]   Bloom was shown this statement plus "certain important
reports...regarding the serious military situation in the Middle East" and
reportedly was "in full accord with the proposed statement and even
suggested that it should be strengthened."   He also advised that a
government official meet with Jewish leaders "to explain to them in
advance the military necessity" of issuing the statement.[46]

Bloom's attitude toward Zionism in general (as a valuable but non-
existential cause) and his knowledge of the administration's attitude toward
Zionist activity during World War II more specifically (as harmful to
prosecuting the war) ultimately determined the fate of resolutions 418 and
419. American Zionists knew of the administration's concerns and tried to
address them at the hearings.   For example, some of the pro-Zionist
witnesses – which included 30 members of Congress[47] – argued that the
Allies had nothing to fear from the Arabs. "[I]f they are faced with a firm
and determined policy, they will back down," said Harvard Professor Carl J.
Friedrich.[48] They also argued that the Arabs – unlike the Jews of Palestine
– had not helped the Allies during the war and therefore did not deserve
their support.[49] The administration, however, was not convinced. In his
memoirs, Secretary of State Cordell Hull recalled:

At the State Department we felt that the passage of these
resolutions, although not binding on the Executive, might
precipitate conflict in Palestine and other parts of the Arab
world, endangering American troops and requiring the
diversion of forces from European and other combat
areas.   It might prejudice or shatter pending negotiations

with [Saudi Arabia's King] Ibn Saud for the construction of a pipeline across Saudi Arabia, which our military leaders felt was of utmost importance to our security.[50]

Reflecting this line of thinking, Secretary of War Henry Stimson sent Bloom a letter on March 17, 1944, stating that "it is the considered judgment of the War Department that without reference to the merits of these resolutions, further action on them at this time would be prejudicial to the successful prosecution of the war."[51] This letter made Bloom's subsequent behavior almost certain: He wasn't going to support a resolution that the war secretary opposed in the middle of a global conflagration. The letter Stimson sent Bloom on March 17 came a month after he had sent a similar letter to Senator Tom Connally, chairman of the Senate foreign Relations Committee, objecting to an identical resolution in the Senate: "I feel that the passage of this resolution at the present time…would be apt to provoke dangerous repercussions in areas where we have many vital military interests. Any conflict between Jews and Arabs would require the retention of troops in the affected areas and thus reduce the total forces that could otherwise be placed in combat against Germany."[52]

In a February 19 memo to Hull, Under Secretary of State Edward Stettinius, Jr., wrote that he discussed Stimson's letter with President Roosevelt, and both agreed that "the War Department would try first to kill the resolution by executive session [i.e., secret] testimony by Army representatives." If that wasn't successful, Stimson would "give consideration to making his letter public."[53] Just a week later, on February 26, Stettinius could already report to the

Sol Bloom and Secretary of War Henry Stimson (1867-1950).

U.S. minister in Iraq that it "now appears unlikely that the Palestine Resolutions will be reported out of either the Senate or the House committee."[54] Assistant Secretary of War John McCloy wrote to Assistant Secretary of State Breckinridge Long that same day enclosing a memorandum he had prepared on the topic, whose contents, he told Bloom, would form the basis of his testimony should he be asked to appear before the Foreign Affairs Committee. The document lists five deleterious effects that passage of the resolution might have on U.S. military efforts. After listing them, McCloy writes, "I do not intend to exaggerate the consequences which would flow from the adoption of this resolution as I can not be certain that all these results will flow, but from the foregoing considerations I think it is quite apparent that from a military point of view we would much prefer to let such sleeping dogs lie."[55]

Bloom hoped that officials at the War Department could amend the resolution in such a manner that would satisfy them,[56] but didn't seem to make much headway.[57] Bloom also suggested an alternate resolution text to Elihu Stone and Leon Feuer of the American Zionist Emergency Council during a meeting on February 21. He showed them Stimson's letter and suggested they eliminate or modify the portion of the resolution calling for a Jewish commonwealth. When they objected that it was "the heart and soul of the measure," he proposed altering the end of the resolution so that it read something like "…so that when the Jewish people shall attain a majority in Palestine, they shall reconstitute Palestine as a free and democratic commonwealth."[58] They were puzzled at how this alternate text would meet the approval of the Foreign Affairs Committee, but Bloom responded that they should "please leave that matter to him." Elihu Stone, who described the meeting in a memo to Abba Hillel Silver, noted, "It was the considered judgment of Mr. Bloom that unless some kind of modification is permitted with reference to the last clause of the Resolution, the views of the War Department will be upheld by the majority of the Committee." He noted that "Mr. Bloom took great pains to make his own position clear to us that he is ready and willing to go along with us," but he asked them to be flexible on the resolution's wording.[59]

No progress, however, was evidently made on this front, and on March 9, both Silver and Wise met with Roosevelt, hoping to secure his endorsement of the resolution. The president at first berated the two, asking them "Do you want to start a Holy Jihad?"[60] But he did permit them to say in his name "that the American government has never given its approval to the White Paper of 1939" and that "when future decisions are reached, full justice will be done to those who seek a Jewish National Home, for which our government and the American people have always had the deepest sympathy."[61] Roosevelt didn't endorse the resolution, however, and, as mentioned above, Stimson subsequently sent Bloom a shortened version of the letter he had sent Connally in early February. On March 17, McCloy testified before the Foreign Affairs Committee in a closed session, and that same day, Bloom released Stimson's second letter to the public, declaring that in light of it "action upon the resolutions at this time would be unwise."[62]

The move apparently caught some leading Zionists by surprise, and in a long letter to Bloom on May 4, Louis Lipsky of the Zionist Organization of America wrote (using language, verbatim, that Silver had supplied to him), "The general impression now being circulated [in Zionist circles] is that while you seemed to favor the resolution, you were in fact working all the while for its defeat." He also complained that "the unexpected vote in Committee, coming a few days after [the pro-Zionist] statement [from Roosevelt] and before we Zionists had a chance to capitalize on it politically in London and in Jerusalem, almost nullified the great value of the President's utterance." Lipsky urged Bloom to report the resolution out of committee and – more importantly – to secure a clear pro-Zionist statement from Roosevelt (who had made an ambivalent comment about Zionism in late March). Otherwise, Lipsky wrote, Silver and others will feel compelled to attack Roosevelt. "I am personally convinced that there will break out a veritable storm of criticism and indignation against the administration, which, you can readily understand, both you and I would regard as being highly undesirable in the critical months ahead [of an election year]," he wrote.[63] Two days later, Bloom responded to this letter in a somewhat evasive fashion, perhaps trying to avoid criticizing Roosevelt:

> …I am just as sympathetic to the cause of which you are so ardent a supporter…
>
> Similarly, it goes without saying that I stand ready in any way within my power, to serve and to be helpful. Just how

far I or anyone, for that matter, can give you an assurance of ability to procure a statement from the President – "clear and definitive" as you phrase it, on the rights of the Jewish people under the Mandate – I am unable to say.

The willingness to help is mine. The outcome rests elsewhere.[64]

Lipsky responded by asking Bloom to speak to Roosevelt personally and to report out resolutions 418 and 419 favorably no later than July 1.[65] In a meeting between the two of them four days later, Bloom voiced a refrain he would use repeatedly over the next half year. As Lipsky reported to Silver: "[Bloom] said that he was willing to do anything we asked of him." Bloom didn't think the resolution would pass if it were "brought up at any time before the invasion [i.e., D-Day], or during the sharpest period of the invasion," but he said he would do whatever the Zionist leaders wanted.[66] In June, Silver wrote to both Lipsky and Rabbi Israel Goldstein of the Synagogue Council of America, urging them to pressure Bloom, who was up for re-election in November. To the former, he wrote:

> Please keep him on the anxious seat. Make him realize that there is a determined group of voters in his district who are very suspicious and resentful of his attitude and who in the months before the election will be watching very carefully his conduct in relation to the resolution.... Bloom should not come to feel, as unfortunately most democratic candidates have been made to feel, that they have the Jewish and Zionist votes in their vest-pocket.[67]

To Goldstein, Silver wrote that Bloom is "still the key man in the entire situation" and Zionists in his district "should tell him that they are making their endorsement conditional upon his piloting the [Palestine] Resolution through the Foreign Affairs Committee." Silver complained that Bloom was misleading the public by publishing thank-you letters that he, Goldstein, and others had sent Bloom in the immediate aftermath of the hearings when Bloom "seemed to be playing ball with [them]."[68] These letters appeared at the back of a 500-page publication that included the official transcript of the hearings and Bloom's 100-page booklet. The publication, which Bloom distributed to key figures in the Jewish community, came out in May and earned him much praise.[69] Silver, though, wasn't impressed. He was upset with Bloom for "rush[ing] through the action of deferment in the Foreign Affairs Committee when he had given [the American Zionist leadership] the clear promise that no action would be taken" and asked Goldstein to apply pressure on Bloom.[70] On June 26, Goldstein, Rabbi Stephen Wise, Rabbi Wolf Gold (of Mizrachi), and two others met with Bloom to discuss the resolution, and Bloom gave them the same reply he had given Lipsky in late May (and two others in the weeks following): "he would bring up the Resolution again at any time that [they] wished."[71] Bloom objected to the words "free immigration" in the resolution, arguing that people are "very sensitive" to such a phrase but said "he would definitely push the Resolution as it stood and would vote for it unamended."[72]

Mid-October 1944 was a turning point for the American Zionist effort: Secretary of War Stimson withdrew his opposition to the Palestine resolution, declaring in a letter to Senator Robert Taft, "I do feel that the military considerations which led to my previous action in opposing the passage of this resolution are not as strong a factor now as they were then." Stimson averred that "political considerations now outweigh the military, and the issue should be determined upon the political rather than the military basis." Taking this statement as a cue, Bloom announced that his committee would consider the resolution again the following month and he was "looking forward to [its] speedy approval."[73]

That next month, both Roosevelt and Bloom won reelection – Roosevelt by 8 percentage points, Bloom by 42 percentage points. Two days after the election, Wise and Silver approached the State Department desiring to know if it would object to the Palestine resolution being reintroduced. Bloom made his own inquiries, and both Wise and Bloom were informed by the State Department that Roosevelt opposed the idea.[74] Wise favored holding off for the time being. In general, he believed, as perhaps Bloom did as well, that "the best way ultimately to secure the Zionist goal [was] by retaining the confidence of the President."[75] As Emanuel Neumann explained the thinking of many people at the time:

"[Roosevelt] might be re-elected, and he was re-elected for a fourth term. His would be the power to shape post-war settlement. To cross him, to offend him, to alienate his affection was to court disaster for the Zionist cause."[76] Silver, however, insisted on forging ahead and submitted a formal letter to Bloom (at the latter's request[77]), declaring, "As chairman of the executive committee of the American Zionist Emergency Council I urge prompt action on the resolution."[78] Bloom acted on this letter, and the resolution was reported out of the Foreign Affairs Committee favorably – by a single vote – on November 30.[79] Bloom pledged to "make every effort to see that the bill [was] passed on the floor of the House" before its next session, and he appeared before the House Rules Committee to facilitate such a vote, arguing vigorously that it would give "a ray of hope to millions of persecuted Jews to whom Palestine stands as the last possible

> "The resolution for the adoption of such a decision is directly opposed to the principles of the Atlantic Charter and violates all the lofty principles of humanity. It undoubtedly arises from the effect of Zionist propaganda on the statesmen in America which leaves no scope for many of them to study, to investigate the justice of the case, and freely to hear the opposite point of view. The principle of interference in the destiny of the countries of others is an extremely dangerous one. This war is raging to exterminate that principle and to bring about justice among the peace-loving nations. It is not reasonable for a Power permeated with the spirit of justice to give Arab Palestine away to the Jews in contravention of these lofty principles. This reassures us that the Palestine cause would inevitably and ultimately be solved in the interest of its Arab inhabitants.
>
> "All the Arabs are completely confident of the justice of their cause in Palestine and of the transgression resulting from Zionist interference therein. Nothing shall, therefore, prevent them from fighting in defense of their legitimate right in Palestine regardless of costs. The Arabs appeal to the leaders of America to weigh the Zionist cause and the benefits which may result from supporting it against the sacrifices and efforts which America has made in the Arab and Islamic countries and the firm traditional friendship and material and moral interests which these sacrifices and efforts have created now and will create in the future in the Arab countries, and also against America's reputation for upholding justice and right. Only then will appear the wide difference between the profit and loss which America will experience in the event she supports the unjust Zionist policy.

Excerpt from a note from the Iraqi Foreign Office, dated December 21, 1944, objecting to a pro-Zionist resolution before Congress.

hope of refuge."[80]   When asked by the committee about the executive branch's opinion on the resolution, Bloom intimated that Roosevelt stood squarely behind it, citing a letter Roosevelt had sent Senator Robert Wagner right before the election "favor[ing] the opening of Palestine to unrestricted Jewish immigration" and "the establishment there of a free and democratic Jewish commonwealth." This reply was seemingly disingenuous since – according to a November 15 government memo – Bloom had been informed three weeks earlier that Roosevelt actually opposed the resolution's passage.[81]

Indeed, opposition from the executive branch ultimately killed the resolution. Like Roosevelt, the new secretary of state, Edward Stettinius, Jr., didn't want the resolution passed[82] having received numerous cables from U.S. officials in the Middle East reporting strenuous Arab opposition to American support for Zionism.[83]   In secret testimony before the Senate Foreign Relations Committee, Stettinius argued that the "situation in the Arab World" was "delicate," and that the resolution "would tie [Roosevelt's] hands."[84] On December 11, the Senate committee voted 10-8 to take no action on the resolution but insisted that the State Department make its opposition to the resolution public so that the public understand why it voted as it did. The department complied, issuing a statement declaring that it viewed passage of the resolution "unwise from the standpoint of the general international situation."[85]

Silver suffered in the aftermath of this vote. His colleagues accused him of telling Bloom to go forward without their approval and despite the group's decision not to push for the resolution's passage until they gained the State Department's backing.[86]   Silver subsequently resigned from his position on the American Zionist Emergency Council,[87] and Bloom complained to Goldstein that he shouldn't have been "placed in this embarrassing position." In a telephone call with Goldstein, he said, "I have been taking it from all angles. I cannot stand any more." Bloom said he wasn't aware that Silver broke rank in asking him to push the resolution through the Foreign Affairs Committee and said, "I do not like all this misunderstanding. From now on I am not going to do anything unless it is kosher." As the conversation drew to a close, Bloom said, "When I am told what to do, it will be done."[88]

However, in pushing the resolution through the Foreign Affairs Committee, Bloom had followed Silver's lead despite knowing the preference of Roosevelt and the State Department to let "sleeping dogs lie." And yet, at that point the war in Europe was nearing completion, which gave Bloom more wiggle room to act, especially since the War Department had retracted its objection to the resolution in October.[89] He thus could satisfy both Zionist demands and his understanding of his duty as chairman of the Foreign Affairs Committee.

~ CHAPTER 10 ~

AFTER THE WAR –
STILL JUGGLING PRIORITIES

This book could end here. Our story about Bloom's behavior during the Holocaust is complete. Yet, it pays to examine the last four years of his life (1945-1949) as they feature interesting historical material – including Bloom's role in the founding of Israel – and provide additional support for our thesis on Bloom's war-time activities.

America's state of emergency lifted with the conclusion of World War II, and in the more relaxed environment of the post-war period, Bloom felt less compelled to toe the administration's line. Indeed, he even helped steer a Zionist resolution through Congress in late 1945 despite opposition by President Truman. Yet, even if the urgency of winning a world war no longer weighed on Bloom's mind, other major foreign policy considerations – such as American interests in the Middle East – did, resulting in Bloom supporting Zionism less robustly than some Jewish leaders would have liked. Bloom may not have admired Truman to the degree he had Roosevelt, but his allegiance to America and his sense of duty as chairman of the House Foreign Affairs Committee remained unaltered. Thus, from 1945-1949, Bloom occasionally fought for Zionist causes, and continued to help individual Jews immigrate to America, but ultimately acted, as he had during the war, in what he deemed the best interests of his country.

Bloom's prestige increased in 1945 when, two weeks before Germany surrendered, he began working on helping draft the charter of the United Nations, an organization designed to oversee a new era of peace.

Appointed by Roosevelt, Bloom served on an eight-member U.S. delegation that traveled to San Francisco to confer with representatives of 50 other nations to create the new body.[1] The work wasn't perfunctory or ceremonial; the U.S. delegates met among themselves no fewer than 77 times,[2] and Bloom proudly signed the UN Charter – a document "drawn to give the world a new start"[3] – on June 26, 1945.

The world, however, had been left a wreck by World War II. Hundreds of thousands of Holocaust survivors, for example, effectively had nowhere to live as they had no desire to remain – and often were unwelcome – in the countries of their birth, countries where their relatives had been murdered by the Nazis and local collaborators. "The civilized world owes it to this handful of survivors to provide them with a home where they can again settle down and begin to live as human beings," wrote Earl Harrison in an official report in August 1945 after visiting displaced persons (DP) camps in Germany and Austria at the request of the U.S. government.[4] Shortly thereafter, Truman called on England to admit

Sol Bloom signing the UN Charter he helped draft on June 26, 1945.

100,000 Jewish refugees into Palestine.[5]   Bloom tried to help these survivors.   He agreed, for example, to be honored by Agudath Israel Youth Council of America in 1947 as part of an effort to raise $500,000 to "provide sorely-needed food supplies for the Passover holiday" to displaced Holocaust survivors.[6]   More importantly, though, he pushed for the creation of a Jewish state, which ultimately provided a home to much of the Jewish displaced persons population.[7] In December 1945, Bloom's Foreign Affairs Committee considered a new pro-Zionist resolution – House Concurrent Resolution 113 – that tied the plight of the displaced persons to the need for a Jewish state. It read in part: "the ruthless persecution of the Jewish people in Europe has clearly demonstrated the need for a Jewish homeland as a haven for the large numbers who have become homeless as a result of this persecution." The resolution called for a "democratic commonwealth" to be created by Jewish immigrants "in association with all elements of the population."[8]

Like the hearings Bloom had presided over in February 1944 for a different Palestine resolution, the hearings for House Concurrent Resolution 113 were clearly tilted in one direction, with pro-Zionist testimony outweighing anti-Zionist testimony by a factor of two to one. And like at the previous hearings, Bloom was clearly biased and interjected on a number of occasions to advance the Zionist cause. For example, in his testimony, Emanuel Neumann of the Zionist Organization of America said he came to Washington directly from Atlantic City where a meeting was being held to raise money for displaced persons in Europe. A couple of minutes later, Bloom says, "You spoke about the meeting in Atlantic City. I wish you would tell the committee the urgency of the situation that called for that meeting." Neumann obliges him and as part of his answer relates that three Jewish organization in tandem were seeking to raise $100 million. In an effort apparently to impress his colleagues, Bloom immediately says, "That is for this year."[9]

In an extended, somewhat hostile exchange with Lessing J. Rosenwald, president of the anti-Zionist American Council for Judaism, Bloom presses him on where displaced Jews should go if not Palestine:

Chairman BLOOM: "[C]ould you mention any other place

throughout the world today where the Jews could be permitted to enter and be safe outside of Palestine?

[…]

Mr. ROSENWALD: I could not say that there are many places.

Chairman BLOOM: Well, is there one place?

Mr. ROSENWALD: Well, I should say one place probably is Russia.

(Soon thereafter, another congressman says to Rosenwald, "Well, this may be an impertinent question, but I will put it, anyway. Would you want to live in Russia?"[10])

Earlier, Bloom had stated that 75-80 percent of American Jews favored passage of the resolution. When Rosenwald doubted this figure, Bloom declared:

> I would like to say this for the record…: That when we had lengthy hearings here with reference to the previous resolution that the committee had under consideration [in February 1944], that we received thousands and thousands and thousands – this table was just covered with them – of letters and telegrams and I do not believe we received a hundred against it.[11]

Unlike the previous resolution, though, this one was reported out of the Foreign Affairs Committee unanimously, and the House of Representatives passed it "overwhelmingly" after hearing speeches from 11 congressmen (eight in favor), including Bloom.[12] In reporting the resolution out favorably, both the House Foreign Affairs Committee and Senate Foreign Relations Committee declared that "the time is at hand when the long-standing pledges to the Jewish people should be fulfilled."[13]

Truman had actually voiced his opposition to the resolution's passage during a press conference on November 29.[14] But with the war long over,

Bloom was less concerned with mild opposition by the administration (it made no vigorous attempt to kill this resolution), especially if it wasn't based on military considerations. It's also possible that Bloom felt slightly less committed to Truman than he had to Roosevelt. Truman, after all, didn't possess the magnetic charisma of Roosevelt and had served with Bloom in Congress so that Bloom probably felt more comfortable disagreeing with him. Furthermore, unlike Roosevelt, Truman had not steered the country through a terrible depression and world war. Perhaps Bloom could also afford to act as he did because an Anglo-American Committee of Inquiry was set to soon study the Palestine question and make recommendations to their respective governments. In other words, Bloom knew Truman could theoretically afford to ignore the resolution and just focus on the committee's recommendations (which came in April 1946) should he so desire. Finally, strictly speaking, the resolution didn't call for a "Jewish commonwealth." The implication was unmistakable, but it technically only called for a "democratic commonwealth" to be created by Jewish immigrants "in association with all elements of the population." This distinction was actually noted in a State Department memorandum.[15] Bloom thus may have felt freer to act than he had in February 1944.

The wishes of the administration, however, did influence Bloom's post-war Zionist-related activity, and the administration's interests often conflicted with those of American Zionists. For decades, America's foreign policy establishment believed the Middle East "was an area of British interests and British responsibility, and that the United States had no direct stake of its own there."[16] That began to change during the war, however, with American businessmen and government officials increasingly concerned about access to oil reserves in the Middle East and fearful of "an imminent drying up of the Texas and Oklahoma oil fields."[17] After the war – with Great Britain's might waning and the Cold War beginning – the U.S. also became increasingly interested in the Middle East "to prevent the Soviet Union from gaining a foothold" in the area.[18] Forming good relations with the Arabs – who opposed the creation of a Jewish state – was thus thought to be crucial.[19]

Thus, while Bloom tried to champion the Zionist cause in the post-war years, he often did so less categorically than some Zionists would have liked. For example, when the Anglo-American Committee of Inquiry submitted its report in April 1946, Bloom, according to the Jewish Telegraphic Agency, "was highly encouraged by the recommendation for immigration of 100,000 Jewish survivors in Europe and for abrogation of the White Paper."[20] Many other American Zionists, however, adopted a less joyous attitude, attacking the report for envisioning a bi-national state rather than a Jewish one. Two months later, British Foreign Secretary Ernest Bevin charged that Americans only supported the migration of 100,000 displaced Jews to Palestine "because they do not want too many of them in New York."[21] Angered by this comment, Bloom introduced a resolution in Congress calling on England to fulfill its 1924 treaty which, according to the interpretation of American Zionists, prohibited England from deviating from its mandate over Palestine without American approval.[22] Bloom, however, did not extend this anger to voting against a $4 billion loan to England in the summer of 1946. Several pro-Zionist congressmen opposed granting England the loan, but Bloom – though calling Bevin's statements "foolish, ridiculous, and asinine" – said they were unrelated to the loan and that granting it would benefit America. "As an American, I am going to vote for that which is to the best interest of my country," he said.[23] Stephen Wise publicly seconded Bloom's position, as did Joseph Proskauer. In a telegram to Bloom whose text was made available to The New York Times, Proskauer wrote that "the American Jewish Committee urges that the question of the British loan must be determined solely from the viewpoint of American policy."[24]

In 1947, however, Bloom did assist the Zionist movement at a key moment, helping it secure enough votes in the United Nations to approve a partition proposal that would create two states in Palestine – one Jewish and one Arab. The proposal was ultimately rejected by the Arabs, but the UN decision is regarded as a seminal moment in the history of Zionism in that the nations of the world collectively voted for the creation of a Jewish state 1,900 years after the destruction of the second Jewish Commonwealth.[25] In at least four private letters, Bloom makes the bold claim that he was responsible for the successful outcome of this vote. "I have the evidence, the letters and telegrams in my file, that will show that they would not have had the partition if it had not been for me," he wrote to an acquaintance in April 1948.[26] In what manner, though, did Bloom secure this victory? In his autobiography, he writes, "I conferred with delegates from a number of...countries and helped to win over enough votes to provide the required two-thirds majority necessary for the United Nations approval of partition."[27] In a statement that Bloom inserted into the Congressional Record, he mentions approaching representatives of "the Philippines, Haiti, Liberia, and others."[28] In a November 10, 1947 letter to Rabbi Israel Goldstein, he also writes that he cabled the presidents of Mexico, Cuba, and Costa Rica.[29]

However, the available evidence of Bloom's activist role – if any – in these countries' votes on the partition plan is limited. Secretary of Defense James Forrestal writes in his diary that Bloom "acknowledged that he had brought great pressure to bear on Liberia, the Philippines and Haiti to change their vote," but it isn't clear from this entry whether Forrestal had independent knowledge of Bloom's behavior or just took his word for it.[30] Historian Ignacio Klich writes that "former US assistant secretary of state Adolf Berle, past New York governor Herbert Lehman and New York Congressman Sol Bloom had various roles in securing Haiti's support" for partition, but Klich's source for this assertion in relation to Bloom is unclear.[31]

Another historian, Peter Hahn, writes without elaboration that Bloom lobbied Liberia's delegate to the UN over the phone, citing a State Department document as his source.[32] William Tubman – whose father was Liberia's president-elect at the time – tells a much more interesting tale. He claims that during a visit to Washington in 1943, his father met Bloom, and Bloom said to him, "[The] Negro and the Jew have been the floor mats of the world. Mr. Tubman, you are about to become President of Liberia. I want us to agree that if there is ever an occasion where you can do something for the Jews, you will do so and if there is anything I can do to better the plight of the Negro I will do so." Tubman and Bloom shook hands on the deal. The next time Tubman heard from Bloom was

William Tubman directed Liberia's representative in the UN to vote for Jewish statehood, apparently thanks to lobbying by Sol Bloom.

four years later when he received the following telegram in advance of the partition vote at the UN: "The Jews need you! Sol Bloom." In response to this telegram, said his son, Tubman instructed Liberia's delegate at the UN to vote yes on partition.[33]

As for the vote of the Philippines: On November 26, Carlos P. Romulo, chief delegate of the Philippines to the UN, delivered a speech indicating that the Philippines intended to vote against partition. The next day, Romulo received many phone calls, urging him to change his position. The very first call, though, came from Bloom who had worked with him at the founding conference of the UN in 1945. "Is there no way of changing the stand you have taken?" Romulo remembers Bloom asking him.[34] According to Charles Malik, a Lebanese diplomat who was with Romulo when he got the call, Bloom "talked with [Romulo] for ½ hour; tried to change his mind; told him last sentence [of his speech] permitted abstention."[35] Years later, Romulo dismissed as "sheer nonsense" reports that "the 'Jewish bloc' brought pressure to bear against" him and threatened him "with dire curtailment of any further aid to the Philippines if [he] did not yield." He writes, "I was under no pressure from any official source, with the exception of Sol Bloom, and his was on a purely personal basis."[36] Filipino president Manuel Roxas ultimately, though, did change his mind, and the Philippines voted for partition. Bloom doesn't appear to have played a role in this vote reversal – although he may have been under the impression that he had.

Bloom's claim that he was responsible for the UN voting to create a Jewish state thus seems tenuous. Yet, the partition plan required a two-thirds majority vote to pass and the final vote at the UN was 33 to 13 with 10 abstentions. That means if

Philippine delegate to the UN Carlos P. Romulo and Sol Bloom. Bloom called him in advance of the UN vote on Jewish statehood, urging him to vote "yes."

Bloom had a hand in changing the "nay" vote of just three countries, he was, in fact, partially responsible for the final outcome. So Boom's claim is at least plausible.

The U.S. was among the 33 nations that voted for partition, but by early 1948, "powerful forces in the U.S. administration…started having second thoughts" thanks in part to violence that erupted in Palestine following the vote.[37]   Truman and other U.S. officials believed that "continued warfare would result in the annihilation of the Yishuv" and were loath to commit U.S. troops to the area.[38]   Bloom supported the Zionist cause, but as a loyal, high-ranking Democrat he also tried to occasionally sugar-coat what many Zionists regarded as the Truman administration's two-faced policy on Zionism. This conduct didn't exactly endear Bloom to many committed Zionist activists who insisted on unequivocal American commitment to Jewish statehood. In February 1948, Bloom wrote a letter to an acquaintance bitterly complaining about Jewish attacks on him in relation to Palestine. Two months later, Bloom was criticized for seeming to support a proposal advanced by Warren Austin, the U.S. ambassador to the UN, who suggested that "a temporary trusteeship for Palestine should be established under the Trusteeship Council of the United Nations."[39] Media outlets reported that Bloom had voiced his support for the suggestion after meeting with Truman, but Bloom vigorously denied the story.[40] He even asked a printing company to make 2,000 copies of a sheet bearing three articles – from The New York Post, The New York Sun, and The Jewish Advocate – which all claimed that he had been misquoted.[41] He sent 50 copies of this sheet to Rabbi Herbert Goldstein and asked him to distribute them to the rabbis of the synagogues in his district with the request that they post them on their bulletin boards.[42]

These three articles painted Bloom in a more positive light. The New York Sun article, for example, reported that Bloom favored creating a Jewish state and had asked Truman to lift the arms embargo. "As it stands now," Bloom said, "arms are going, indirectly at least, to only one side in the controversy, and the Jews are unable to obtain them." A month earlier, on March 12, The New York Times reported on a letter sent by 41 "predominantly Administration stalwarts" – including Bloom – voicing their "profound misgivings" about the United States' Palestine policy.[43]

And a week later, on March 20, in reporting on Austin's trusteeship plan, the Times quoted Bloom as saying, "I can't agree to that proposal in any way, shape or form."[44]

As the British mandate for Palestine wound down, it became increasingly clear that Palestine's Jews would proclaim the founding of a Jewish state, and Bloom – in person and in writing – urged Truman several times to be the first world leader to recognize it (in part to stave off any goodwill the Soviet Union might enjoy with the new state should it recognize it first).[45] Even after the U.S. recognized Israel, however – 11 minutes after its creation – the battle for its viable birth was not over. The arms embargo (against a country fighting for its life) remained in place and the U.S. had only recognized Israel *de facto*, not *de jure*. On May 19, Bloom begged out of attending a dinner in honor of humorist Harry Hirschfield in New York, explaining, "If I should leave Washington at this time and something should come up on the Palestine situation and I were not here, I would be very worried and more concerned than words can explain to you.... [W]ith my connection[s] here and abroad, I think that my place is in Washington until things are settled in Israel."[46] A week later, Bloom agreed to head a committee organizing an "American Friendship Train to Israel" that would tour the country soliciting food and supplies for the Jews in Israel.[47] "Like our own great republic in its early years of struggle for independence, Israel today represents more than merely a refuge for the physically and spiritually displaced persons of Europe. It represents a moral force in the world that must not be allowed to flounder through apathy or inaction on our part," Bloom proclaimed in a press release.[48] Several months later, on August 4, Bloom met with Truman and urged him to amend the arms embargo, grant complete recognition to Israel, secure Israel's admittance to the UN, and extend a $100 million loan to the fledgling country.[49] Two weeks later, he proposed a six-point plan that included these four items plus calls for the withdrawal of Arab troops from Israel and the monitoring of U.S. dollars and arms to prevent them from falling into Arab hands via Great Britain.[50]

Notwithstanding this activity, Bloom's Palestine record was attacked in the months prior to the 1948 elections, and Bloom frantically defended himself in what he regarded as his "first real [electoral] fight" since 1923.[51] He inserted a statement in the Congressional Record on August 7 touting his Zionist achievements, which he then published in pamphlet form under the title "My Efforts in Behalf of Palestine" and distributed in his district. He also published the statement as a full-page ad in The New York Times on October 19 above letters of praise from Zionist figures like Chaim Weizmann and Eliahu Epstein, who became Israel's first ambassador to the United States.[52] The basis of the attacks against Bloom was his loyalty to the administration. In April, New York Post editor Ted Thackrey asked him whom he would support in the upcoming elections, to which Bloom responded, "I intend to support the Democratic candidate for the Presidency, whoever it may be."[53] Thackrey wasn't pleased. "I am amazed that you continue to pledge your support…to the author of the most immoral foreign policy undertaken in our history," he replied.[54] Bloom was also criticized by Leo Sack of the American Zionist Emergency Council. In a memo to Abba Hillel Silver, Sack enclosed a short article from the Washington Evening Star that quoted Bloom as saying that Truman was

"My Efforts in Behalf of Palestine"

Remarks of CONGRESSMAN SOL BLOOM of New York

From the Congressional Record, House of Representatives, August 7, 1948

A STATEMENT ON ISRAEL

THE STRUGGLE for ISRAEL IS NOT OVER. The infant Jewish state in Palestine is still experiencing a precarious existence hanging in the balance between war and peace. There is still much that the United States, with its great international prestige and influence, could do to assure the existence of Israel as a state and to help bring peace to its war-tormented people and to all the people of the Near East. Our country can be helpful in the following ways:

MY SIX POINTS FOR ISRAEL

1.
Extend de jure or full recognition to the Jewish state of Israel.

2.
Grant a loan of $100,000,000 to Israel to aid in the resettlement of displaced persons, in the reconstruction of war-devastated areas and in bolstering the economy of the country.

3.
Sponsor and support Israel's admission to the United Nations as an equal member of the family of nations.

4.
Remove the embargo on arms shipments because its further continuance places the United States in the unneutral position of indirectly supporting the Arabs.

5.
End Arab aggression and obtain the withdrawal of foreign Arab troops from the Holy Land whose presence there is threatening the prestige of the United Nations and the peace of the world.

6.
Finally, the United States must be on the alert at all times that the Marshall Plan funds advanced to Britain and surplus United States military equipment which remained in British hands should not be diverted to Arab countries for possible use against Israel now or in the future.

This is my six point program and my outline for continued efforts in behalf of Palestine in the months ahead. This is what I shall continue to fight for in the next Congress.

Sol Bloom

Upper half of full-page ad Sol Bloom placed in The New York Times on Oct. 19, 1948.

"on the right track" in solving the Palestine problem and commented: "It is horrible that a Jewish member of Congress, who should be so intimately aware of the double-cross that this Administration has given the Jews, should publicly declare that 'President Truman is on the right track' in the settlement of the Palestine problem."[55] Bloom, however, was trying to respond to the "larger" picture; he was thinking, not just of the future of Zionism, but of the future of the United States, in whose legislature he served. In a May 24, 1948 letter, he wrote: "The situation that exists today...must be handled very diplomatically and very carefully. There is one thing that we all are trying to avoid and that is to have a clash that would destroy the United Nations or isolate us from other countries throughout the world that we might need in case of trouble."[56]

In July, Bloom wrote to an acquaintance about the upcoming elections, "The Communists and the Wallace group are making a special attack upon me," referring to his opponent Eugene Connolly (of the American Labor Party) and former Vice President Henry Wallace, who in February had accused Truman of "laying the foundations" for war with the Soviet Union.[57] Bloom was also running against a Republican, Jules Justin, and, according to The New York Times, all three candidates considered Palestine the "leading issue" in the campaign.[58] If it was, though, the electorate gave Bloom a vote of confidence on his Palestine activities as he won 59 percent of the vote – Justin winning 28 percent and Connolly just 13 percent.[59] In a story published a week before the election, Douglas Dales of The New York Times wrote about Bloom, "Although he disagrees wholeheartedly with President Truman's activities on Palestine, he is, however, supporting Mr. Truman, otherwise, up to the hilt."[60] Perhaps the little distance Bloom put between himself and Truman helped him in November. In any event, his relatively close ties with the Truman administration didn't seem to ultimately hurt him.

These ties also helped him assist European Jews who wished to immigrate to the United States just as his government ties had helped him do so over the previous 10 years.[61] Like he did in the late 1930s and early to mid-1940s, Bloom assisted several famous European rabbis and individuals from prominent rabbinic families settle in America. For example, he helped the Bobover Rebbe, Rabbi Shlomo Halberstam, settle in the U.S. after he came to the country on a visitor's visa.[62] He later worked to bring the Rebbe's brother and sisters to the U.S. as well.[63]

Additionally, Bloom helped the future Lubavitcher Rebbe, Rabbi Menachem Mendel Schneerson, secure an immigration visa for his mother[64] and helped the Kolbushover Rav, Rabbi Alexander Teitelbaum, and his family move to the United States. In an advertisement in The Morning Journal, Rabbi Teitelbaum publicly thanked Bloom for his efforts and wished him "healthy years so that he [could] continue his work of self-sacrifice on behalf of the oppressed."[65] Dr. Gisela Perl, who is credited with saving numerous lives at Auschwitz, is another distinguished personality Bloom helped. She arrived in the U.S. on a lecture tour in 1946 on a temporary visa. Upon its expiration, U.S. officials threatened to deport her to her native country, Romania – even though she hadn't lived there since the war and feared the Soviets who had since taken control of the country.[66] Numerous people wrote to Bloom on her behalf, including Eleanor Roosevelt and Rabbi Moshe Teitelbaum, the future Satmar Rebbe, who knew Dr. Perl in Europe and whom he credited with saving his sister's life in Auschwitz.[67]

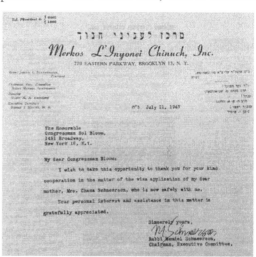

Letter and advertisement of thanks, respectively, from the seventh Lubavitcher Rebbe and the Kolbushover Rav.

Bloom lobbied extensively for her to remain in America – "I have worked harder on this case and fought harder than on any other," he wrote to an intercessor on her behalf[68] – and, ultimately, when he couldn't convince the Justice Department to let her stay, he introduced a special bill in Congress directing the attorney general to admit her as a citizen. Truman signed this bill on March 11, and Dr. Perl remained in the U.S., sending Bloom a letter of profuse thanks."[69]

Bloom helped many less famous people as well. One couple, Mr. and Mrs. Kornel Bernatsky, fled Hungary in 1945 and made their way to Germany but were unable to secure visas to America until Bloom involved himself in their case. "As it turned out, it was just your letter written to the Munich Consulate that [gave] the decisive push to our case," the husband wrote to Bloom once they arrived in America.[70] In another instance, a young woman, Nelly Blumner, secured a visa to America after the war

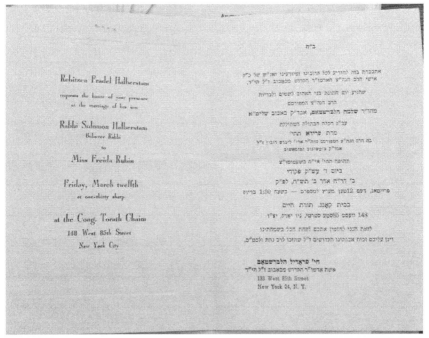

An invitation to the Bobover Rebbe's second wedding in 1948. (The Rebbe lost his first wife in the Holocaust.) The invitation was extended to Bloom presumably because he helped the Rebbe and several members of his family secure refuge and citizenship in the U.S.

under the German quota, but her husband, a Polish national, remained without a visa until Bloom interceded on her behalf.[71] Bloom intervened on behalf of another person, Rabbi Herman Fekete, who left Hungary for America with eight of his 10 children; the oldest two were over 18 and therefore could not obtain non-quota visas. Bloom, however, wrote to the State Department and obtained visas for them.[72]

In 1947, Sumner Welles wrote to Bloom: "Public opinion does not realize how difficult the problems which you have had to handle have been nor how much you have been able to accomplish behind the scenes and without publicity in your quiet and effective way in the interest of this country, but I do believe that all of this will be more widely appreciated as time goes on."[73] The subject matter of this letter isn't clear, but it does highlight a key point – that while Bloom may not have championed some of the more aggressive campaigns against the Roosevelt and Truman administrations relating to rescue and Zionism, he did much behind the scenes for which he has not received enough credit.

Bloom died on March 8, 1949, having lived a life that was quintessentially American. "His rise from an impoverished home to great wealth in the music business and the theatrical world is as American as baseball, apple pie and hot dogs," wrote journalist Hope Ridings Miller a year before his passing.[74] Brash and bold, Bloom had entered Congress in a special election in 1923 and fought successfully on behalf of his co-religionists in the early years of his congressional career. He publicly attacked Henry Ford for publishing anti-Semitic comments in his newspaper and fought a calendar reform scheme that would have undermined the sanctity of the Jewish Sabbath. But with the rise of Nazi Germany – and Bloom's elevation to the chairmanship of the House Foreign Affairs Committee – his focus narrowed. The future and safety of America was now his utmost concern, and he stayed far from anything that might undermine it.

This decision dictated his approach to immigration policy, his actions at the Bermuda Conference, his position on the Bergson-backed resolution calling for the creation of a government rescue commission, and his response to Zionist activism during the war. To a large extent, it also dictated his relationship with Roosevelt. During the Holocaust, America was fighting a war to defend itself from a maniacal dictator and Bloom felt it his duty to remain loyal to the country's commander in chief. Not only was Roosevelt leading the fight against Germany, he appreciated the Nazi threat long before others did and prepared the country to combat it. Bloom had, in fact, helped the president pass crucial legislation in 1939-1941 without which hundreds of thousands – if not millions – of additional Jews may well have died. To castigate Bloom, therefore, for not turning on Roosevelt in the middle of World War II is to be a harsh judge of persons. Of course Bloom could have broken rank. But he was a patriotic and dutiful American congressman and acted in accordance with the constraints patriotism and duty placed upon him as he understood them. These constraints may have prevented him from advocating for large-scale, vigorous rescue activity, but they also enabled him to help many individual Jews behind the scenes.

Sol Bloom's gravestone in Mount Eden cemetery in Westchester County, NY.

Multiple smaller factors influenced Bloom's behavior during his years in Congress. He sometimes received mixed messages from the American Jewish community, he may not have appreciated the enormity of the Holocaust, and he could be petty. Yet, more important than all these was his sense of obligation. Bloom was an energetic and proud Jew and certainly wished to help his brethren when he could. But Bloom was not a Jewish leader; he was an American congressman, and his primary duty was serving his country. Towards the end of the war, Bloom enjoyed more leeway to advance Jewish causes, but even then he only did so to the extent that it didn't conflict with vital U.S. interests. For at the end of the day, Bloom was an American congressman and attended to America's interests first. At Bloom's funeral, attended by 3,000 people at the West Side Institutional Synagogue,[75] his coffin was draped in an American flag. It was only fitting.

APPENDIX

In addition to mischaracterizing Bloom, several Holocaust historians have made at least two major and two minor factual errors in writing about this colorful congressman. These mistakes could be glossed over but for the fact that they appear in numerous books and will likely appear in still others unless someone highlights them. (Besides, if they aren't noted, some readers might wonder why certain "facts" about Bloom that appear in other books don't appear in this one.) Below is a brief discussion of the four errors:

1) Several historians write that Assistant Secretary of State Breckinridge Long wanted Bloom to represent the U.S. at the Bermuda Conference because he was "easy to handle" and "terribly ambitious for publicity." For this assertion, they rely on Henry Feingold's work *The Politics of Rescue* (p. 195). But Feingold misquotes Long. Long never said Bloom was "easy to handle," and he certainly didn't make this remark in relation to Bloom attending the Bermuda Conference (nor does Feingold claim he did; historians have misread his words). In attributing this remark to Long, Feingold cites an entry from Long's diary dated "June 20, 1940" – in other words, an entry written *three years before* the Bermuda Conference and thus obviously unconnected with it. It actually concerns a quarrel between Bloom and Senator Key Pittman, chairman of the Senate Foreign Relations Committee, and, of the two of them, Long said he found Bloom "*easier* to handle" (emphasis added), which – in context – is a compliment rather than a put-down. Long does say that Bloom was terribly ambitious for publicity, but, again, this comment was made in relation to a specific incident. It wasn't a comment on Bloom's overall character.[1]

2) Several Holocaust historians write that Stephen Wise called Bloom "the State Department's Jew." The true source for this designation, however,

seems to be historian Henry Feingold.[2] In attributing this moniker to Wise, one prominent historian cites Melvin I. Urofsky's *A Voice That Spoke for Justice* (p. 305),[3] but Urofsky appears to have misread Feingold.[4] (In a footnote, Urofsky cites a letter in the Central Zionist Archives that Wise wrote to Harry Friedenwald on August 18, 1938, but no such letter appears to exist in these archives. The only letter in the relevant folder of the Harry Friedenwald Papers in the Central Zionist Archives between Wise and Friedenwald on that date was written *by* Friedenwald *to* Wise.) Moreover, the passage in which Urofsky credits Wise for calling Bloom the "State Department's Jew" is riddled with other errors. (This author counted at least four.)

3) Several historians claim that Peter Bergson was the only witness required to testify under oath during the congressional hearings on creating a government commission to rescue European Jewry. In fact, Arthur Hale, a radio broadcaster, was also asked to testify under oath.[5]

4) At least two prominent Holocaust historians write that Rep. Emanuel Celler called the Bermuda Conference a "bloomin' fiasco." That's not technically accurate. What Celler actually said on May 3, 1943 was: "Unless some concrete action is set in motion, the Bermuda Conference will be another 'bloomin'' fiasco like the Evian Conference on Refugees."[6] So, he didn't call it a "bloomin' fiasco." He said it will *turn out* to be another "bloomin' fiasco" if no action is taken. There's a difference between the two. Not a huge difference, but a difference nonetheless.

FOOTNOTES

Introduction *(pages 1-8)*

[1] Between five and eight Jews sat in Congress at any given time between 1939-1945.

[2] Arthur T. Weil, "The Stone the Builders Rejected," *The American Hebrew*, July 7, 1939, pg. 18. See also "Sol Bloom, Great American" *The Sioux City Journal*, March 9, 1949, pg. 6: "He was a Jew and extremely proud of it."

[3] *Memorial Services Held in the House of Representatives of the United States, Together with Remarks Presented in Eulogy of Sol Bloom, Late a Representative from New York, Proceedings in the House* (Washington: Government Printing Office, 1950), 79. In 1926, Bloom proposed building a grand "model synagogue" in Washington, DC, and 20 years later advocated erecting a Jewish museum in the nation's capital. Jews who prefer keeping a low profile tend not to champion such projects. See "National Synagogue Proposed by Bloom," *The New York Times*, January 26, 1926, pg. 5, and the June 13, 1944 letter from Sholem Asch to Bloom in Sol Bloom Papers, New York Public Library, Box 61.

[4] *The Jewish National Home in Palestine: Hearings Before the Committee on Foreign Affairs, House of Representatives, Seventy-Eighth Congress, Second Session, on H. Res. 418 and H. Res. 419* (Washington: Government Printing Office, 1944), 229.

[5] David Wyman and Rafael Medoff, *A Race Against Death: Peter Bergson, America, and the Holocaust* (New York: The New Press, 2002), 149-150. Activist Peter Bergson recalled, "[Bloom] told me...that all the ambassadors knew he was a Jew and that he didn't smoke on the Sabbath. He said...to him the most important part of a meal was not what you ate, but the cigar afterwards." Interview with Peter Bergson, p. 56HK, personal collection of Rafael Medoff. See also the remarks of Rabbi Goldstein in *Memorial Services*, 62.

[6] Sol Bloom, *The Autobiography of Sol Bloom* (New York: G. P. Putnam's Sons, 1948), 53 and 200.

[7] Ibid., 302-303.

[8] Oliver McKee, Jr., "Super-Salesman of Patriotism," *Outlook and Independent*, February 3, 1932, p. 158

[9] Richard Breitman and Alan M. Kraut, *American Refugee Policy and European Jewry, 1933-1945* (Bloomington: Indiana University Press, 1988), 140; Monty Noam Penkower,

The Jews Were Expendable: Free World Diplomacy and the Holocaust (Chicago: University of Illinois, 1983), 108; and Lucy S. Dawidowicz, "American Jews and the Holocaust," *The New York Times Magazine*, April 18, 1982, p. 109.

[10] David S. Wyman, *The Abandonment of the Jews: America and the Holocaust, 1941-1945* (New York: Pantheon, 1984), 202. See also ibid., 317, and *Race Against Death*, 144-145.

[11] In their respective tributes, the Hebrew Convalescent Home called Bloom a "great man," Agudath Israel Youth Council of America hailed Bloom's "historic efforts for persecuted people," and the American Jewish Congress tagged Bloom as a "great leader of Jewry."

[12] The honor paid Bloom by Agudath Israel can perhaps be cynically dismissed as an attempt to strengthen ties with a powerful congressman, but why would 17 Jewish organizations honor him *after he died* if he had failed his people at the hour of their greatest need?

[13] Of course, even if they had wanted to, it's not clear that American Jewry could have successfully pressured Roosevelt to save their brethren. According to historian Henry Feingold, "American Jewry simply did not possess the power to change foreign policy priorities during hostilities." *Bearing Witness: How America and Its Jews Responded to the Holocaust* (Syracuse: Syracuse University Press, 1995), 221. See also ibid., 223 and 231, and *The Politics of Rescue: The Roosevelt Administration and the Holocaust, 1938-1945* (New York: Waldon, 1970), 302, and "Did American Jewry Do Enough During the Holocaust?" The B.G. Rudolph Lectures in Judaic Studies (Syracuse: Syracuse University Press, 1985), 4: "So much of the judgment of those anxious to indict [American Jewry] is based on reading our comparative effectiveness today back into the history of that tragic period where it does not belong."

[14] This phrase comes from Rabbi Milton Steinberg (1903-1950). Qtd. in Laurel Leff, *Buried by the Times: The Holocaust and America's Most Important Newspaper* (Cambridge: Cambridge University Press, 2005), 325.

Chapter 1 *(pages 9-15)*

[1] *Autobiography*, 10 and 18. Bloom celebrated his birthday on March 9, but his true birth date is unknown. In his autobiography, he explains that his family marked time by the Jewish calendar and didn't particularly take note of birthdays.

[2] Ibid., 6 and 10. According to Brooklyn College's Robert Shapiro, Szyrpcz is probably "Sierpc (pronounced Sherpts), a town located about 125 km...northwest of Warsaw" (e-mail correspondence with author, January 25, 2018).

[3] *Autobiography*, 10 and 13.

[4] Harriet and Fred Rochlin, *Pioneer Jews: A New Life in the Far West* (Boston: Houghton Mifflin, 1984), 44. This figure is based on a national Jewish census conducted between 1876-1878 under the auspices of the Board of Delegates of American Israelites and the Union of American Hebrew Congregations. The total Jewish population of the United States according to the census was 230,000.

⁵ Fred Rosenbaum, *Cosmopolitans: A Social and Cultural History of the Jews of the San Francisco Bay Area* (Berkley: University of California Press, 2009), 50.

⁶ Edward Zerin, *Jewish San Francisco* (Charleston: Arcadia Publishing, 2006), 9 and *Encyclopedia Britannica*, s.v. "San Francisco," https://www.britannica.com/place/San-Francisco-California (accessed February 2, 2018).

⁷ *Cosmopolitans*, 1.

⁸ Ibid. 34. See also ibid., 59; Bruce Phillips, "The Challenge of Family, Identity, and Affiliations" in *California Jews*, eds. Ava F. Kahn and Marc Dollinger (Lebanon: Brandeis University Press, 2003), 17; Ava F. Kahn, "Joining the Rush" in *California Jews*, 29; and Irena Narell, *Our City: The Jews of San Francisco* (San Diego: Howell North, 1981), 12.

⁹ See Ava Kahn's comments in *American Jerusalem: Jews and the Making of San Francisco*, directed by Marc Shaffer (Actual Film, 2013), DVD; Earl Raab "There's No City Like San Francisco," *Commentary* 10 (October 1950), 371; and Narell, 12: "[Jews] were not newcomers...it was *their* City."

¹⁰ Rochlin, 49, and Phillips, 17.

¹¹ Narell, 11. See also *Cosmopolitans*, 29, 37, 38, 42, 55, and 62, and Leonard Dinnerstein, *Anti-Semitism in America* (New York: Oxford University Press, 1994), 51.

¹² Narell, 11. See also Kahn and Dollinger, 1.

¹³ See *Cosmopolitans* 28. Rochlin, 144, writes that "the political welcome accorded Jews in the Far West [was] unmatched anywhere else." 157.

¹⁴ *Cosmopolitans*, 72. The last phrase comes from Norman Bentwich, qtd. in Fred Rosenbaum, "San Francisco-Oakland Son," in *Like All the Nations? The Life and Legacy of Judah L. Magnes*, ed. William M. Brinner and Moses Rischin (Albany: SUNY Press, 1987), 66.

¹⁵ *Cosmopolitans*, xvi, 36, and 37. See also Kahn and Dollinger, 10.

¹⁶ *Cosmopolitans*, 35 and 37.

¹⁷ Narell, 380.

¹⁸ Rochlin, 220, and *Cosmopolitans*, 95 and 97.

¹⁹ He later "dropped the last title because in his own words, 'It is impossible to protect such an unsettled nation.'" Narell, 78-79.

²⁰ Rochlin, 169, 183, and 189, and *Cosmopolitans*, 68 and 122.

²¹ http://worldpopulationreview.com/us-cities/san-francisco-population (accessed February 11, 2018) and other sources – all based on U.S. census figures.

²² *Autobiography*, 89 and 212. D. W. Brogan writes in "The British Looked Us Over," *New York Times*, August 29, 1948, pg. BR1, that Bloom "expressed at times the spirit of northern California."

²³ SB Papers, Box 34. See also the October 5, 1940 letter to Judge H. Grossman in ibid., Box 2.

[24] See Letter to Judge Grossman and *Autobiography* 4, 10, 15-17, 19, 29, 51, and 69.

[25] *Autobiography*, 17. His mother evidently didn't push the matter and taught him to read and write herself. Ibid., 49.

[26] Ibid., 18 and 20, and the clipping from the March 5, 1946, edition of The Evening Star in SB Papers, Boxes 60-62.

[27] *Autobiography*, 29-31, 32, 57-58, 94, 97-98, and 101.

[28] Ibid., 31, 34-35, and 67.

[29] Calculated using: http://www.in2013dollars.com (accessed June 19, 2022).

[30] *Autobiography*, 96.

[31] Normon Bolotin and Christine Lang, *The World's Columbian Exposition* (Chicago: University of Illinois Press, 2002), 3 and 8. See also ibid., vii. The fair's chief of construction, Daniel H. Burnham, once said, "Make no little plans; they have no magic to stir men's blood." Qtd. in ibid., 5. Antonin Dvořák actually originally composed his "New World Symphony" for the fair. "It was to be enacted in a 12,000-seat 'Spectatorium,' with twenty-five moving stages…. Unfortunately, the sponsor ran out of money after spending $500,000, the building was never finished and the symphony was never heard – at least not at the fair." Ibid., 157-158.

[32] Ibid., 158.

[33] Erik Larson, *The Devil in the White City: Murder, Magic, and Madness at the Fair That Changed America* (New York: Vintage, 2003), 179. The Ferris Wheel stood 264 feet tall and could hold a total of 1,440 people in its 36 cars. See *Autobiography*, 138-139 and Bolotin and Lang, vii, 22, 28, and 131.

[34] *Autobiography* 135-136. Bloom insists the dance at the fair was not the "crude, suggestive dance" it later became. Ibid., 135. See also the June 23, 1939 letter to Hal Watkins, Jr. in SB Papers, Box 24.

[35] Bolotin and Lang, 127-139. Bloom also promoted other elements of the fair due to his "flair for…spectacular advertising" *Autobiography*, 120.

[36] *Autobiography*, 157-159. See also "The Music Man Vs. The Orator" and the scrapbook of articles and ads related to Bloom's music career in SB Papers, Box 62.

[37] *Autobiography*, 165. The date this copyright appears in the government's official records is January 4, 1900. See *Catalogue of Title Entries of Books and Other Articles, Vol. 22, no. 11, Whole no. 454 – March 15, 1900* (Washington: Government Printing Office, 1900), 768. In response to an official inquiry, a worker at the United States Copyright office stated that the government doesn't file copyright requests in a manner "that it is [clear] that a specific claim was the first one in a specific year" (e-mail correspondence, November 22, 2019). Only the "date of registration" is recorded, he explained. In other words, Bloom may have been the first to request a copyright in the 20th century, but not the first to technically receive one.

[38] *Autobiography*, 165 and 183.

[39] "Corners are scarce in and around Times Square and you can't make any more of

them," Bloom said. "Times Square Business Never Stops, Says Buyer of $450,000 Corner," *The New York Times*, February 4, 1917, pg. XX7. For other examples of his activity, see "Times Square Realty Deal: Sol Bloom Pays $500,000 for 42nd Street Lease – To Build 12 Story, Structure," *The New York Times*, Aug. 23, 1910, pg. 13; and "Big Theatre Lease Above Columbus Circle," *The New York Times*, November 19, 1913, p. 22 (always thinking big, Bloom aimed to convert the first floor of the leased building into "a sort of indoor Fifth Avenue" – qtd. in "Plan New House of Amusement," *The New York Times*, December 10, 1913).

[40] *Autobiography*, 185-186. See, for example, "The Real Estate Field: 46th Street Deal Near Times Square," *The New York Times*, July 1, 1914, pg. 19 and "Selwyn and Co. to Build: Plans for Three Theatres in 42nd St. Near Times Square," *The New York Times*, September 17, 1917, pg. 13.

[41] *Autobiography*, 185.

Chapter 2 *(pages 16-21)*

[1] This district was "bounded on the south by Eighty-sixth Street, on the west by the Hudson River, on the north by 125th Street, and on the east by a waggly line that went over as far as Madison Avenue." *Autobiography*, 201. For details on this "waggly line," see Ernest Havier, "The Music Man Vs. The Orator: Sol Bloom and W. M. Chandler to Contest Congressional Seat in the Nineteenth District," *The New York Times*, January 28, 1923, pg. E3, and Ira E. Bennett, "Biographical Sketch," in Sol Bloom, *Our Heritage: George Washington and the Establishment of the American Union* (New York: G. P. Putnam's Sons, 1944), 7. Starting in 1945, due to redistricting, Bloom represented New York's 20th congressional district, which a *New York Times* journalist characterized as a "district of cosmopolitan character that runs up the West Side of Manhattan from Twenty-sixth to 116th Street through a rough area once known as 'Hell's Kitchen' and on to an area of well-to-do homes along Riverside Drive." Douglas Dales, "Bloom, 78, Waging a Brisk Campaign," *The New York Times*, October 27, 1948, pg. 14. Jews comprised roughly half of the 20th district's 140,000 voters; another 30 percent, approximately, were Irish-Catholic. Ibid.

[2] "Samuel Marx Dies, Congressman-Elect," *The New York Times*, December 1, 1922, pg. 17.

[3] *Autobiography*, 199 and 200.

[4] Ibid., 198.

[5] His daughter writes that her father gave "eight or nine speeches" every evening of the campaign. Vera Bloom, *There's No Place Like Washington* (New York: G. P. Putnam's Sons, 1948), 8. See also *Autobiography*, 200-202.

[6] "Bloom Wins Seat in House Contest," *The New York Times*, April 11, 1924, pg. 1, and *Speech of Hon. John M. Nelson (Republican) in Favor of Representative Sol Bloom in the Chandler-Bloom Contest in the House of Representatives* (Washington: Government Printing Office, 1924), 4. The Republicans contested the final result, but Congress

essentially recognized Bloom as the legitimate winner a year later when it voted 210-198 not to unseat him. See "House Committee Votes Bloom Out," *The New York Times*, February 22, 1924, pg. 1, and "Bloom Wins Seat in House Contest."

[7] Bennett, 9. See also *Autobiography*, 208.

[8] "Sol Bloom Elected, But Faces Recount," *The New York Times*, January 31, 1923, pg. 1.

[9] "Sol Bloom to Open Day and Night Office; Interpreters to Aid Poor in Congress Pleas," *The New York Times*, February 5, 1923, pg.1. See also *Autobiography*, 207, and his March 28, 1927, letter to the editor in *The New York Times*, "Mr. Bloom and the Radio," pg. 20, in which he writes that he is trying to help "the little fellow."

[10] *Autobiography*, 306.

[11] New members of Congress were expected to be "seen but not heard," writes his daughter. *There's No Place*, 13.

[12] See "Statistics of the Congressional and Presidential Election of November 4, 1924" and "Statistics of the Congressional Election of November 2, 1926" – both available at https://history.house.gov/Institution/Election-Statistics (accessed March 20, 2020). According to one New York Times writer, Bloom was one of the "two most popular 'freshman'" members of the House of Representatives in 1923-24. "Who's Who Among the Convention Leaders," *The New York Times*, June 22, 1924, pg. XX5.

[13] The official election returns for all his races can be found at https://history.house.gov/Institution/Election-Statistics/ (accessed July 11, 2021).

[14] Thomas J. Campanella, "Playground of the Century: A Political and Design History of New York City's Greatest Unbuilt Park," *Journal of the Society of Architectural Historians*, 72:2 (2013), 192. In a footnote, ibid., 203, Campanella writes that the projected searchlight "was, of course, a figment of Bloom's fertile imagination – curvature of the earth would curtail the distance even a very powerful light could be seen...to some fifty miles at best." See also "Wants World Fair on Jamaica Bay," *The New York Times*, December 1, 1925, pg. 2, and "Brooklyn As Site for "World's Fair," *The New York Times*, December 13, 1925, pg. RE1.

[15] Bennett, 11, and *Autobiography* 215-216.

[16] "Invitation to American Farmers," radio address, August 15, 1931, printed in *Our Heritage*, 101. In another radio address, he promised to "stage the greatest celebration ever held in the history of civilization" ("George Washington, the Builder," in *Our Heritage*, 112-113). At one point, Bloom reportedly approved of a plan to build a "colossal statue" of George Washington on Staten Island that "would be visible to all travelers entering or leaving New York Harbor" ("Huge Statue Urged of First President," *The New York Times*, May 22, 1932, pg. 10).

[17] On that day, among other things, President Herbert Hoover, delivered an address about Washington to a joint session of Congress. The speech is reproduced in *Report of the United States George Washington Bicentennial Commission* (Washington: George Washington Bicentennial Commission, 1932), 47-49.

[18] *Report of the Bicentennial Commission*, 2.

[19] *Our Heritage*, 14; *Autobiography*, 217. One historian writes that in 1932 "no sentient American could enter a public building, go to school, attend a lodge meeting, mail a letter, or open a newspaper without meditating on the personhood of the First President; his picture was everywhere – on posters, stamps, ads, booklets, calendars from the butcher, and all manner of patriotic bric-a-brac." Karal Ann Marling, "A 'New Historical Whopper': Creating the Art of the Constitutional Sesquicentennial," *A Bicentennial Chronicle* (Spring 1987, no. 14), 15-16.

[20] *Report of the Bicentennial Commission*, 5.

[21] *Our Heritage*, 13. Indeed, no member of the House of Representatives spoke more often on the radio in 1932 than Sol Bloom. "Panorama of Broadcasting," *The New York Times*, December 25, 1932, pg. XX6.

[22] *Our Heritage*, 14. The final volume was published in 1944.

[23] *Report of the Bicentennial Commission*, 2.

[24] See ibid., 175-176. See also "Washington Coin Bill Approved by Mellon," *The New York Times*, February 10, 1931, pg. 2.

[25] "Informs President of Bridge Naming," *The New York Times*, January 15, 1931, pg. 14.

[26] "Johnson Twice Throws a Dollar Across the Turbid Rappahannock," Charles McLean, *The New York Times*, February 23, 1936, pg. 1. Bloom insisted that the river was four times wider in Washington's day and refused to concede defeat. "Mr. Bloom Widens River to 1,300 Feet," *The New York Times*, February 20, 1936, pg. 21. See also Bloom's letters to Charles A. Higley and A. Atalas Leve in SB Papers, Box 6.

[27] The speech is printed in *Our Heritage*, 302-305.

[28] Under Bloom's direction, two books were published and widely distributed by the sesquicentennial commission: *The Story of the Constitution* (Washington: U.S. Constitution Sesquicentennial Commission, 1937) and *History of the Formation of the Union Under the Constitution* (Washington: U.S. Government Printing Office, 1941). The former was apparently one of only seven books that sat on President Roosevelt's desk. See Bloom's November 29, 1943 letter to Melville Minton in SB Papers, Box 11; see also "Political Leaders at Rites for Bloom," *The New York Times*, March 11, 1949, pg. 25.

[29] Thomas J. Campanella, "Washington's New York Monument," *The Wall Street Journal*, May 14, 2004.

[30] Marling, 21. See also *There's No Place Like Washington*, 164-168.

[31] "The News of the Week in Review," *The New York Times*, March 20, 1938, pg. 59.

Chapter 3 *(pages 22-36)*

[1] Qtd. in "Ford Weekly Replies to Strauss Speech," *The New York Times*, December 12, 1926, pg. E1.

[2] In 1927, Ford, issued an apology in which he claimed to be "deeply mortified" to learn

that his newspaper had been used to slander Jews. This plea of ignorance, however, stretches credulity. Indeed, historians Allan Nevins and Frank Ernest Hill call the proposition that Ford didn't know that anti-Semitic articles were appearing in his own newspaper "absurd." See Allan Nevins and Frank Ernest Hill, *Ford: Expansion and Challenge, 1915-1933* (New York: Charles Scribner's Sons, 1962), 321. It's not even clear if Ford read the apology issued in his name. See Neil Baldwin, *Henry Ford and the Jews: The Mass Production of Hate* (New York: PublicAffairs, 2001), 237.

[3] Bloom wasn't the first Jew to publicly attack Ford for being anti-Semitic. Another man who was "neither timid nor insecure" and was "confidently at home both as an American and a Jew" – Louis Marshall, president of the American Jewish Committee from 1912-1929 – launched a public relations campaign against Ford in late 1920. Robert S. Rifkind, "Confronting Antisemitism in America: Louis Marshall and Henry Ford," *American Jewish History* 94, no. 1-2 (March-June 2008), 71 and 73. See also Baldwin, 120-121, and *Louis Marshall, Champion of Liberty: Selected Papers and Addresses*, ed. Charles Reznikoff (Philadelphia: Jewish Publication Society, 1957), 330.

[4] "Asks House Inquiry on Ford's Charges," *The New York Times*, December 15, 1926, pg. 27. See also "Wants Congressional Inquiry into Ford's Charges Against Jews," *Jewish Daily Bulletin*, December 15, 1926, pg. 1.

[5] Qtd. in "Wants Ford Called to Give His 'Facts,'" *The New York Times*, December 20, 1926, pg. 16.

[6] *Autobiography*, 315-316.

[7] "Asks House," *New York Times*.

[8] "Ford Indiscreetly Definite," *The New York Times*, December 16, 1926, pg. 26.

[9] "On the Proposal for a Congressional Inquiry Into Ford's Charges," *Jewish Daily Bulletin*, December 17, 1926, pg. 2-4.

[10] *Cyrus Adler: Selected letters, Volume II*, ed. Ira Robinson (Philadelphia: Jewish Publication Society of America, 1941), 137-138.

[11] "Bloom Urges Ford to Submit Facts," *The New York Times*, December 26, 1926, pg. 27.

[12] "Bloom Retorts to Ford," *The New York Times*, January 7, 1927, pg. 9. See also "Ford Evades Reply to Bloom's Challenge," *Jewish Daily Bulletin*, January 9, 1927, pg. 3.

[13] "Calls Ford Charges False," *The New York Times*, February 7, 1927, pg. 21.

[14] Qtd. in "Congress Leaders Do Not Approve Committee of Inquiry on Ford's Charges," *Jewish Daily Bulletin*, December 27, 1926, pg. 3.

[15] "No Action Likely by U.S. Congress on Bloom Resolution, Is Prediction," *Jewish Daily Bulletin*, December 28, 1926, pg. 1.

[16] *Autobiography*, 316.

[17] Napoleon discarded this calendar in 1805.

[18] See E. G. Richards, *Mapping Time: The Calendar and its History* (Oxford: Oxford University Press, 1998), 112-118 and Eviatar Zerubavel, *The Seven Day Circle: The History and Meaning of the Week* (New York, The Free Press, 1985), 74-81. This blank

day has been given different names over the years – e.g., *dies non*, year day, zero day, no man's day, and World Day.

[19] Joseph H. Hertz, *The Battle for the Sabbath at Geneva* (London: Oxford University Press, 1932), 18.

[20] "Asks World Parley on Calendar Shift," *The New York Times*, December 3, 1928, p. 24.

[21] See George Eastman's testimony in *Simplification of the Calendar: Hearings Before the Committee on Foreign Affairs, House of Representatives, Seventieth Congress, Second Session, on H. J. Res. 334* (Washington: Government Printing Office, 1934), 10.

[22] Christie Davies, Eugene Trivizas, and Roy Wolfe, "The Failure of Calendar Reform (1922-1931): Religious Minorities, Businessmen, Scientists, and Bureaucrats," *Journal of Historical Sociology*, 12:3 (1999), 253. "It is clear from the correspondence in the files of the League of Nations that....the funds for the printing and translation of pro-calendar reform propaganda sent out by the League, the salaries and expenses of extra assistants taken on by the League, and the fees and expenses of many of the organizers of the national committees were paid for by George Eastman." Ibid., 257.

[23] Exodus 20:9-11.

[24] Jeffrey S. Gurock, *Orthodox Jews in America* (Bloomington: Indiana University Press, 2009), 98. See also ibid., 149.

[25] Henry L. Feingold, *A Time for Searching: Entering the Mainstream, 1920-1945* (Baltimore, Johns Hopkins University Press, 1992), 58. See also ibid., 107.

[26] *Orthodox Jews in America*, 94.

[27] *A Time for Searching*, 106-107. See also Samuel Friedman "The Five-Day Week and the Proposed Calendar Reform," *The Jewish Forum*, September 1931, 296: "Most Jews who do work on the Sabbath, nevertheless revere that day as holy; their reason for violating it being one of economic necessity, and not of indifference."

[28] *Orthodox Jews in America*, 99-100.

[29] Hertz, 12 and 38.

[30] *Simplification*, 2.

[31] *Simplification*, 46. See also ibid., 209.

[32] Ibid., 20, 151, 12, 158, and 148. For other examples, see ibid., 187-188 and 221.

[33] Rabbis Bernard Drachman, Mortimer Cohen, David de Sola Pool, Moses Hyamson, and Abram Simon.

[34] "Around and About Washington," *The Jewish Tribune*, January 4, 1929, p. 29. See also "Congressman Sol Bloom Explains," p. 5.

[35] Hertz, 15.

[36] "Yeshiva to Hear Fess," *The New York Times*, March 11, 1929, p. 35

[37] See Volume 43 of the American Jewish Year Book (Philadelphia: Jewish Publication Society, 1941), p. 567, and subsequent volumes.

[38] *Autobiography*, 311. For more of Bloom's recollections of this saga, see *Autobiography* 308-314.

[39] *Congressional Record*, 71st Cong., 1st Sess., p. 2698-2715.

[40] Ibid., 2707, 2708, and 2699. See also *Simplification*, 180. Opponents of the Eastman plan also argued that businesses could adopt the 13-month calendar for their own internal accountings without burdening the rest of the population. A number of businesses, in fact, had already done so by the 1920s.

[41] *Congressional Record*, 2706 and 2707.

[42] *Simplification*, 113. See also Friedman, 295.

[43] *Congressional Record* 2704 and 2710.

[44] Ibid., 2701. See also *Autobiography*, 312 and 313.

[45] *Congressional Record*, 2701. See also ibid., 2704.

[46] Representatives of all three Jewish denominations testified before Congress against the Eastman plan with equal vigor, and the main organizations of all three passed resolutions against it. See "Fess Sees America in the World Court," *The New York Times*, March 18, 1929, p. 19; "Topic of Interest to the Churchgoer," *The New York Times*, September 19, 1931, p. 20; "Synagogue Fights Calendar Reform," *The New York Times*, May 22, 1928, p. 28; and *Central Conference of American Rabbis, Fortieth Annual Convention (June 27-30, 1929), Volume XXXIX,* ed. Rabbi Isaac E. Marcuson, p. 62-63 and 111. Rabbi Stephen Wise, America's most prominent Reform leader at the time, wrote, "If there were but a thousand Jews left in the world to preserve the Sabbath, I would go through fire and water to help them keep their religion." Qtd. in *Simplification*, 109. Not every Reform rabbi, however, opposed the Eastman plan. Rabbi (Ephraim?) Frisch of the CCAR stated, "We [Reform Jews] are interested in a great institution and idea [i.e., the Sabbath], and not in its geography or its time location; and I do not think we would suffer any serious consequences if once a year the Sabbath was an Elijah – a wanderer." *Central Conference of American Rabbis, Fortieth Annual Convention*, 65.

[47] "Calendar Reform Put Off in Geneva," *The New York Times*, October 17, 1931, p.6.

[48] Qtd. in Hertz, 33.

[49] Davies, Trivizas, and Wolfe, 252. See the four letters between Bloom and Rabbi Herbert S. Goldstein in SB Papers, Box 41, about efforts to introduce calendar reform legislation in 1947. As late as 1963, calendar reform was apparently enough of a concern for Rabbi Abraham Joshua Heschel to raise the issue during an important meeting with Cardinal Augustin Bea. See the Memorandum from Simon Segal to Marc Tanenbaum, April 5, 1963 (available on the American Jewish Committee's online archives, http://www.ajcarchives.org/ajcarchive/DigitalArchive.aspx [accessed May 17, 2020]).

[50] Indeed, according to Eastman's National Committee on Calendar Simplification, 82 percent of Protestant clergymen replied "No" when asked, "Do you see any objection on religious grounds to such a calendar causing the occurrence of one 8-day week each year and two such weeks in leap years?" *Supplementary Report of the National Committee on Calendar Simplification for the United States* (U.S.: Office of the Chair-

man, 1931), 40-41.

[51] *Congressional Record*, 2699. See also ibid., 2701.

Chapter 4 *(pages 37-46)*

[1] *Autobiography* 245-246.

[2] "Footnotes on Headliners," *The New York Times*, July 23, 1939, pg. E2, and "Bloom, Veteran of House 16 Years, New Chairman of Foreign Relations Body," *Jewish Telegraphic Agency*, July 12, 1939.

[3] Robert Dallek, *Franklin D. Roosevelt: A Political Life* (New York: Penguin Books, 2017), 378.

[4] Alonzo Hamby, *Man of Destiny: FDR and the Making of the American Century* (New York: Basic Books, 2015), 284. See also Lynne Olson, *Those Angry Days: Roosevelt, Lindbergh, and America's Fight Over World War II, 1939-1941* (New York: Random House, 2013), xvii. A French journalist in New York during this time period described the United States as "literally drunk with pacifism." Qtd. in ibid., 54.

[5] Hamby, 287. In 1939, Roosevelt saw talk of "entering the conflict as domestic political poison." Dallek, 335.

[6] Hamilton Fish, *FDR: The Other Side of the Coin* (Torrance: Institute for Historical Review, 1976), 21. See also *Lend-Lease Bill: Hearings Before the Committee on Foreign Affairs, House of Representatives, Seventy-Seventh Congress, First Session, on H.R. 1776: A Bill Further to Promote the Defense of the United States, and for Other Purposes* (Washington: Government Printing Office, 1941), 6, and *There's No Place*, 273.

[7] See Alan Brinkley, *Franklin Delano Roosevelt* (Oxford: Oxford University Press, 2010), 64. See also Hamby, 321; Dallek, 329; and Warren E. Kimball, *The Most Unsordid Act: Lend-Lease, 1939-1941* (Baltimore: The Johns Hopkins Press, 1969), 9 and 239.

[8] Qtd. in Dallek, 425. See also Jean Edward Smith, *FDR* (New York: Random House, 2007), 448. In testimony before Congress, Secretary of State Cordell Hull predicted what America would face should Europe and the Atlantic Ocean come under Hitler's control: "Under these conditions our national security would require the continuous devotion of a very great part of all our work and wealth for defense production, prolonged universal military service, extremely burdensome taxation, unending vigilance against enemies within our borders, and complete involvement in power diplomacy." *Lend-Lease Bill*, 6. Noted columnist Dorothy Thompson predicted economic blackmail of the U.S. if Hitler defeated England: "German-dominated Eurasia will offer to buy our cotton, wheat, oil, and so forth, provided – provided we have a president in the White House who suits them." *Lend-Lease Bill*, 645. See also ibid., 652.

[9] Dallek, 362, 377, and 420.

[10] Qtd. in ibid., 334.

[11] Qtd. in Olson 90. Already in 1937, Roosevelt wrote, "I am fighting against a public

psychology of long standing. A psychology which comes very close to saying, 'Peace at any price.'" Qtd. in Smith, 420.

[12] Joseph P. Lash, *Roosevelt and Churchill – 1939-1941: The Partnership That Saved the West* (New York: W. W. Norton, 1976), 477.

[13] Qtd. in Olson, xviii.

[14] *There's No Place Like Washington*, 269. See also ibid., 93.

[15] See Olson, 277 and 357.

[16] Ibid., 64. See also Hamby, 293, and Smith, 427.

[17] Dinnerstein, 105-127.

[18] See "H. R. 1776 Becomes Law," editorial, *New York Daily News*, March 13, 1941, pg. 31: "[A] whispering campaign [is] now going on to the effect that the Jews are mainly to blame for our being as deep in the war as we now are, and are moving heaven and earth to push us all the way in." See also the December 31, 1940 letter by America First leader General Robert E. Wood published in Ruth Sarles, *A Story of America First: The Men and Women Who Opposed U.S. Intervention in World War II* (Westport: Praeger, 2003), 52, in which he writes, "There is persistent propaganda all over this country to the effect that the Jews here are trying to get us into the war."

[19] "Des Moines Speech," www.charleslindbergh.com/americanfirst/speech.asp (accessed July 11, 2020).

[20] Edward S. Shapiro, "The Approach of War: Congressional Isolationism and Anti-Semitism, 1939-1941" *American Jewish History* 74 (1984), 49.

[21] Qtd. in ibid., 48.

[22] Ibid., 55-61, 63-64.

[23] See Wayne S. Cole, *America First: The Battle Against Intervention, 1940-1941* (Madison: University of Wisconsin, 1953), 141.

[24] Ibid., 51. See also Olson, 370. In Congress, Nye said, "[Many Americans think] our Jewish citizenry would willingly have our country and its sons taken into this foreign war." Ibid., 372. Aware of anti-Semitic sentiment in society, studio heads actually feared making anti-Nazi films – lest they inspire talk of "Jewish warmongers" – and when they did make such films, they refrained from indicating that Jews were the primary victims of Nazi oppression. Ibid., 364 and 368.

[25] Shapiro, 51. "The sub-committee adjourned early and never submitted any report, in part because of charges of anti-Semitism." Ibid., 53. See also Wayne S. Cole, *Roosevelt & the Isolationists, 1932-45* (Lincoln: University of Nebraska Press, 1983), 476.

[26] Anne Lindbergh, *War Within and Without: Diaries and Letters of Anne Morrow Lindbergh – 1939-1944* (New York: Harcourt Brace, 1980), 227. Socialist leader Norman Thomas, who severed ties with Lindbergh after the speech, also didn't regard him as anti-Semitic. Olson, 388.

[27] Reeve Lindbergh, *Under a Wing: A Memoir* (New York: Simon & Schuster, 1998), 201 and 203.

²⁸ Shapiro, 64.

²⁹ Ibid., 46, and Henry L. Feingold, "'Courage First and Intelligence Second': The American Jewish Secular Elite, Roosevelt and the Failure to Rescue," *American Jewish History* LXXII (June 1983), 428-429. However, the "isolationist focus on the Jews was singularly misplaced" as "Jewish influence on American foreign policy during this period was virtually nonexistent." Furthermore, the "most influential element within the interventionist camp was the South which contained relatively few Jews." Shapiro, 64.

³⁰ "Des Moines Speech."

³¹ Qtd. in Olson, 380. See also *America First*, 149.

³² After the Central Conference of American Rabbis called for government recognition of Jewish conscientious objectors to war, one man wrote the following in a newspaper's "Readers' Forum": "Under these conditions, it would seem that Bernard M. Baruch, Solomon Bloom and other Jewish leaders ought to be more careful about urging steps that will plunge our Republic into war, with inevitable mass slaughter of Christian youth, while Jewish youth are being kept from jeopardy." "An Attorney Writes Ex-Governor Smith," *The Tablet*, October 7, 1939, pg. 8. See also Ariel Hurwitz, *Jews Without Power: American Jewry During the Holocaust* (New Rochelle: MultiEducator, 2011), 23.

³³ Olson, 385.

³⁴ Qtd. in ibid., 384. In September 1939, Rabbi Stephen Wise wrote to a colleague, "We Jews are in a peculiarly difficult position…. We do not want to give anyone, even the bitterest and most mendacious of our foes, the right to charge us with war-mongering. We Jews must not give the appearance of seeking to rush America into war." Qtd. in Rafael Medoff, *The Jews Should Keep Quiet: Franklin D. Roosevelt, Rabbi Stephen S. Wise, and the Holocaust* (Philadelphia: Jewish Publication Society, 2019), 93.

³⁵ "John W. McCormack Oral History Interview – 3/30/1977," John F. Kennedy Presidential Library and Museum, page 34, available at www.jfklibrary.org/sites/default/files/archives/JFKOH/McCormack%2C%20John%20W/JFKOH-JOWM-01/JFKOH-JOWM-01-TR.pdf (accessed July 19, 2020). See also Kimball, 141, citing the diary of Henry Morgenthau, and two *New York Times* articles in the summer of 1939 that referred to the original Cash-and-Carry legislation as "the Bloom resolution": "New Fight Looms on Foreign Policy," *The New York Times*, June 18, 1939, pg. 1, and "Debate on Neutrality," *The New York Times*, July 2, 1939, pg. E1. McCormack regarded Bloom as "a man of guts and courage and of energy….a great American and a great legislator." "Oral History Interview," 34.

³⁶ "WMCA Picketing Limited," *The New York Times*, June 19, 1939, pg. 8. A year later, a "delegation representing the West Side Mothers Peace Committee of New York City, presented petitions signed by 10,000 mothers to Reps. Solomon Bloom and Barton of New York, against any participation of [the U.S.] in the war abroad." "Mothers Plea For Peace," *The Berkshire Eagle*, May 31, 1940, pg. 7.

³⁷ *Congressional Record*, 76th Congress, 2nd Session, October 10, 1939, p. 261, and Shapiro, 55. The second name is a reference to Bernard Baruch, a prominent American

Jewish financier.

[38] "Seek to Inject Anti-Semitism Into Hearings on Lend-Lease Bill," *News from All Over the World – by the Jewish Telegraph Agency*, February 14, 1941, pg. 3-4. *The New York Times* quoted Mynnie Fischer, chairman of the Mothers Mobilization Committee Against War, making a similar statement: "[We want to learn] why this man Sol Bloom and his henchmen are being permitted to run the country." "Women Hang Effigy Near British Embassy; Other Anti-Aid Crusaders Storm Capitol," *The New York Times*, February 14, 1941, pg. 5.

[39] *Jewish Telegraph Agency*, February 14, 1941.

[40] "Women Protest Bill," *The New York Times*, February 23, 1941, pg. 36.

[41] "Effigy of Writer Seized in Capital," *The New York Times*, February 24, 1941, pg. 7.

[42] "Protest Against War Staged by Women: 150 Parade in Streets – Seek to Impress Sol Bloom," *The New York Times*, May 11, 1941, pg. 7.

[43] *There's No Place Like Washington*, 204-206. Bloom's daughter, Vera, writes that her father and other non-isolationist members of Congress were regularly "swamped with scurrilous mail and besieged by high-sounding isolationist delegations." Ibid., 206.

[44] *Autobiography*, 243. See also Kurt F. Stone, *The Jews of Capitol Hill: A Compendium of Jewish Congressional Members* (Plymouth: Scarecrow Press, 2011), 129: "Bloom was vilified as a 'Jewish warmonger'…; he received enough death threats that J. Edgar Hoover assigned him a personal retinue of bodyguards" and Ray Hill, "Sol Bloom of New York," *The Knoxville Focus*, May 19, 2019, available at http://knoxfocus.com/archives/this-weeks-focus/sol-bloom-new-york (accessed July 19, 2020).

[45] Dallek, 347; *Autobiography*, 235. Kimball, 141, writes that this defeat was Bloom's fault: "Bloom had badly botched the floor fight to repeal the Neutrality Act."

[46] Letter dated November 3, 1939. SB Papers, Boxes 60-61.

[47] Letters dated November 3, 1939, and November 22, 1939, respectively. Ibid.

[48] February 1, 1941 letter to Louis H. Markowitz in SB Papers, Box 10. See also the February 21, 1941 letter to Louis Hart in ibid., Box 3.

[49] *Autobiography*, 251.

[50] August 6, 1941 letter to Sara Paul, SB Papers, Box 13. See also Bloom's letter to Rev. Dr. Jacob L. Gabel, superintendent of the Hebrew Convalescent Home, in which he writes, "[E]very time I try to talk about my dear wife, I lose control of myself completely." Ibid., Box 40.

[51] *Autobiography*, 251. See also, ibid., 156.

[52] "How Mr. Sam Saved the Draft," *The Washington Post*, August 18, 1991, available at www.washingtonpost.com/archive/opinions/1991/08/18/how-mr-sam-saved-the-draft/40056dca-450a-4dce-b1cd-cb123ef36139/ (accessed July 19, 2020).

[53] *Autobiography*, 243-244.

[54] British Prime Minister Harold Macmillan (1957-1963) wrote in 1966, "The provision of American aid in the shape of Lend-Lease saved us from something like disaster." Qtd. in

Kimball, 229.

[55] The Neutrality Act of 1939 and Lend-Lease, for example, outfitted the U.S. arms industry for war, while the draft bills took a U.S. army that was ranked 18th in the world in 1939 with 200,000 men and transformed it into a more battle-ready army of 1.4 million men by mid-1941. Smith, 425 and 467. See also Olson, 219, and Hill, 778.

[56] See Stephen Bungay, *The Most Dangerous Enemy: A History of the Battle of Britain* (London: Aurum Press, 2000), 29-31, 111, and 307.

[57] The British "kept the Nazis from taking Egypt and then overrunning Palestine and killing Jewish settlers there. Without FDR's policies and leadership there may well have been no Jewish communities left in Palestine, no Jewish state, no Israel." Richard Breitman and Allan J. Lichtman in *FDR and the Jews* (Cambridge: Belknap, 2013), 318. See also Gerhard L. Weinberg, "Foreword," in Robert Rosen, *Saving the Jews: Franklin D. Roosevelt and the Holocaust* (New York: Thunder's Mouth, 2006), xv-xvi: "The Germans did not send the Afrika Korps into Egypt to dismantle the pyramids for shipment to Berlin but rather to make possible the killing of the Jewish inhabitants of the Palestine mandate, as Hitler promised the grand mufti of Jerusalem."

[58] The Soviet Union also received war material from the U.S. and England thanks to Lend-Lease. See Albert L. Week, *Russia's Life-Saver: Lend-Lease Aid to the U.S.S.R. in World War II* (Plymouth: Lexington Books, 2004), 9, and Alexander Hill, "British Lend Lease Aid and the Soviet War Effort: June 1941-June 1942," *The Journal of Military History*, vol. 71, no. 3 (July 2007).

[59] Rosen, xxv. For a breakdown by country of the 11 million Jews the Nazis hoped to exterminate, see the Nazis' "Wannsee Protocols," available at www.jewishvirtuallibrary. org/the-wannsee-protocol (accessed July 5, 2020).

Chapter 5 *(pages 47-54)*

[1] See below, page 50.

[2] "Bloom Bill to Permit German Aliens' Stay Here," *Jewish Daily Bulletin*, May 11, 1933, pg. 3 and "Blocks Mercy-Ship Bill," *The New York Times*, August 6, 1940, pg. 21. For the text of the first bill, see the press release related to it in SB Papers, Box 40.

[3] See "Seek to Appeal Consular Immigration Decisions," *Jewish Daily Bulletin*, May 25, 1933, pg. 3.

[4] Hurwitz, 35. They did, however, attempt some "backdoor diplomacy." Ibid., 37, and Breitman and Lichtman, 89.

[5] Rafael Medoff, *The Deafening Silence: American Jewish Leaders and the Holocaust* (New York: Shapolsky, 1987), 22-27.

[6] Qtd. in ibid. See also Breitman and Lichtman, 71, and "Did American Jewry Do Enough?" 12.

[7] Qtd. in *The Deafening Silence*, 33.

8 See https://u-s-history.com/pages/h1528.html (accessed December 20, 2020) among other places.

9 *The Deafening Silence*, 28, 32-33, 43, and 53, and *The Jews Should Keep Quiet*, 29. In addition to the fear of economic displacement, "nativists whipped up fears that immigrants would bring radical foreign ideologies with them." *The Jews Should Keep Quiet*, xiii. Considering the disproportionate number of Jews among American socialists, these fears were not entirely irrational. In *A Fire in Their Hearts: Yiddish Socialists in New York* (Cambridge: Harvard University Press, 2005), 2, Tony Michels writes, "The stereotype of the radical Jew was fairly accurate, as stereotypes go."

10 Dinnerstein, 105 and 126-127.

11 Qtd. in *The Deafening Silence*, 34. Fear of anti-Semitism led Wise to oppose other immigration initiatives as well, including a plan to settle Jewish refugees in Alaska. See *The Anguish of a Jewish Leader*, 45. Commissioner of Immigration and Naturalization Daniel MacCormack told Judge Julian Mack "that American Jews had to choose between protecting 4.5 million Jews in the United States or aiding many fewer German Jews." Breitman and Lichtman, 74.

12 Breitman and Lichtman, 102. "Roosevelt knew...that any congressional review of the immigration law during the 1930s was certain to lead to even further restrictions, if not a complete closure of the country." Weinberg, "Foreword," xiii-xiv. See also Feingold, "Did American Jewry Do Enough?" 4. One bill that called for cutting all immigration quotas by 90 percent actually passed the House of Representatives in the early 1930s. Peter Novick, *The Holocaust in American Life* (New York: Houghton Mifflin, 1999), 51.

13 Henry L. Feingold, *Jewish Power in America: Myth and Reality* (New Brunswick, New Jersey: Transaction, 2008), 25. See also *The Politics of Rescue*, 15. In early 1939, Bloom wrote to a Dr. Jakob Hoffman, "Whenever it is suggested in Washington to change the present [immigration] law, you would be surprised to learn of the tremendous opposition." Increasing immigration quotas at this time is "impossible," he argued. SB Papers, Box 5.

14 Breitman and Lichtman, 116.

15 Two-thirds of Americans opposed the bill, according to a Gallup poll in March 1939. Ibid., 149.

16 Novick, 50-51; Breitman and Lichtman, 151 and 160; and Rosen, 86. See also Saul S. Friedman, *No Haven for the Oppressed: United States Policy Toward Jewish Refugees, 1938-1945* (Detroit: Wayne State University Press, 1973), 50, and *The Jews Should Keep Quiet*, 313. As noted in chapter 4, Roosevelt was politically weaker in 1938 than he had ever been during his presidency. Olson, 64.

17 *The Deafening Silence*, 56-59. See also *Bearing Witness*, 231.

18 Weinberg, "Foreword," xiv. Walter Laqueur wrote years later, "No one in his right mind thought that Hitler actually intended to kill all Jews." *The Terrible Secret: Suppression of the Truth About Hitler's 'Final Solution'* (New York: Routledge, 2017), 123. See also Rosen, 26; *Bearing Witness*, 229; and *The Deafening Silence*, 28.

19 David S. Wyman, *Paper Walls: America and the Refugee Crisis, 1938-1941* (New York:

Pantheon Books, 1985), 35. See also Novick, 50, and *The Politics of Rescue*, 69 and 82.

[20] Rosen, xxvii, 103.

[21] Qtd. in Breitman and Lichtman, 138. See also Rachel Erbelding, *Rescue Board: The Untold Story of America's Efforts to Save the Jews of Europe* (New York: Anchor, 2018), 14.

[22] Increasingly, but not immediately. The Nazis' Final Solution had not yet begun, which is why Jewish religious leaders like Rabbi Chaim Ozer Grodzinski actually *opposed* leaving Lithuania in early 1940, believing it would remain independent – "neither red nor black," in his words. Qtd. in Efraim Zuroff, *The Response of Orthodox Jewry in the United States to the Holocaust: The Activities of the Vaad Ha-Hatzala Rescue Committee, 1939-1945* (Hoboken, Yeshiva University Press, 2000), 49. An American health specialist, Dr. Samuel Schmidt – who traveled to Lithuania on a fact-finding mission for an American rescue group – concurred in a letter he wrote to his wife on March 17, 1940. Ibid., 58.

[23] Furthermore, Jews were hardly the only group whose lives were at risk once war broke out, and Americans may have feared that opening the country's doors to Jews would only invite numerous other populations to clamor for permission to immigrate to the U.S. as well.

[24] *The Politics of Rescue*, 128 and 130, and Breitman and Lichtman, 166.

[25] Friedman, 117.

[26] *The Jews Should Keep Quiet*, 66. Additionally, a non-Jewish refugee to the U.S was caught spying for Germany in 1941. The New York Times carried this story on its front page. Breitman and Lichtman, 193.

[27] *The Jews Should Keep Quiet*, 93. See also Breitman and Lichtman, 161-164 and 169, and *Rescue Board*, 16.

[28] Qtd. in *The Jews Should Keep Quiet*, 93. See also Breitman and Lichtman, 167.

[29] SB Papers, Box 1. See also the April 4, 1942 letter to Cobina Wright in SB Papers, Box 26.

[30] July 13, 1940 letter to James H. McDonough, SB Papers, Box 10. See also "Bloom Charges Nazis Looting Internees in Occupied Countries," *Jewish Telegraphic Agency*, December 15, 1940, in which Bloom defends the government against critics of its attitude toward Jewish refugees: "This Government is fully aware of the fact that Hitler [h]as seized upon refugee movements to cloak the infiltration of subversive agents into the democratic countries of the world and we are taking every precaution to see that our aid for refugees does not result in damage to our own country."

[31] Letter to secretary Beth Flegelman about Fred Herrmann, SB Papers, Box 4. One cannot plausibly argue that Bloom was fibbing in all these letters and using "national security" as an excuse not to help. First, as we will see in the following chapter, Bloom was more than happy to help people when he could. Second, at least one of these letters was written to a friend. Third, Bloom would have no reason to lie to his own

longtime secretary in an internal office correspondence.

[32] *The Politics of Rescue*, 160

[33] See Breitman and Lichtman, 166, 175, and 177.

[34] *The Abandonment of the Jews*, 8.

[35] See *The Deafening Silence*, 99 and 125-126.

[36] "Did American Jewry Do Enough?" 24. See also *The Politics of Rescue*, 128, 131, and 146.

[37] David Riesman, "The Politics of Persecution," *Public Opinion Quarterly* 6, no. 1 (Spring 1942), 56. Riesman's comment was made in 1942. According to polls between 1938 and 1945, 15 percent of Americans would have supported an anti-Jewish campaign in the United States and 20-25 percent would have sympathized with a movement of this nature. *The Abandonment of the Jews*, 15.

[38] Considering the intense opposition toward increasing America's immigration quotas, historian Peter Novick wonders: "Were [the] initiatives [of Celler and Dickstein] serious or were they grandstanding for their largely Jewish constituencies?" Novick, 292.

[39] In general, Bloom was – as The New York Times wrote on at least three occasions – a "party man" (or a "strict party man"). See "Bloom, 78, Waging a Brisk Campaign," by Douglas Dales, *The New York Times*, October 27, 1948, pg. 14; "Bloom an Expert on Foreign Affairs," *The New York Times*, November 3, 1948, pg. 16; and "Representative Sol Bloom Dies of Heart Attack," *The New York Times*, March 8, 1949, pg. 1.

[40] July 27, 1939 letter. FDR Presidential Library and Museum, "PPF 1138: Sol Bloom."

[41] Letter to Samuel Null, May 6, 1939. SB Papers, Box 13. In 1944, one New York Democratic official went so far as to call Bloom "the right hand of the president." See "Tammany Revolt Ends in Harmony," *The New York Times*, May 18, 1944, pg. 15.

[42] Roosevelt was of course also idolized by millions of non-Jewish Americans as well. When Rep. Robert Ramspeck, the Democratic House Whip, learned of Roosevelt's death, he responded, "My God, how terrible! The greatest man in the world." Few men inspire such comments. Frederick R. Barkley, "Shock, Disbelief Echo in Congress," *The New York Times*, April 13, 1945, pg. 4.

[43] *The Politics of Rescue*, 8.

[44] Historian Monty Noam Penkower refers to Roosevelt as American Jews' "mortal savior." Penkower, 83. Admiration for Roosevelt wasn't restricted to America; historian Saul Friedman writes, "No man in the twentieth century was more idolized by Jews throughout the world than Roosevelt." *No Haven for the Oppressed*, 226.

[45] Smith, x. See also Naomi W. Cohen, *American Jews and the Zionist Idea* (United States: Ktav, 1975), 56: "[Jews] saw Roosevelt as the omnipotent champion of the common man, the protector of the insecure and not-quite-accepted."

[46] Breitman and Lichtman, 5. See also ibid., 42. He was the only world leader to recall his country's ambassador to Germany after Kristallnacht. Ibid., 114.

[47] *The Politics of Rescue*, 9; Breitman and Lichtman, 65.

[48] Ibid., 90. Bloom had his own run-ins with Coughlin whose followers tried to defeat him in the 1936 election. See "O'Connor Renomination Is Opposed by Coughlin," *The New York Times*, July 16, 1936, pg. 5; "Lemke Endorsed by Coughlinites; Vote Is 8,152 to 1," *The New York Times*, August 16, 1936, pg. 1; letter to George Gordon Rattle, dated August 25, 1936, SB Papers, Box 30; and letter to Norman C. Epstein, dated August 4, 1936, ibid., Box 37. Coughlinites worked against Bloom's re-election in 1940 as well. See Bloom's September 6, 1940 letters to Lou Smith and Stephen S. Wise. Ibid., Boxes 17 and 26, respectively.

[49] William E. Leuchtenberg, *Franklin D. Roosevelt and the New Deal: 1932-1940* (New York: Harper & Row, 1963), 24-25. See also Breitman and Lichtman, 67.

[50] Qtd. in Leuchtenberg, 25, footnote 22.

[51] Qtd. in Arthur M. Schlesinger, Jr., *The Age of Roosevelt: The Crisis of the Old Order: 1919-1933* (Cambridge: Riverside Press, 1957), 185.

[52] *Autobiography*, 228.

[53] "Franklin D. Roosevelt," editorial, *The New York Times,* April 13, 1945, pg. 16. See also Breitman and Lichtman, 2.

[54] Breitman and Lichtman, 182. Besides, on "every matter of concern to Jews FDR eclipsed his Republican and conservative Democratic rivals." Ibid. See also *The Politics of Rescue*, 8.

[55] See Breitman and Lichtman, 125-141. "Ironically, FDR overlooked [Dominican Republic President Rafael] Trujillo's mass murder of Haitians in part so that the United States could work with him on plans to resettle Jews in the Dominican Republic." See ibid., 325.

[56] *The Politics of Rescue*, 116. Ultimately, the project's staff "produced 666 studies of possible resettlement options," but "nothing was ever done with the material they compiled." Ibid.

[57] Plus: "In the six months from the Evian Conference until the end of the year, members of the Roosevelt administration from the president to the most experienced American diplomat in Berlin put serious time and energy into the long-shot effort of removing hundreds of thousands of Jews in an orderly fashion from Germany and Austria." Breitman and Lichtman, 122.

[58] Ibid., 108.

Chapter 6 *(pages 55-72)*

[1] David Biale et al., *Hasidism: A New History* (Princeton: Princeton University Press, 2018), 600 and 601. See also Arthur Green, "Ger Hasidic Dynasty," in *The YIVO Encyclopedia of Jews in Eastern Europe*, https://yivoencyclopedia.org/article.aspx/ Ger_Hasidic_Dynasty (accessed December 23, 2020).

[2] Bloom actually sat on the Board of Directors of the Institutional Synagogue (the parent

body of the West Side Institutional Synagogue); contributed $100 to its founding (the equivalent of $2,300 in 2022); and was honored at its "bar mitzvah" anniversary dinner in 1930. Aaron I. Reichel, *The Maverick Rabbi* (Norfolk: Donning, 1986), 162-163.

[3] Bloom first met Goldstein at Congregation Kehilath Jeshurun when the latter was a child. Reichel, 162. In a telegram to Goldstein on May 6, 1939, Bloom writes, "I remember as though it were yesterday a little boy who used to sit next to me in schule long before you were a rabbi and who used to help me find my place in the good book." SB Papers, Box 41. In his unpublished and unfinished autobiography (page 72), Goldstein refers to Bloom as "a very dear friend." The autobiography is in the possession of his grandson, Rabbi Aaron I. Reichel.

[4] Letter to Goldstein, March 23, 1933. SB Papers, Box 41.

[5] Letter to Messersmith, September 26, 1939. SB Papers, Box 28.

[6] See Bloom's September 29, 1939 letter to Goldstein. SB Papers, Box 28.

[7] Letter from Warren to Bloom, September 30, 1939. SB Papers, Box 28.

[8] Letter dated October 4, 1939. SB Papers, Box 28.

[9] Monty Noam Penkower, *Twentieth Century Jews: Forging Identity in the Land of Promise and in the Promised Land* (Boston: Academic Studies Press, 2010), 57. See Moshe Yechezkieli, *The Miracle of the Rescue of the Gerrer Rebbe* (Hebrew) (Jerusalem: Yeshurun, 1959), 29-30. Penkower, 56, also writes that Bloom didn't agree to take any steps to help the Gerrer Rebbe until convinced to do so by Justice Louis Brandeis. This assertion seems improbable as Bloom constantly sent letters to various government officials on behalf of his constituents – even, it seems, when he surely knew the answer would be no. He was especially eager to help if a request came through a friend (such as Rabbi Goldstein) or a prominent Jewish group (such as the Agudas Harabonim). Bloom didn't exert himself in every single case, but his papers give no indication that he ever refused to help someone if asked (assuming the request was reasonable).

[10] SB Papers, Box 41.

[11] SB Papers, Box 28.

[12] Ibid.

[13] See his January 6, 1940 letter to Eugene Bonardelli, Counselor of Emigration at the Italian Embassy in Washington. SB Papers, Box 1.

[14] SB Papers, Box 1.

[15] January 15, 1940 letter to Kasher. SB Papers, Box 1. The following day, Bloom wrote to Goldstein and two other people involved in the case identical short letters about the same matter. All three documents are in SB Papers, Box 1.

[16] February 16, 1940 letter to Julius A. Bernstein. SB Papers, Box 1. "I do not believe that anyone has a right to interfere with what I requested the Italian Government to do for me," he wrote to Rabbi L. Feltzer of the Orthodox Union three days later. SB Papers, Box 1.

[17] Letter to Rabbi L. Feltzer. Ibid.

[18] SB Papers, Box 1. In a letter two days earlier to Bernstein, Bloom writes, "It is just as I said. If they had not interfered with the arrangements that I made and tried to increase the number of transit visas, the Gerrer Rabbi and his family would have been out of Poland and in Palestine by this time." Ibid.

[19] SB Papers, Box 61. A 13th household member (an orphaned grandson) was later added to the list illegally. See "The Rescue of My Father," *Ami-Living Magazine*, June 20, 2018, pg. 45-46.

[20] SB Papers, Boxes 60-61. For further details on the rescue, see Ruth Lichtenstein, ed., *Witness to History* (Brooklyn: Project Witness, 2009), 424-427, and Esther Farbstein, *Hidden in Thunder: Perspectives on Faith, Halacha and Leadership During the Holocaust*, trans. Deborah Stern (Jerusalem: Mossad Harav Kook, 2007), 83-85.

[21] Death Notice of Yeshvath Sfath Emeth of Jerusalem in *The New York Times*, March 10, 1949, pg. 27.

[22] Bloom seems to point to the importance of maintaining friendly relations in government in a September 30, 1948 letter (to a person named Samuel Beier). Complaining that a certain case was handled improperly, Bloom writes, "We cannot afford to lose our friendship with people connected with the Government." SB Papers, Box 3.

[23] March 31, 1949 letter to "Rose." SB Papers, Box 5.

[24] January 14, 1949 letter to Larry Levin. SB Papers, Box 46.

[25] "Puts 'Social Lobby' Under Inspection," *The New York Times*, August 11, 1935, pg. RE18. Importantly, the article notes that at "all diplomatic functions great consideration is shown the members of the Senate Foreign Affairs Committee and the House Foreign Affairs Committee." It also relates that President Coolidge's secretary "scanned the society columns just as carefully as the political news. It was important, he felt, to know who went where."

[26] "Sol Bloom Honors German Envoy," *The New York Times*, January 17, 1931, pg. 22; "Notes of Social Activities in New York and Elsewhere," *The New York Times*, January 27, 1931, pg. 26; ibid., *The New York Times*, January 28, 1931, pg. 23; and ibid., *The New York Times*, January 29, 1931, pg. 25.

[27] "New Book Covers Career – From First Muscle Dance to Recent Publicity Stunts," by Hope Ridings Miller, *The Washington Post*, in SB Papers, Box 62.

[28] Rep. Emanuel Celler recalled with criticism years later, "[Bloom] liked to attend the state dinners and he liked the diplomacy that the State Department could accord him. He had a daughter of whom he was very proud, and the daughter attended these sumptuous dinners at the State Department." *Race Against Death*, 144.

[29] Letter dated May 26, 1943. SB Papers, Boxes 60-61.

[30] See Rachel Altein, ed., *Out of the Inferno: The Efforts That Led to the Rescue of Rabbi Yosef Yitzchak Schneersohn of Lubavitch from War Torn Europe in 1939-40* (New York: Kehot, 2002), 71, 105, 175, 179, 233, and (especially) 274. In trying to help the

Lubavitcher Rebbe, Bloom contacted the Lithuanian Minister in Washington (ibid., 71 and 105) and sent letters to the Minister of Sweden on September 29, 1939 ("I am greatly and personally interested in this case.... I shall appreciate any cooperation you can render as a great personal favor"); and the United States Minister in Riga, Latvia on December 29, 1939. Both letters as well as other documents related to this case are in SB Papers, Box 18. See also Bryan Mark Rigg, *Rescued from the Reich: How One of Hitler's Soldiers Saved the Lubavitcher Rebbe* (New Haven: Yale University Press, 2004), 105.

[31] See the July 18, 1940 letter from Bloom to Bernard Gufler at the American Consul in Kaunas, Lithuania, and an official offer to Kotler from Yeshiva College to serve as an instructor of Talmud at a salary of $2,000, dated July 10, 1940. SB Papers, Box 8. This job offer may have been the basis of the original visa granted to Kotler to come to America; the full details of Kotler's escape to America are unknown (November 5, 2017 and September 9, 2021 e-mails to this author from Rabbi Dovid Reidel, director of Research & Archive Division at the Amud Aish Memorial Museum).

[32] See the 13 documents related to Rabbi Shapiro in SB Papers, Box 19. The earliest ones date to July and August 1939, before the war began. Agudas Harabonim hoped to obtain a visa for him by inviting him to head its rabbinical court. Efforts to save him continued for at least another three years as Bloom – at the instigation of Rabbi Herbert S. Goldstein – wrote to the Minister of Switzerland at the Swiss Legation in Washington about saving him as late as June 15, 1942. Bloom was also involved in trying to save his son, Nachman Shapiro, a linguist. SB Papers, Box 19.

[33] See the eight documents related to Rabbi Wasserman and "his associates" in SB Papers, Box 24. Rabbi Goldstein seems to have been the "go-between" in this case, making requests of Bloom and Bloom reporting back to him after contacting the State Department or officials elsewhere. See Bloom's April 4, 1941 letter to A. M. Warren, chief of the State Department's Visa Division, in ibid. Yonason Rosenblum, author of *They Called Him Mike: Reb Elimelech Tress – His Era, Hatzalah, and the Building of an American Orthodoxy* (New York: Mesorah, 1995), 258, writes that "Bloom was unquestionably helpful in a number of cases involving leading rabbinic figures."

[34] Program for "Testimonial and 77th Birthday Dinner in Honor of Congressman Sol Bloom," in SB Papers, Box 62.

[35] Farbstein, 74, citing the Babylonian Talmud, *Gittin* 56b. In a December 1, 1943, letter to Lord Halifax, Rabbi Kalmanowitz writes that the group of rabbis and yeshiva students in Shanghai he hopes to save may be "a small remnant" of the devastated Jewish communities of Europe, but they are "a remnant which, nevertheless, is vitally necessary to the rebirth of spiritual Jewry." SB Papers, Boxes 60-61.

[36] Farbstein, 77. See also ibid., 80.

[37] See Zuroff, 35 and 89-90.

[38] See ibid., 231.

[39] See, for example, the November 5, 1943 memorandum signed by Kalmanowitz and Goldstein on behalf of the Agudas Harabonim: "The latest reports, received through the International Red Cross, confirm their danger and urge their immediate evacuation." SB

Papers, Boxes 60-61.

[40] Unpublished autobiography, page 73. See also ibid., 74-75; the April 10, 1941 letter from Bloom to Goldstein, the June 7, 1941 letter from Bloom to Goldstein (both in SB Papers, Box 41); the June 27, 1941 letter from Bloom to Kalmanowitz; and the November 11, 1943 letter from Bloom to Goldstein ("I spoke again last Sunday to Lord Halifax about the Shanghai matter and he promised to do everything possible to help further"). The latter two documents are in SB Papers, Box 15.

[41] November 2, 1943 letter from Bloom to Halifax and November 3, 1943 letter from Bloom to Kalmanowitz. SB Papers, Box 15. See also Zuroff, 248-249, and the November 7, 1943 letters from Kalmanowitz to Bloom and Goldstein to Bloom. SB Papers, Boxes 60-61. Subsequent to the meeting, Bloom followed up with Halifax personally, according to letters he wrote to Kalmanowitz and Goldstein on November 11, 1943. SB Papers, Box 15. In response to a request from Kalmanowitz a month later, Bloom again promised to speak to Halifax. Ibid.

[42] May 12, 1943 letter from Bloom to Goldstein and the May 18, 1943 letter from Seltzer to Bloom. SB Papers, Boxes 41 and 60-61, respectively.

[43] January 17, 1944 telegram from Bloom to Kalmanowitz and January 19, 1944 letter from Kalmanowitz to Bloom, SB Papers, Boxes 15 and 60-61, respectively. See also the August 1, 1944 letter from Bloom to Goldstein, SB Papers, Box 41.

[44] See the February 7, 1944 telegrams from Bloom to Kalmanowitz and Goldstein. SB Papers, Box 15.

[45] March 14, 1944 telegram from Bloom to Kalmanowitz. SB Papers, Box 15.

[46] See the September 17, 1943 letter from Rabbi L. Seltzer to Bloom in Yeshiva University's Vaad Hahatzala collection. Seltzer writes that Bloom's rescue work "will be immortalized in the annals of our people." See also Zuroff, 249.

[47] See the May 27, 1943 telegram from Davies (probably Joseph E. Davies, the former ambassador to the Soviet Union), in National Archives and Records Administration (NARA), RG-59, War Refugee Board, Box 1. See also the May 21, 1943 telegram from Secretary of State Cordell Hull to U.S. Ambassador William Harrison Standley in *Foreign Relations of the United States: Diplomatic Papers, 1943, the British Commonwealth, Eastern Europe, the Far East, vol. III*, available online at https://history.state.gov/historicaldocuments/frus1943v03/d504 (accessed April 2, 2021) and the May 25, 1943 letter from Davies to Bloom quoted in *Problems of World War II and Its Aftermath: Part 2* (Washington: U.S. Government Printing Office, 1976), 66.

[48] *Autobiography*, 12 and 53; Rosenbaum, 49; and Norton B. Stern, "An Orthodox Rabbi and a Reforming Congregation in Nineteenth Century San Francisco," *Western States Jewish Historical Quarterly* 15 (April 1983).

[49] He did try to keep some rituals, however. A daughter of Rabbi Herbert S. Goldstein wrote to this author, "I recall my father having said that when in Sol Bloom's office in Washington, he opened a cabinet door and showed my father Shabbat candlesticks, presumably used when necessary" (e-mail correspondence, January 20, 2015). See also

Autobiography, 53, and the remarks of Rabbi Goldstein in *Memorial Services*, 62. One of Bloom's secretaries wrote about him, "I think that Mr. Bloom is one of the most devout Orthodox Jews that I have ever met." March 17, 1943 letter from Boyd Crawford to A. Lincoln Nathan, in SB Papers, Box 12.

[50] In the 1930s, "Orthodox" often just meant belonging to an Orthodox synagogue. It did not mean, as it generally does today, religiously observant. For just one example of Bloom's non-observance, see "Dictators Assailed By Bishop At Mass Attended By Envoys," *The New York Times*, March 4, 1940, pg. 6.

[51] *Jewish National Home*, 498.

[52] June 13, 1939 letter. SB Papers, Box 24.

[53] March 25, 1942 letter. SB Papers, Box 18.

[54] October 31, 1940 letter from Goldstein to Flegelman (Bloom's secretary). SB Papers, Box 21. Bloom responded two days later suggesting that Rabbi Stam visit his office to provide more details. "[W]e will be pleased to do whatever we can to assist," he concludes. Ibid.

[55] The details of the case can be found in an internal office correspondence from Flegelman to Bloom on the same day of August 8. On August 19, Bloom wrote to Fisch, assuring him that he had contacted the State Department and urged that the case be expedited. All three documents are in SB Papers, Box 39.

[56] Page 73. Goldstein also writes, "Congressman Bloom opened the doors for me to the most prominent men visiting the United States." Ibid.

[57] Letter from Jung to Bloom. Bloom responded on December 15 that he would "do everything [he could] to assist." These two letters, plus an internal office correspondence about this case between two of Bloom's secretaries, dated December 13, 1939, are in SB Papers, Box 40.

[58] See the October 12, 1940 letter from Bloom to Secretary of State Cordell Hull and the October 31, 1940 thank-you letter from Jung to Bloom in SB Papers, Boxes 45 and 20, respectively.

[59] See the June 2, 1941 letter from Bloom to the American Consul General in Zurich, Switzerland. SB Papers, Box 17.

[60] SB Papers, Box 2. Bloom's April 28 letter to the State Department asking about the mother-in-law is in Box 2 as well.

[61] See *Autobiography*, 250, where Bloom writes that one of his secretaries took "care of things for [him]; she could do everything, including the signing as well as the writing of most of [his] letters."

[62] The documents related to this case are in SB Papers, Box 2.

[63] Letter to Samuel K. Beier. SB Papers, Box 31.

[64] All three documents are in SB Papers, Box 14.

[65] SB Papers, Box 2. Bloom received a letter from the Labor Department on January 3, 1940 informing him that the petition had been approved. Ibid.

[66] The six documents related to this case are in ibid.

[67] SB Papers, Boxes 60-61.

[68] SB Papers, Box 4. Another man, Frederick Stern, in an undated telegram, writes to Bloom, "You have done for our family what I never thought possible for anyone to do. Due to your kindness and continuous efforts...ten members [of my family] are already here and two more out of danger and en route to New York. We have towards you the feeling of thanks that words will never be able to express." SB Papers, Boxes 60-61.

[69] December 30, 1943 letter from Leopold Steinreich to Bloom. SB Papers, Boxes 60-61. See also the September 16, 1940 telegram he and his wife sent Bloom (ibid.) and the September 12, 1940 memo on the *S.S. Quanza* from Breckinridge Long (in NARA), which notes Bloom's support of the Steinreichs. This author would like to thank Dr. Stephen Morewitz for graciously sharing a digital copy of this document with him.

[70] Letter to Jacob L. Gabel. SB Papers, Box 41.

[71] Letter to Lester Udell. SB Papers, Box 38.

[72] May 4, 1939 letter from Bloom to Reginald Seger, SB Papers, Box 1. The case concerned a young man, Alfred Bloch of Lwow, Poland, who wished to come to the U.S. temporarily for a "special course of study" at the Horace Mann School in New York. See Bloom's June 1, 1939 letter to John K. Davis of the American Consul General in Warsaw, Poland. Ibid.

[73] January 14, 1942 letter to Simon Hirschler. SB Papers, Box 2.

[74] October 28, 1943 letter to Benjamin Shalleck. SB Papers, Box 4.

[75] Letter dated April 25, 1940. SB Papers, Box 4.

[76] Letter dated June 30, 1937. SB Papers, Box 17. A year earlier, he wrote to Rabbi Israel Goldstein: "if you have any proposition in which I could assist you, personally, I want you to feel and know that you can call on me at any time and under any circumstances or conditions." February 17, 1936 letter in SB Papers, Box 2.

[77] February 23, 1948 letter to H. I. Mantell, SB Papers, Box 10. See also Richard P. Stevens, *American Zionism and U.S. Foreign Policy, 1942-1947* (Lebanon: Institute for Palestine Studies, 1970), 44: "Bloom's labors in the securing of entrance visas for hapless European Jews were extensively recognized."

Chapter 7 *(pages 73-93)*

[1] The Nazis, however, had already killed three-quarters of the Holocaust's victims by this point. Christopher R. Browning, *Ordinary Men: Reserve Police Battalion 101 and the Final Solution in Poland* (New York: Harper Perennial, 2017), xv.

[2] *The Abandonment of the Jews*, quoting Richard Law, head of the British delegation at Bermuda. In *Saving the Jews: Franklin D. Roosevelt and the Holocaust* (New York: Thunder's Mouth, 2006), 461, Robert Rosen questions the authenticity of this quote. Even if accurate, he argues, it was made in 1965 – 22 years after the fact – and is

inconsistent with Law's correspondence from the time of the conference.

[3] The text of this telegram appears in numerous places, including in *The Jews Should Keep Quiet*, 102-103.

[4] Richard C. Lukas, *The Forgotten Holocaust: The Poles Under German Occupation, 1939-1944* (New York: Hippocrene Books, 2012), 34. See also ibid., 9, and Timothy Snyder, *Bloodlands: Europe Between Hitler and Stalin* (New York: Basic Books, 2010), 132-133 and 153-154.

[5] Novick, 26. See also Snyder, x, 155, and 180. The Nazis ultimately killed three million Soviet prisoners of war from 1941-1945. In German prisoner-of-war camps for Soviet soldiers, the death rate was 58 percent. In their camps for Western soldiers, it was less than five percent. Ibid. 181.

[6] Anna Reid, *Leningrad: The Epic Siege of World War II, 1941-1944*, (New York: Walker, 2011), 3. Ultimately, a million people died in the siege. Snyder, 173.

[7] *The Abandonment of the Jews*, 28. Historian Peter Novick writes, "[F]rom early 1933 to late 1942 – more than three quarters of the twelve years of Hitler's thousand-Year Reich – Jews were, quite reasonably, seen as among but by no means as the singled-out victims of the Nazis regime. This was the all-but-universal perception of American gentiles; it was the perception of many American Jews as well." Novick, 21. See also Hurwitz, 85 and 285: "There was a general feeling that the entire war was one immense atrocity perpetrated by the Germans and Japanese on all the occupied nations."

[8] *The Abandonment of the Jews*, 27.

[9] Ibid., 27 and 41.

[10] "Allied Declaration on the Persecution of the Jews (December 17, 1942)," *Jewish Virtual Library*, www.jewishvirtuallibrary.org/allied-declaration-on-persecution-of-the-jews (accessed February 11, 2021). The statement was "broadcast in twenty-three languages to all countries in Nazi-occupied Europe." "Bermuda Conference," 145.

[11] "Bermuda Conference," 148, 151, 152, and 153; *No Haven for the Oppressed*, 156; and *The Politics of Rescue*, 193.

[12] Formal discussions between the two delegations only took place over five days: April 20-24.

[13] Lucas, for health reasons, missed the first three days of discussions, only arriving at Bermuda on April 23.

[14] On April 3, 1943, Long wrote in his diary: "Rabbi Wise and a few of his colleagues object to Sol Bloom – as not being a representative of Jewry. I reacted that he was a representative of America." *The War Diary of Breckinridge Long: Selections from the Years 1939-1944*, ed., Fred L. Israel (Lincoln: University of Nebraska, 1966), 306. Nahum Goldman, representing the Jewish Agency in America, claimed the administration intended to use Bloom as its "alibi" should no significant rescue proposal emerge from Bermuda. *The Abandonment of the Jews*, 110.

[15] Foreign Secretary Anthony Eden believed "no differentiation should be made between Jews and other refugees in all rescue efforts" and, on January 11, England's

Cabinet formally agreed. "Bermuda Conference," 148. See also ibid., 149, 153.

[16] The document, dated April 7, 1943 is in Breckinridge Long Papers at the Library of Congress, Box 203. See also Roosevelt's letter asking Bloom to go to Bermuda in SB Papers, Boxes 60-61, which begins, "A very serious situation exists in many parts of this world because of the policies so viciously prosecuted by Nazi governments to persecute religious, racial and political groups who have incurred their wrath." Jews are not mentioned.

[17] BL Papers, Box 203.

[18] Breckinridge Long was "particularly anxious lest the conference's possible aid to Jews...be exploited by the Nazi propaganda office as proof positive that Jews commandeered the country's military drive." "Bermuda Conference," 156.

[19] See *The Politics of Rescue*, 197, citing Long's diary.

[20] Richard Lucas, *Axis Sally: The American Voice of Nazi Germany* (Havertown: Casemate, 2010), 58 and 266. See also, ibid., 45, 96, 175, 261, 264, 265 and 269.

[21] See chapter 3 of this dissertation, 36-38.

[22] See pages 2 and 3 of the report of "United Kingdom Delegates to the Bermuda Conference on the Refugee Problem to Mr. Eden," June 28, 1943, in "Conference in Bermuda: Proceedings," *The National Archives* (of the British Government), Ref.: CO 323/1846/14: "The members of the American delegation more than once emphasized their anxiety that everything should be done to remove the impression that the refugee problem was exclusively Jewish in scope." Paradoxically, at the same time, "they showed constant interest in any plan which could assist Jewish refugees." (All further citations to *The National Archives* in this chapter are to the same reference number.)

[23] January 20, 1943 "Aide-Memoire" from the British Embassy to the U.S. State Department, *Foreign Relations of the United States: Diplomatic Papers, 1943, General, vol. I*, available at https://history.state.gov/historicaldocuments/frus1943v01/d103 (accessed November 21, 2021).

[24] *The Politics of Rescue*, 190 and 193: "The planners of the conference thus went on record beforehand as not favoring any significant action for the overwhelming majority of the people who were either in camps or ghettos."

[25] "Bermuda Conference," 156. See also "Three Members of Congress Included in U.S. Delegation to Bermuda Conference," *Jewish Telegraphic Agency*, April 8, 1943.

[26] Letter dated March 29, 1943. SB Papers, Boxes 60-61. The letter was drafted by the State Department. See the "Memorandum for the President" in BL Papers, Box 203. Secretary of State Cordell Hull's April 8, 1943 letter to the president of Yale University, asking him to lead the American delegation at Bermuda (before Dodds was selected), reads similarly: "The American and British governments have agreed to a preliminary conference to make recommendations to [the Intergovernmental Committee on Political refugees'] Executive committee." Ibid. See also Breckinridge Long's April 7, 1943 memorandum in ibid.

[27] *The Politics of Rescue*, 194, and *The Abandonment of the Jews*, 108.

[28] Page 1 of the report.

[29] Bermuda Conference Minutes in *The Mock Rescue Conference: Bermuda*, ed. David S. Wyman, "Archives of the Holocaust" (New York: Garland, 1990), 133. During a meeting at Bermuda, George Backer, a member of the Executive Committee of the Refugee Economic Corporation, addressed the three main American delegates at great length and the contrast between his knowledge and theirs is striking at times. See also *The Politics of Rescue*, 204.

[30] April 21, 1943 telegram. Law also writes that the conference "is bound to be (in greater or lesser degree) abortive." Ibid.

[31] Ibid.

[32] The letter is reproduced in *The Mock Rescue Conference*, 40.

[33] "Program For The Rescue Of Jews From Nazi Occupied Europe," April 14, 1943, *American Jewish Committee Archives*, available at www.ajcarchives.org/ajcarchive/ DigitalArchive.aspx (accessed March 1, 2021). This 12-point plan was discussed at some length by the American group at Bermuda on April 25.

[34] Advertisement, *The Washington Post*, April 20, 1943; a copy appears in *The Mock Rescue Conference* between pages 64 and 65. In early 1943, no Jewish group had yet suggested the idea of bombing Auschwitz. Whether this idea was, in any event, practical – considering, among other things, the sorry state of the Allies' "precision bombing" – is the subject of fierce debate. See *The Bombing of Auschwitz: Should the Allies Have Attempted It?*, eds., Michael J. Neufeld and Michael Berenbaum (Lawrence: University Press of Kansas, 2003). Only 2-3 percent of bombs dropped by heavy bombers in World War II directly hit their target. Michael J. Neufeld, "Introduction to the Controversy," in ibid., 7.

[35] Also writing to Bloom was Rabbi Kalmanowitz of the Vaad Hahatzala who sought his help in bringing various Polish rabbis stuck in the Soviet Union to the U.S. Bloom did, in fact, "press for action" on the issue. See the U.K.'s post-conference report, page 2, and *The Politics of Rescue*, 198.

[36] Letter dated April 16, 1943. Reproduced in *The Mock Rescue Conference*, 36-37.

[37] Minutes of a "Meeting of the Joint Emergency Committee for European Jewish Affairs," April 18, 1943. *American Jewish Committee Archives*, available at www.ajcarchives.org/ajcarchive/DigitalArchive.aspx (accessed February 28, 2021).

[38] Bermuda Conference Minutes, 77. Eden had earlier called the idea of asking Hitler to release all Jews in his control "fantastically impossible" as did, apparently, Sumner Welles. "Bermuda Conference," 155, and Jacob Rosenheim Diary in the Amud Aish Memorial Museum archives, p. 64.

[39] Bermuda Conference Minutes, 78. Eden said the same thing to Hull before the conference began. "Bermuda Conference," 155.

[40] Bermuda Conference Minutes, 78-81. See also ibid., 168.

[41] Page 2 of the U.K. delegation's post-conference report to Eden. See also an April 21,

1943 telegram (No. 8) from Law to the Secretary of State of Colonies, "Mr. Sol Bloom was inclined to argue that approach to the enemy should not be excluded but his fellow delegates overruled him." *The National Archives.*

[42] "Memorandum on Bermuda Conference on the Refugee Problem," reproduced in *The Mock Rescue Conference*, 20. It notes that on "Bloom's insistence, the matter was left open."

[43] Bermuda Conference Minutes, 81-82.

[44] Penkower, 295, writes that "public opinion agreed with Winston Churchill's publicly expressed conviction that '[any form of relief would] directly or indirectly assist the enemy's war effort.'"

[45] Bermuda Conference Minutes, 99 and 108.

[46] Sir Herbert Emerson, director of the ICR, wrote in a memorandum before the conference, "So far the Spanish Government has been very helpful.... But unless she is ready to keep an indefinite number [of refugees], the time will come when she will have to tighten her preventative measures unless the outflow of refugees approximates to the inflow." BL Papers, Box 203.

[47] Qtd. in Bermuda Conference Minutes, 118. See also, ibid., 98.

[48] Minutes of Meeting of American Delegation, in *The Mock Rescue Conference*, 180.

[49] Ibid., 179-180. See also ibid., 237; Bermuda Conference Minutes, 98, 102, 138, and 139; April 22, 1943 telegram (No. 13) from Law to the Secretary of State for the Colonies in *The National Archives*; and Final Report, in *The Mock Rescue Conference*, 270.

[50] See his remarks in Minutes of Meeting of American Delegation, 200 and 202.

[51] Bermuda Conference Minutes, 82-83.

[52] BL Papers, Box 203.

[53] Bermuda Conference Minutes, 86.

[54] Ibid., 90.

[55] Strictly Confidential Memorandum, 2-3, in BL Papers, Box 203.

[56] Ibid., 6.

[57] Bermuda Conference Minutes, 157. See, also, the post-conference British report's comment on the U.S. delegation "being careful to do nothing to stir up Congress's agitation (a very important consideration with them)." Page 1. See also page 2 of Law's annexed note on the conference (addressed to Anthony Eden and dated May 3, 1943); commenting on the position of the American government, he writes, "I think that they are genuinely anxious to play their part. They want to appease the Jewish organisations if they can do so without causing mortal offense to domestic American opinion. If, however, it came to a showdown, Jew and Gentile, I am satisfied that their internal position is such that they would have to tell the Jewish organisations to go to hell." The document is in *The National Archives* of the British government (Cabinet Office), W.P. (43) 191.

58 Bermuda Conference Minutes, 157.

59 Rebecca Erbelding points out the hypothetical basis of this memo in her *Rescue Board*, 292. She correctly notes that many historians fail to mention this critical fact.

60 June 26, 1940 memorandum in NARA, RG-59, General Visa Correspondence, Box 220, 811.111/107.

61 Minutes of a "Meeting of the Joint Emergency Committee on European Jewish Affairs," April 10, 1943. *American Jewish Committee Archives*, available at www.ajcarchives.org/ajcarchive/DigitalArchive.aspx (accessed June 17, 2022). Roosevelt apparently later changed his mind, writing on the side of a May 7, 1943 memorandum that Hull submitted to him, "I agree with you [about not] bringing in temporary visitors. We have already brought in a large number." BL Papers, Box 203. (According to Rep. Daniel Ellison [R-Md.], Bloom was most unhelpful at the meeting with Roosevelt and said nothing the entire time. See the March 24, 1944 memorandum from Rabbi Leon I. Feuer to Abba Hillel Silver, AZEC Papers, Central Zionist Archives, F39/24.)

62 Bermuda Conference Minutes, 160. See also ibid., 156.

63 Minutes of Meeting of American Delegation, 191-194.

64 April 22, 1943 telegram from Law to the Secretary of State for the Colonies (No. 13), in *The National Archives*.

65 Bermuda Conference Minutes, 105-108.

66 April 22, 1943 telegram from Law to the Secretary of State for the Colonies (No. 12), in *The National Archives*.

67 Bermuda Conference Minutes, 108.

68 Ibid., 97. See also ibid., 108.

69 Ibid., 108.

70 April 22, 1943 telegram (No. 13). See also Bermuda Conference Minutes, 119.

71 Bermuda Conference Minutes, 118-119. Law writes in an April 22 telegram (No. 12) that the proposal "clearly shook the American delegation."

72 BL Papers, Box 203.

73 Bermuda Conference Minutes, 125.

74 In its post-conference report (page 3), the British delegation wrote: "This habit of putting on the Inter-governmental Committee difficult or disagreeable tasks which the United States Government was clearly unwilling to carry out alone, was a constant feature of the discussions. The American delegates, who admitted very little knowledge of the previous history of the Inter-governmental Committee, made frequent references to that body as if it were a kind of *deus ex machine*, to be produced on the stage whenever any apparently insoluble problem of finance, shipping or politics confronted us."

75 BL Papers, Box 203. See also page 2 of the annexed note on the conference.

76 See Judith Tydor Baumel, "Bermuda Conference," in *The Holocaust Encyclopedia*, ed.,

Walter Laqueur (New Haven: Yale University Press, 2001), 76.

[77] Minutes of Meeting of American Delegation, 216. Backer envisioned 20,000 of them coming from Bulgaria and an additional 70,000 from Romania. Bulgarian Jewry wound up surviving the Holocaust intact, so, in retrospect, Backer's plan to save Bulgarian Jews wasn't necessary. Ibid., 217-218.

[78] Bloom later put it as follows: "we can not say everything that we are trying to do...because if we did we would just give evidence to Mr. Hitler...to stop us from doing it." He claimed a U.S. official was actually arrested in Romania trying to help Jews due to lack of discretion, and Breckinridge Long claimed that a plan to save 5,000 Jewish children was thwarted because word of it reached the Nazis. *Problems of World War II*, 31 and 180. The Red Cross (and the World Jewish Congress) complained in late 1943 when a plan for it to collaborate with the ICR on distributing food was made public: "We feel that publicity to our efforts will compromise our slender chances...extreme discretion is essential." Qtd. in Rachel Erbelding, "About Time: The History of the War Refugee Board," PhD dissertation (George Mason University, 2015), 122.

[79] April 27, 1943 telegram from Law to the Secretary of State for the Colonies, in *The National Archives*. Law added, "On the other hand delegates are all agreed that the sooner the first installment of news (i.e. the joint declaration on North Africa, if that can be agreed, or resurrection of Inter-Governmental Committee) can be released the better."

[80] *The New York Times*, April 29, 1943, pg. 9.

[81] Full-page ad, May 4, 1943, *The New York Times*, pg. 17. Seven months later, it would even suggest that Bloom should "feel blood, Jewish blood on [his] hands." Qtd. by *No Haven for the Oppressed*, 163.

[82] In addition to the sources cited earlier, see page 2 of the British delegation's post-conference report.

[83] Bloom did try to get the British to commit to extend the expiration date of its restrictionist White Paper so that more Jews could enter Palestine. Both Law and Dodds cut the conversation short. See Bermuda Conference Minutes, 115, and the U.K.'s post-conference report, page 3 ("Mr. Bloom was inclined to press us for some assurance regarding admissions after the expiry of the White Paper period").

[84] See *The Abandonment of the Jews*, 266 and 336, and "About Time," 72.

[85] "Memorandum by President Roosevelt to the Secretary of State," May 14, 1943, *Foreign Relations of the United States,* available online at https://history.state.gov/historicaldocuments/frus1943v01/d143 (accessed February 28, 2021).

[86] The main objections concerned the Muslim reaction to an increased Jewish presence in the area. See *The Politics of Rescue*, 202 and *No Haven for the Oppressed*, 177. In relation to other objections, historian Rebecca Erbelding writes: "it is difficult to escape the conclusion that the [State] Department allowed itself to be stymied by them, rather than re-approaching the problems creatively." "About Time," 62.

[87] "Bermuda Conference," 165-170.

[88] Law wrote that "the strongly-pressed United States argument that it was easier to revive an established body than create a new one was impossible to resist." April 25, 1943 telegram to the Secretary of State for the Colonies, in *The National Archives*.

[89] David Nasaw, *The Last Million: Europe's Displaced Persons from World War to Cold War* (New York: Penguin, 2020), 183. See also "Bermuda Conference," 148, note 9, and *The Abandonment of the Jews*, 141. Erbelding writes that for the ICR to do even "[s]mall things took months." "About Time," 76.

[90] Minutes of American Delegation, 186. See also Bermuda Conference Minutes, 145.

[91] BL Papers, Box 203. Historians Henry Feingold and David Wyman claim that Long "seized upon the agency as a ready instrument to go through the motions of doing something without actually doing anything." *The Politics of Rescue*, 201, and *The Abandonment of the Jews*, 141. Perhaps, but it's highly doubtful that Bloom or the other delegates knew this. In his annexed note on the conference, Law writes, "If you *can* get the Committee going I believe that it can do a great deal for refugees" (emphasis in original). It should also be noted that while the ICR did not live up to its revivers' hopes, it wasn't completely useless. For example, the State Department tried to help Sweden rescue children at the behest of the ICR. *The Politics of Rescue*, 224. The ICR also "transferred $1.28 million to the JDC for...projects in France, Rumania, Hungary, and northern Italy. *The Abandonment of the Jews*, 141. See also ibid., 140.

[92] "Bloom 'Satisfied' on Refugee Talks," *The New York Times*, May 24, 1943, pg. 15. At a meeting of the Joint Emergency Committee the following day, Rabbi Israel Goldstein "suggested that Bloom be publicly disavowed." Proskauer agreed "that this action should be taken, but at the right time and place." Minutes of a "Meeting of the Joint Emergency Committee on European Jewish Affairs," May 24, 1943, *American Jewish Committee Archives*, available at www.ajcarchives.org/ajcarchive/DigitalArchive.aspx (accessed March 1, 2021).

[93] "Former Governor Returns From Abroad," *The New York Times*, May 3, 1943, pg. 5.

[94] May 3, 1943 letter to Dr. Benjamin Salzer. SB Papers, Box 17. "Complete success" is the phrase Bloom uses in another letter (to William B. Thalheimer, Sr.) that he wrote that day. SB Papers, Box 23. Months later, Bloom would offer another reason for keeping silent on the results of the Bermuda Conference: "If we give out too much information it might hurt instead of help. If [someone] should say that we are planning to get a thousand into one country, that country might say, 'Here, we can't allow this.' We do not want to do that." When asked to explain, Bloom said, "[A]ll of these countries are suffering today for lack of food for their own nationals, and they have quotas and they have immigration laws.... But if they think we are going to bring some Jews into a certain country and the people of those different countries are starving or have lack of food, they are apt to get up in arms and say, 'Well now, this is going to stop right now! We are not going to let any Jews or any refugees into this country.'" *Problems of World War II*, 63-64. See also ibid., 68.

[95] May 4, 1943 letter to Walter Newman. SB Papers, Box 12.

[96] May 4, 1943 letter to J. Sidney Bernstein. SB Papers, Box 1.

[97] May 15, 1943 letter to Meyer Epstein, SB Papers, Box 37.

[98] June 14, 1943 letter to Mone Anathon. SB Papers, Box 28. Over the ensuing few days, on June 16 and 18, Bloom sent more than 150 copies of a laudatory article about the Bermuda Conference that appeared in The Sentinel to friends (100 copies went to his campaign manager). June 16, 1943 letters to E. I. Kaufmann and J. Sidney Bernstein and June 18, 1943 letters to Jacob L. Gabel, Max Manischewitz, and Morris Engelman. SB Papers, Boxes 7, 1, 40, 10, and 37, respectively. On June 15, he sent copies of a different article apparently to R. Abraham and Jacob L. Gabel. SB Papers, Boxes 27 and 40, respectively.

[99] June 25, 1943 letter. SB Papers, Box 9.

[100] Minutes of June 30, 1943 meeting in the Central Zionist Archives, Z6/282. One government official in July wrote that Bloom was "extremely upset" at the criticism leveled at him for his role in the Bermuda Conference. See Showdown in Washington: State, Treasury, and Congress, vol. 6 of America and the Holocaust: The Abandonment of the Jews, ed. David S. Wyman (New York: Garland, 1990), document 10.

[101] July 20, 1943 letter. SB Papers, Boxes 60-61. See also the laudatory letters to Bloom from Arthur L. Malkenson, publisher of the Jewish Journal and Daily News, and Herman Younglieb, president of the American-Jewish Broadcasting Co., written that same day. NARA, RG-233, Box 66.

[102] Perhaps they felt ill-equipped to comment on the conference considering that its recommendations remained secret.

[103] The Abandonment of the Jews, 121.

[104] Leff, 205.

[105] No Haven for the Oppressed, 159, and "Bermuda Conference," 170.

[106] Page 4 of the U.K. delegation's post-conference report.

[107] Page 4.

[108] The Letters and Papers of Chaim Weizmann: Series B – Papers, Volume II, ed., Barnet Litvinoff (New Brunswick: Transaction, 1984), 102.

[109] Neufeld, 9.

[110] Minutes of American Delegation, 229-230.

[111] Ibid., 245.

[112] During the same meeting, Lucas noted that "plenty" of American Jews also "have boys in the front and plenty more [are] going." Ibid., 231. Indeed, like "in the population as a whole, scarcely a Jewish family existed that did not have a son or a brother, father or an uncle, in the service." Deborah Dash Moore, GI Jews: How World War II Changed a Generation (Cambridge, Belknap Press, 2004), 46.

[113] Minutes of American Delegation, 243-244. "[T]here were, as is well known, thousands of deaths every day into the final days of the war.... In this connection, it might be worthwhile to consider how many more Jews would have survived had the war ended even a week or ten days earlier – and conversely, how many more would have

died had the war lasted an additional week or ten days. Whatever numbers one might put forward in such speculations, one thing is or ought to be reasonably clear: the number would be greater that the total number of Jews saved by the various rescue efforts in 1943-1945." Gerhard L. Weinberg, "The Allies and the Holocaust," in *The Bombing of Auschwitz*, 26.

[114] *Autobiography*, 273. Law, interestingly, took a different point of view in terms of rescuing at least some Jews. In his annexed note to Eden on the conference, he writes, "If neutral shipping is unobtainable, is it really beyond the bounds of possibility that we should find *one* ship? I know all the arguments, but I believe, too, that bread *does* return from the waters and that the story of the Good Samaritan is still valid" (emphasis in original).

[115] *No Haven for the Oppressed*, 162 and 163. Dodds wrote to Bloom the week after the conference, "You were in a more difficult position than any other member of the conference. Knowing as I do how keenly you feel for the persecuted peoples of Europe, it is with great satisfaction that I express to you my admiration for the reasonable and straightforward course you pursued throughout the deliberations of the conference." May 3, 1943 letter in SB Papers, Boxes 60-61.

[116] "Bermuda Conference," 170.

Chapter 8 *(pages 94-113)*

[1] Bergson changed his name to protect his family (his uncle was Rabbi Abraham Isaac Kook, the first Ashkenazic chief rabbi of Palestine) from any fallout resulting from his controversial activities. *The Abandonment of the Jews*, 85.

[2] May 4, 1943, *The New York Times*, pg. 17.

[3] Bergson "apprehended...that the way to the American public's heart in general and to American Jewry's in particular was via newspaper, leaflets, theater, and radio. The more bombastic the headline and the more tearjerking the accompanying illustration, the greater chance the ad had of catching the public's eye." Judith Tydor Baumel, *The "Bergson Boys" and the Origins of Contemporary Zionist Militancy*, trans., Dena Ordan (Syracuse: Syracuse University Press, 2005), 131. See also ibid., 132 and 142.

[4] See the August 1, 1944 letter from Senator Guy M Gillette to Harry Louis Selden in the appendix to *Race Against Death*, 223; ibid., 43; *Problems of World War II*, 40, 103-104, and 120; and *The Abandonment of the Jews*, 155 and 193.

[5] *Problems of World War II*, 16.

[6] "Introduction" in *Problems of World War II*, 10.

[7] Many credit the WRB with helping save 200,000 lives, but Rebecca Erbelding, the foremost expert on this government agency, deems this figure "a vast overestimation" and argues that the true number is "impossible" to know. She notes, "Many small acts of 'rescue' were needed to save one person. To presume that 'being saved' is a singular act is to ignore the complicated nature of the Holocaust." She also notes, "[A] person could be saved and still be murdered in the Holocaust. In the fall of 1944, a group of

Slovak Jews holding Latin American protective papers saw their papers torn up prior to the group's deportation. Does this mean the WRB's intervention with Latin American countries to recognize those papers did not work?" She argues that there is also "no way to quantify how many people survived because of the Board's psychological warfare campaign." "About Time," 709 and 713-715.

[8] See, for example, *Problems of World War II*, 32, 39, 76, and 136.

[9] Ibid., 36-37, 96-103.

[10] *Problems of World War II*, 107. He made $45 a week, the equivalent of $760 a week – or $39,500 a year – in 2022. Francer Gunther, the organization's treasurer, said she found Bergson's salary "very embarrassing" but said Bergson refused an offer by the organization's financial committee to increase it. Ibid., 146.

[11] Ibid., 105. Bergson wondered the same thing. See ibid., 100.

[12] Ibid., 77-80, 83-84, 93-95, and 212-216. Bloom wrote to the broadcaster and two others: "You say further that 'large Jewish groups are said to be identified with the attitude of Congressman Bloom in opposing any action by the United States Government to help rescue their compatriots.' If there ever was a lie, that statement is the biggest lie I have ever heard in my life, and you know it." November 23, 1943 letter to Herbert S. Moore, et al., NARA, RG-233, Box 67.

[13] At a later point, someone accused Bloom of telling Rep. Joseph C. Baldwin, one of the bill's co-sponsors, "Only over my dead body will any help, other than provided by the Bermuda Conference, be extended for the saving of the Jews of the war-stricken areas." Made aware of the accusation, Baldwin wrote to Bloom, "For the record, I would like to emphasize now that no such statement was ever made by you to me. I would also like to add as a matter of personal knowledge I know that you have done a valiant job in behalf of the stricken Jews, not only at the Bermuda Conference but subsequently in achieving the aims we both have in view for these unfortunate people. In your own quiet way you have been as effective as anyone I know in this regard and I hope someday the Jewish people will realize it." January 26, 1944 letter, SB Papers, Box 61. For background on this story, see NARA, RG-233, Box 66.

[14] *Problems of World War II*, 37 and 79-80. See also ibid., 39 and 101, and letter to Herbert S. Moore, et al., pg 2.

[15] *Problems of World War II*, 137-138. "Mr. Bergson, I want you to know that this has never happened before.... I say it is wrong and is going too far," Bloom said. Ibid., 138.

[16] Bloom actually told New York Post editor Ted Thackrey he supported the resolution. See his November 24, 1943 letter to Thackrey in NARA, RG-233, Box 67, and the subsequent article in the Post quoting this letter (a clipping of which is in ibid.). See also *The Abandonment of the Jews*, 195.

[17] See, for example, *Problems of World War II*, 57, 110, and 236.

[18] See ibid., 154, 182, 196, and 199.

[19] Ibid., 90-91. See also ibid., 87. Long actually told the committee, "Everybody that I

know, everybody in the Department of State, and everybody that I have come in contact with is interested, and a lot of them have been active in endeavoring to save the Jewish people from the terrorism of the Nazis." Ibid., 181.

[20] A copy of the booklet – *Rescue of the Jewish and Other Peoples in Nazi-Occupied Territory* (United States: Government Printing Office, 1943) – is in NARA, RG-233, Box 67. On November 20, Bloom wrote to Assistant Secretary of State Adolf A. Berle, Jr., "This [booklet] was printed for the specific purpose of showing the Committee, the witnesses and the sponsors of these Resolutions, the great amount of work that has been done by the State Department on the refugee problem."   NARA, RG-59, 840.48/Refugee/4807. Four days later, Berle responded, in part, "I think that the State Department has done a good deal more work on the refugee problem than it gets credit for, and some of the things it has done cannot be told even yet lest they prejudice the fate of refugees still in Europe." Ibid.

[21] *Rescue of the Jewish and Other Peoples*, 7.

[22] Bergson was not entirely correct. The aim of setting up a refugee camp in North Africa, for example, was to initiate a flow of refugees from Spain so that new refugees from occupied Europe could replace the old ones. The report from the Bermuda Conference, however, had not yet been released, so Bergson may not have known this fact.

[23] *Problems of World War II*, 134. See also, ibid., 63. It's difficult to know if Bergson was being serious or just trying to make a polemical point. After all, the Bergson group had published a full-age ad in The New York Times in May calling the Bermuda Conference a "cruel mockery."

[24] Ibid., 111, 114, and 116. See also, ibid., 119: "We exist in order to save the Jews of Europe."

[25] Qtd. in *The Jews Should Be Quiet*, 298.

[26] *Problems of World War II*, 110. See also ibid., 121.

[27] Also testifying in behalf of the resolution was Mayor Fiorello La Guardia, Kermit Eby of the Congress of Industrial Organizations, Lewis Hines of the American Federation of Labor, Rep. Joseph C. Baldwin, Rep. Will Rogers, Jr., New York gubernatorial candidate Dean Alfange, and author Frances Gunther. The latter four all belonged to the Bergson group, which at this point was called the Emergency Committee to Save the Jewish People of Europe.

[28] Ibid., 47-48.

[29] Ibid., 109.

[30] Ibid., 218 and 220. See also ibid., 235.

[31] Ibid., 220.

[32] Ibid., 219 and 221. He said it represented 60-70 percent of American Jewry. Ibid., 234. Years later, Bergson dryly remarked, "'Responsible' means do nothing." *Race Against Death*, 64.

[33] *Problems of World War II*, 221 and 240. In a press release issued that same day by the

American Jewish Conference, Rabbi Wise makes it clear that he, in fact, did *not* support the resolution. NARA, RG-233, Box 67.

[34] Ibid., 122.

[35] *The Jews Should Keep Quiet*, 203. See also Baumel, 143.

[36] *Problems of World War II*, 235-236. Bloom seemed to endorse Bergson's view, saying on the first day of the hearings, "I think we had better stay off the Palestine question if we want to get this resolution through." Ibid., 68.

[37] Long evidently met with Bloom the day before he testified – presumably to discuss his upcoming testimony. See the November 25, 1943 entry in Breckinridge Long's date book in BL Papers, Box 6. Bloom also said he spoke to Long over the phone on November 23 about testifying. *Problems of World War II*, 157.

[38] *Problems of World War II*, 183, 185, 196, 197, 205. At one point, he actually said voting *against* the resolution would be "very dangerous" and "very unwise." Ibid., 184.

[39] Ibid., 171.

[40] Almost every single member of the committee showered Long with praise after his testimony. One congressman said the next day that the committee was "rather astounded at the extent" of the State Department's efforts to rescue Jews. Ibid., 240.

[41] Rep. Rogers, Jr., one of the bill's sponsors, told Long, "There has been an impression around that the State Department and the Intergovernmental Committee had not been active, and I think that that is false and fallacious. I think a statement such as you have just made, if it could be printed…[and] known to the general public, it would do a great deal toward allaying fears. I think it is an excellent statement and an excellent record and one which you and this country should be proud of." Ibid., 199. See also ibid., 201. Long had actually wanted to publicize what he saw as the State Department's accomplishments vis-à-vis saving Jews as early as May 1943. See his letter to Howard K. Travers on May 4, 1943. BL Papers, Box 203.

[42] Bloom also said that just publicizing the ICR's official mandate – which was secret at the time – would in itself "answer the entire question" of whether a new entity was needed to rescue Europe's Jews. *Problems of World War II*, 207. In a letter to Long after the publication of his testimony, Jacob Rosenheim, president of Agudath Israel World Organization, wrote that if Long's understanding of the ICR's mission was correct, "a new commission on basis of the House Resolution 350 would, in fact, be superfluous." December 19, 1943 letter in NARA, RG-59, 840.48/Refugees/4930.

[43] Description of December 8, 1943 meeting between Bloom and Goldmann and Shulman, in *America and the Holocaust, vol. 6*, 354.

[44] Press release, December 12, 1943. NARA, RG-233, Box 67.

[45] "About Time," 121.

[46] "Congressional Committee Suspends Hearing on Resolution to Rescue Jews from Europe," *Jewish Telegraphic Agency*, December 19, 1943. (The dateline of this story on page 4 of the hard copy of the "JTA Daily News Bulletin" for December 19 reads "Dec. 17.")

[47] "Hearings to Reopen on Bill Urging U.S. Commission to Rescue Jews; Senate May Act Soon," *Jewish Telegraphic Agency*, January 7, 1944.

[48] Treasury Department official Ansel Luxford told his boss, Henry Morgenthau, Jr., that Bloom was doing "everything he [could] possibly do to keep that resolution from being reported out." Minutes of January 13, 1944 meeting at 11:00 a.m. in "Diaries of Henry Morgenthau, Jr." vol. 693, p. 198, in the FDR Library, available at www.fdrlibrary.marist. edu/_resources/images/morg/md0978.pdf (accessed April 1, 2021).

[49] Memorandum from Hodel to Luxford in "Diaries of Henry Morgenthau, Jr." vol. 693, p. 236.

[50] See the December 28, 1943 letter from Cox to Bloom in Oscar Cox Papers, Box 101, and the phone logs of Cox for December 28 and 29, 1943, in ibid., Box 144.

[51] "Diaries of Henry Morgenthau, Jr." vol. 693, p. 236.

[52] *Autobiography*, 275.

[53] Baumel, 105-106. Bergson believed Bloom was "the biggest block in the way of the Jewish Army idea." Minutes of Meeting Held on April 25, 1943, page 2. Palestine Statehood Committee papers, Reel 4, Folder 9, frame 319. In 1940, Bloom called the proposal to form a Jewish army "fantastic" (in a pejorative sense) and said he didn't "believe in [Jews] segregating" themselves. "Plan Jewish Army to Battle Hitlerism," *The New York Times*, September 3, 1940, pg. 7.

[54] October 12, 1943 letter from Jabotinsky to "Dr. Altman" reproduced in *America and the Holocaust, vol. 6*, ed. David S. Wyman, document 59. Erbelding casts doubt on the accuracy of this report as it appears in a letter that she says is "filled with demonstrable exaggerations and inaccuracies." *Rescue Board*, 297. If Bloom did have reservations about the march, though, he was hardly the only one. Stephen Wise also opposed the march as did some Orthodox leaders. For example, J. David Delman, president of the National Council of Young Israel, wrote that the march was not "proper or dignified" and "Washington had enough turmoil...without the confusion caused by a mass march on the White House." Qtd. in Jeffrey S. Gurock, *Jews in Gotham: New York Jews in a Changing City, 1920-2010* (New York: New York University Press, 2012), 92. The sixth Lubavitcher Rebbe, Rabbi Joseph Isaac Schneersohn, also opposed public demonstrations for rescue efforts during the Holocaust. See Rigg, 174-176.

[55] October 8, 1943 letter to Max Manischewitz, SB Papers, Box 10. For a description of the dignified impression the march made on bystanders, see *A Year in the Service of Humanity: A Survey of the Activities of the Emergency Committee to Save the Jewish People of Europe, July 1943-August 1944* (New York: Emergency Committee, 1944), 17-19.

[56] Interview with Benzion Netanyahu by Rafael Medoff, "'FDR Used the Jews,'" *The Jerusalem Post*, May 3, 2012, available at www.jpost.com/features/in-thespotlight/fdr-

used-the-jews (accessed March 26, 2021).

[57] July 12, 1939 letter from Bloom to Gustavus A. Rogers, SB Papers, Box 15. See also Bloom's comments in a 1948 radio interview on the difference between a politician and a statesman: "A politician is a vote getter. He's interested only in his own district, because that's the district that elects him. A statesman is interested in his whole country. Suppose some legislation came up which benefited his district 75 percent, the country 25 percent; suppose there was other legislation which would benefit the district 25 percent and the country 75, you could tell by the way he votes if a fellow's a politician or a statesman." Qtd. *Memorial Services*, 41.

[58] *Problems of World War II*, 42.

[59] Qtd. in Breitman and Lichtman, 56.

[60] Stephen Wise, *Challenging Years: The Autobiography of Stephen Wise* (New York: Putnam's, 1949), 216. Zionist leader Eliahu Golomb wrote during the war period, "The American Jew thinks of himself first and foremost as an American. This is a fact, whether we like it or not." Quoted in Melvin I. Urofsky, *American Zionism from Herzl to the Holocaust* (Garden City: Anchor Books, 1976), 393. See also Rosen, 497, Hurwitz, 19, and Novick, 34.

[61] *The Deafening Silence*, 187.

[62] Baumel, 159.

[63] Qtd. in Erna Kaplan, "A Rebel with a Cause: Hillel Kook, Begin and Jabotinsky's Ideological Legacy," *Israel Studies*, vol. 10. no. 3 (fall), 93. See also "About Time," 70-71.

[64] See Kaplan, 90-91. Bergson understood why American Jews would be hesitant to lobby the American government to save European Jews and thus tried to argue that American Jews were actually *not* Jews but rather "Americans of Hebrew descent." Minutes of April 25, 1943 meeting in Palestine Statehood Committee papers, reel 4, folder 9. He thought their inhibitions would disappear on their own accord by adopting this alternative identity. For more on Bergson's idiosyncratic beliefs on Jewish identity and nationality, see Kaplan, 93-100.

[65] Eric L. Goldstein, *The Price of Whiteness: Jews, Race, and American Identity* (Princeton: Princeton University Press, 2006), 213. Elsewhere, Goldstein refers to this view as "integrationist liberalism." Ibid., 215. See also Novick, 178 and 188-189.

[66] Ibid., 212.

[67] Qtd. in *We Who Dared to Say No to War: American Antiwar Writing from 1812 to Now*, ed. Murray Polner and Thomas E. Woods, Jr. (New York: Basic Books, 2008), 296. His father, John Adams, argued that "we should separate ourselves as far as possible and as long as possible from all European politics and wars" and "it ought to be our rule not to meddle." Qtd. in Charles A. Beard, *A Foreign Policy for America* (New York: Alfred A. Knopf, 1940), 16 and 19. In 1863, Abraham Lincoln's secretary of state, William Seward, wrote, "Our policy of non-intervention, straight, absolute, and peculiar as it may seem to other nations, has...become a traditional one, which could not be abandoned without the most urgent occasion." Qtd. in ibid., 31. Many similar

quotations can be adduced.

[68] Thus, for example, the State Department instructed a U.S. representative in Egypt in 1840 to interfere diplomatically when a blood libel was leveled at a number of Jews in Damascus, Syria. Cyrus Adler and Aaron Margalith, *With Firmness in the Right: American Diplomatic Action Affecting Jews, 1840-1945* (New York: American Jewish Committee, 1946), 3-5. Over the next hundred years, it issued similar instructions on behalf of persecuted Jews in such countries as Turkey, Iran, Morocco, Romania, Poland, and Russia. See Adler and Margalith's book for numerous examples.

[69] "Previously, non-involvement in European politics and wars had been a given," even a "hallowed tradition." Herring, 406. See also ibid., 412. Indeed, no sitting president even visited Europe before Woodrow Wilson.

[70] Arthur Schlesinger, Jr. "Back to the Womb?: Isolationism's Renewed Threat," *Foreign Affairs*, July/August (1995), 3. See also Martin Folly, *The United States and World War II: The Awakening Giant* (Edinburgh: Edinburgh University Press, 2002), 3; Kaufman, 56 and 61; and Adler, 39.

[71] "Nanjing Massacre," *Encyclopedia Britannica*, https://www.britannica.com/event/Nanjing-Massacre (accessed October 30, 2020). "The Rape of Nanking was front-page news across the world, and yet most of the world stood by and did nothing while an entire city was butchered," writes historian Iris Chang. Qtd. in Rosen, 58. The U.S. also did nothing to stop the Armenian genocide in World War I.

[72] See the "Amazon Exclusive interview with author George C. Herring," second answer, available at www.amazon.com/Colony-Superpower-Foreign-Relations-History-dp-195078225/dp/0195078225/ref=mt_other?_encoding= UTF8&me=&qid= (accessed October 30, 2020). See also Kaufman, 16.

[73] Cole, 94. See also Mark Lincoln Chadwin, *The Warhawks: American Interventionists Before Pearl Harbor* (New York: W. W. Norton, 1968), 52, 54, 71-72, 228, 259, and 269.

[74] Henry Feingold notes, as a general matter, that humanitarian responses on the part of governments "are rare in history and practically nonexistent during wartime." *The Politics of Rescue*, xiii. See also Novick, 59: "The notion that the rescue of threatened foreign civilian populations was an obligation of a country involved in total war didn't occur to Americans during World War II or its immediate aftermath." Indeed, the War Refugee Board's ultimate creation was "an anomaly, an unexpected deviation, a sudden and surprising altruistic moment." *Rescue Board*, 273. For more on isolationism as an explanation for America's actions during the Holocaust, see my forthcoming article in *Haikrah*, "Why Didn't America Save the Six Million?"

[75] The two even shared a personal relationship. Roosevelt wrote to Bloom's wife during her final illness in 1941 and a condolence letter to Bloom following her passing. June 20 and June 25, 1941 letters, in the FDR Library. Roosevelt also occasionally sent Bloom "Happy Birthday" wishes (see the March 9, 1943 and March 9, 1944 telegrams to Bloom in the FDR Library) and wrote to him in May 1944 to congratulate him on the publication of *Our Heritage*, prompting Bloom to write to Roosevelt's secretary, "I can't think of anything else that has happened to me that has given me so much pleasure as reading [Roosevelt's letter]." May 31, 1944 letter to William D. Hassett. Both letters are in the

FDR Library. In general, Roosevelt was "replete with charm" and had a mesmerizing effect on people. Writing about his meetings with Roosevelt, Rep. Emanuel Celler recalls, "At the end of each visit I realized that I had been hypnotized." Emanuel Celler, *You Can Never Leave Brooklyn: The Autobiography of Emanuel Celler* (New York: John Day, 1953), 12.

[76] Hull called Bloom a "very old and very dear friend." See his inscription in Bloom's copy of *Charter of the United Nations: Report to the President on the Results of the San Francisco Conference*, June 26, 1945 (Department of State, Publication 2349), in SB Papers, Box 62. Bloom's daughter writes that the Hulls were "warm friends" of the family. *There's No Place Like Washington*, 101. See also *Our Heritage*, 450-451.

[77] Long is often regarded as an anti-Semite, but not all historians agree with this appraisal. Saul Friedman, for example, writes that "it is difficult to find a single anti-Semitic statement in any of [Long's] personal notes or memorandums" and "[f]ar from being the anti-Semite suggested by [author Arthur] Morse...Long was extremely cordial to the Jews and opened his office on repeated occasions to spokesmen of every faction." Friedman, 116. (See, however, his later book, *A History of the Holocaust* [London: Vallentine Mitchell, 2004], 347.) Treasury Secretary Henry Morgenthau apparently regarded Long as "genuinely sympathetic to the plight of the Jews." Ibid., 137. So did the Vaad Hahatzala rescue organization. Zuroff, 111. Peter Bergson called Long "hostile" but said he didn't know if he was an anti-Semite. *Race Against Death*, 151. Even Wyman writes, "Whether Long was...anti-Semitic is not clear." *The Abandonment of the Jews*, 191.

[78] Thomas E. Hachey, "American Profiles on Capitol Hill: A Confidential Study for the British Foreign Office in 1943," *The Wisconsin Magazine of History*, Vol. 57, No. 2 (Winter, 1973-1974), 150.

[79] "Representative Sol Bloom Dies of Heart Attack," *The New York Times*, March 8, 1949, pg. 1.

[80] "President Tells War Plans Secretly to Congress Group," *The New York Times*, February 2, 1943, pg. 1. See also "Representative Sol Bloom Dies of Heart Attack."

[81] "It will not be any pleasant thing," Luxford said. Minutes of January 13, 1944 meeting at 11:00 a.m. in "Diaries of Henry Morgenthau, Jr." vol. 693, p. 198. See also the comment of Henry Morgenthau recorded in the Minutes of a May 24, 1944 meeting at 11:00 a.m. in "Diaries of Henry Morgenthau, Jr." vol. 735, p. 30, in the FDR Library, available at www.fdrlibrary.marist.edu/_resources/images/morg/md1022.pdf (accessed April 14, 2021). Historian Saul Friedman writes about people like Bloom and Stephen Wise that "proximity to power may compromise." By the middle of the war, Bloom had been a congressman for 20 years – five of them as head of the House Foreign Affairs Committee – and he may have grown too close to Roosevelt, too close to his administration, and, in general, too close to official government sources at the expense of ordinary people. See *Problems of World War II*, 87, 90, 157, and 187 for examples of Bloom demonstrating perhaps excessive trust in government.

[82] Minutes of January 15, 1944 meeting at 9:30 a.m. in "Diaries of Henry Morgenthau,

Jr." vol. 694, p. 88, in the FDR Library, available at www.fdrlibrary.marist.edu/ _resources/images/morg/md0979.pdf (accessed November 30, 2021)

[83] See the July 14, 1943 letter to Sam Dickstein in SB Papers, Box 2.

[84] See the letter dated April 5, 1943 in SB Papers, Box 33. Butler thought the idea "excellent" and "hope[d] that the Columbia University Press might publish it." April 6, 1943 letter from Butler to Bloom, SB Papers, Boxes 60-61.

[85] See Bloom's letters on June 6, 1944 to Max Manischewitz, Nat B. Jacoby, and M. J. Hays. All three are in SB Papers, Box 10.

[86] M. J. Nurenberger, *The Scared and the Doomed: The Jewish Establishment vs. the Six Million* (New York: Mosaic Press, 1985), 190. Bergson also believed that Bloom failed to grasp the "emergency" of European Jewry's situation. *Race Against Death*, 151. Nurenberger writes that Bloom was "what one calls 'a very good Jew'" but criticizes him in his book for failing to push Roosevelt on rescue efforts. "[N]o matter how profoundly I feel for the man — and he was a good man — I must say that he was one of the two American Jews who held the key to the salvation of European Jewry."

[87] Qtd. in Hurwitz, 87-88.

[88] Zuroff, 230.

[89] West Side Institutional Review, May 7, 1943. A copy is available in the private collection of Rabbi Aaron I. Reichel.

[90] Private collection of Rabbi Reichel. The authors of articles in this newsletter also found time to focus on *post*-war problems. See, for example, "Germany's Youth: A Post-War Problem" (April 30, 1943 issue) and "Jews in a Post-War World" (January 5, 1945 issue). Agudath Israel's Jacob Rosenheim held a meeting with a government official on "Jewish post-war relief" as early as April 10, 1943. Rosenheim Diary, p. 74. See also, "Representatives of Jewish Organizations Discuss Post-war Problems in Geneva," *Jewish Telegraphic Agency*, August 12, 1943.

[91] *Jews in Gotham*, 93.

[92] Letter from Rabbi Chaim Heller to Bloom, July 8, 1942. SB Papers, Box 4.

[93] See the July 7, 1942 letter from Bloom to Rabbi Herbert S. Goldstein; the July 8, 1942 letter from Bloom to Major General James A. Ulio, adjutant general of the War Department; the September 8, 1942 letter from Bloom to Rev. Louis Novick, and the September 1, 1942 letter from Bloom to Milo Perkins, executive director of the Board of Economic Warfare. All four letters are in SB Papers, Box 21.

[94] See Bloom's letters to Hirschel Revel dated September 27, 1943; November 4, 1943; and January 10, 1944, and Bloom's letter to Byron B. Lindsley dated June 13, 1944. All four letters are in SB Papers, Box 15. Bloom was also asked to obtain "air priority" for Rabbi Sidney B. Hoenig "to visit Latin American countries on behalf of the Yeshiva College of New York." December 16, 1944 letter from Bloom to Maj. Gen. Harold L. George, SB Papers, Box 4-5.

[95] See Rabbi Wolf Gold's July 1, 1942 letter to Goldstein and Bloom's July 7, 1942 letter to Rabbi Wolf Gold, SB Papers, Box 13.

[96] See also Leon I. Feuer, "The Birth of the Jewish Lobby: A Reminiscence," *American Jewish Archives* (Nov. 1976), p. 112. He recalls Bloom "expressing skepticism about the extent of the Holocaust" in a meeting.

[97] See *The Jews Should Keep Quiet*, 115-122 for examples of Wise and other American Jewish leaders "behaving in a business-as-usual fashion" during the Holocaust years.

[98] *Jews in Gotham*, 80. "It was unthinkable that a government in the very heart of civilized Europe...should openly hold as its main political goal the physical extermination of an entire people." Isaiah Trunk, *Judenrat: The Jewish Councils in Eastern Europe Under Nazi Occupation* (New York: Stein, 1972), 453.

[99] See Yosef Gorny, *The Jewish Press and the Holocaust, 1939-1945: Palestine, Britain, the United States and the Soviet Union*, trans. Naftali Greenwood (Cambridge: Cambridge University Press, 2012), 165, and Novick, 45. That would also explain why so many American Jews concentrated on supporting the troops and community matters that seem so unimportant in retrospect. In these areas they felt they could make a difference. See Rigg, 164 and 167-168.

[100] "The Allies and the Holocaust," 26. See also Baumel, xx: "[E]ven taking into account David Wyman's claims regarding the impact of the [Bergson group's] activities on the establishment of the War Refugee Board, there is little debate that the remnants of European Jewry were ultimately rescued by the advancing Allied armies and not by any American Jewish or Zionist organization."

[101] Qtd. in *The Jews Should Be Quiet*, 202. See also Rafael Medoff, *Blowing the Whistle on Genocide: Josiah E. DuBois, Jr. and the Struggle for a U.S. Response to the Holocaust* (West Lafayette, Indiana: Purdue University Press, 2009), 60.

[102] Wise wrote, "One good term deserves another, – and you have had a good, serviceable, fruitful first term. If you do as well in your second term, the District ought to make it unanimous the third time!" Letter from Wise to Bloom, October 14, 1924, SB Papers, Box 26. Letters from Bloom soliciting and thanking Wise for the endorsement are in the same box.

[103] Ibid.

[104] See, for example, Wise's October 11, 1928 letter to Bloom, in ibid. (about securing tickets to Army-Navy football games), and the May 9 and May 15, 1941 letters from Bloom to Wise in SB Papers, Box 22. In 1926, Wise also extended a personal invitation to Bloom to attend a meeting of select individuals on the welfare of Eastern European Jewry. See his October 7, 1926 letter to Bloom in SB Papers, Box 26, and "Rabbi Wise Presents Plea to Queen Marie for Jews in Roumania," *Jewish Daily Bulletin*, October 21, 1926, p. 3.

[105] January 2, 1936 letter in SB Papers, Box 26. Bloom's opinion of Wise may have soured over time; he called him a "racketeer" in conversation with Vice President Henry Wallace in 1943. See *The Price of Vision: The Diary of Henry A. Wallace, 1942-1946*, ed., John Morton Blum (Boston: Houghton Mifflin, 1973), 193. Wise, for his part, made "acerbic comments about Bloom (behind his back)." *They Should Be Quiet*, 309.

[106] See, for example, *Problems of World War II*, 218 ("Take all the time that you want") and 220 ("Pardon me for interrupting"). The only person from the Bergson group to whom Bloom showed as much courtesy was Frances Gunther. See ibid., 144 and 146. Perhaps she elicited his chivalric spirit; perhaps Bloom also appreciated her celebrity status as the wife of noted author John Gunther.

[107] *Bearing Witness*, 232.

[108] June 23, 1943 letter to Max Manischewitz, in SB Papers, Box 10. Cf. Bloom's July 9, 1943 letter to Nat Jacoby regarding criticism from Emanuel Celler (presumably in relation to the Bermuda Conference), "I do not believe that any benefit will be gained for the Jews, of not only this country, but of the world, if the Jews, especially members of Congress, shall begin to fight among themselves. I have always said that I will be one Jew who will never fight another Jew, especially in public." He concludes the letter with what is apparently an explanation for his stance: "I think that everything possible should be done not to encourage or give comfort to the enemies of religious and racial tolerance." SB Papers, Box 6.

[109] January 29, 1947 letter to Morris Engelman, SB Papers, Box 37. See also *The Jews Should Be Quiet*, 28.

[110] Historian Rafael Medoff attributes Bloom's behavior to this cause. "Bloom felt personally stung by the Bergson-led criticism of his role" at the Bermuda Conference. Rafael Medoff, *FDR and the Holocaust: A Breach of Faith* (Washington: Wyman, 2013), 87.

[111] See "Bloom, 78, Waging a Brisk Campaign," by Douglas Dales, *The New York Times*, October 27, 1948, pg. 14. See also Abba Hillel Silver's comment to Bloom in a March 2, 1944 letter: "I trust that you are...in your usual good spirits." SB Papers, Boxes 60-61.

[112] *Autobiography*, 131.

[113] William "Fishbait" Miller, *Fishbait: The Memoirs of the Congressional Gatekeeper* (New York: Warner Books, 1977) 500. This same story appears in slightly modified form in "New Book Covers Career" by Hope Ridings Miller. See also the comments on Bloom in Louis Nizer, *Between You and Me* (New York: Pyramid Books, 1964), 187-188.

[114] Samuel Dickson, *Tales of San Francisco* (Stanford: Stanford University Press, 1957), 685.

[115] January 28, 1948 letter to Bloom, in SB Papers, Box 41.

[116] "Congressman Sol Bloom Marks 75th Birthday; Arranges Parties for Needy," *Jewish Telegraphic Agency*, March 11, 1945. Among these institutions was St. Ann's Roman Catholic Infant Asylum. Bloom would buy the asylum's children ice cream and cake. "Asylum Has Service in Memory of Bloom," *the New York Times*, March 10, 1949, pg. 28.

[117] Bloom goes on to write, "I feel that I will be unfaithful to my trust if I should not do whatever comes to my notice, so as to spread a little joy and happiness, and faith and love in the world." March 19, 1948 letter to Rabbi Jonathan Steif, SB Papers, Box 22. See also Bloom's August 19, 1943 letter to Sylvain Coblentz, in which he writes "I also like to go through the world thinking that the sun is shining all the time, and it is our duty to bring happiness and contentment to all the world whenever we can." Ibid.,

Box 34.

[118] Eleanor Roosevelt wrote to a friend about Bloom in 1946, "Sol Bloom is able and petty and vain and yet in ways I like him." Joseph P. Lash, *A World of Love: Eleanor Roosevelt and Her Friends, 1943-1962* (Garden City: Doubleday, 1984), 214. See also Eleanor Roosevelt, *On My Own* (New York: Harper & Brothers, 1958), 52.

[119] "Oral History Interview with Charles Burton Marshall," by Niel M. Johnson, June 21 and 23, 1989, available at www.trumanlibrary.gov/library/oral-histories/marshall (accessed March 25, 2021). According to Marshall, the members of the Foreign Affairs Committee "personally just didn't care a damn for Bloom" – an estimation largely shared by Rep. Karl Mundt, who served on the committee. See also Kimball, 160, who writes that Bloom was considered "pompous" and "an inveterate publicity hound." Most sources, though, indicate that Bloom generally enjoyed a good reputation. In a report for the British Foreign Office, Isaiah Berlin sized Bloom up as an "easy-going, superficial, glad-handish type." Hachey, 150. See also "Sol Bloom, Great American" *The Sioux City Journal*, March 9, 1949, pg. 6: "Few members of congress were more loved and respected than 'Sol,' as he affectionately was called by his host of friends from the White House to New York's east side." One colleague, Daniel J. Flood, remembered him 21 years later as "great, beloved, and revered." *Cuba and the Caribbean: Hearings Before the Subcommittee on Inter-American Affairs of the Committee on Foreign Affairs, House of Representatives, Ninety-First Congress, Second Session* (Washington: U.S. Government Printing Office, 1970), 204. See also the tributes in the booklet on the luncheon held in honor of Bloom's 74th birthday in SB Papers, Box 62.

[120] *Race Against Death*, 154. Bloom therefore seems to have been exaggerating when he wrote to a friend, "I have never personally had a falling out with anyone" and when he told his colleagues at his 74th birthday celebration, "I have never left a scar in any of my debates or any of my battles or controversies. If any one has scarred me, the scar has immediately healed and vanished." July 9, 1943 letter to Nat Jacoby and birthday booklet, p. 34.

[121] "Oral History Interview with Durward V. Sandifer," by Richard D. McKinzie, Marc 15 and May 29, 1973, available at www.trumanlibrary.gov/library/oral-histories/sandifer (accessed March 25, 2021).

[122] Interestingly, while historians partial to the Bergson group write about Bloom with hostility, Bergson himself didn't seem to share their categorical rancor. "[Bloom] was sympathetic and cautious, sort of neutral," Bergson said in an interview 30 years after the war. "And he was trying to calm down the Zionists. He was really better than I thought.... there was no conflict between us." *Race Against Death*, 99. Bergson didn't regard Bloom as "bright" or "impressive" and thought Bloom displayed a great measure of "nastiness" toward him at the hearings. But Bergson subsequently asked for a meeting with Bloom, and the two seem to have parted on relatively cordial terms. Ibid., 144 and 149.

[123] May 24, 1944 meeting at 11:00 a.m. in "Diaries of Henry Morgenthau, Jr." vol. 735, p. 29-30. Bloom also publicly criticized Bergson in September 1944. See "Bergson Admits

His Committee Has No Right to Collect Funds," by Gloria Lubar and Edward P. van der Veen, *The Washington Post*, September(?) 4, 1944, in War Refugee Board Papers, reel 5, folder 35, US Holocaust Memorial Museum.

[124] Rafael Medoff, *Militant Zionism in America: The Rise and Impact of the Jabotinsky Movement in the United States, 1926-1948* (Tuscaloosa: Univ. of Alabama Press, 2002), 188, quoting a statement from Bloom that appears "prominently in FBI memoranda on the subject." Other people who pressured the government to deport Bergson include Nachum Goldmann and Morris Waldman, executive director of the American Jewish Committee. Ibid., 188. Rep. Dickstein, ostensibly a supporter of rescue efforts, once threatened to deport Bergson as well. According to Bergson, "he more or less said, 'You either behave, or we'll deport you.' He didn't say it in so many words, but he couldn't have been more explicit." See *A Race Against Death*, 98-99.

[125] "Hungary Is Warned by House Committee," *The New York Times*, June 22, 1944, pg. 9.

[126] See "House Foreign Affairs Committee Gets Resolution Urging Turkey to Admit More Refugees," *Jewish Telegraphic Agency*, June 25, 1944.

[127] June 23, 1944 letter from Pehle to Morgenthau with accompanying documents in "Diaries of Henry Morgenthau, Jr." vol. 746, p. 294-296, in the FDR Library, available at www.fdrlibrary.marist.edu/_resources/images/morg/md1034.pdf (accessed April 14, 2021). The resolution numbers are 610 and 615, respectively.

[128] See the "paraphrase of telegram received," July 10, 1944, from the American legation in Bern to Secretary of State Hull and accompanying documents in War Refugee Board Papers, reel 35, folder 2.

[129] See "official text of telegram sent" from Hull to "Amlegation, Bern," dated June 30, 1944, in ibid., reel 32, folder 8.

[130] See the July 3, 1944 telegram (sections one and two) from Steinhardt to Hull, in ibid., reel 55, folder 12, and the July 6, 1944 letter from Friedman to Pehle in ibid.

[131] August 21, 1944 letter in ibid., reel 32, folder 8.

[132] August 25, 1944 letter from Bloom to Pehle in ibid.

[133] Letter with accompanying documents in ibid., reel 35, folder 2.

[134] Letter dated September 4, 1944, in ibid.

Chapter 9 *(pages 114-130)*

[1] Aaron Berman, "American Zionism and the Rescue of European Jewry: An Ideological Perspective," *American Jewish History* 70, no. 3 (March 1981), 316. See also the statement of Louis Lipsky quoted in Samuel Halperin, *The Political World of American Zionism* (Silver Spring: Information Dynamics, 1985), 32: "It is now appreciated – as never before – that the homelessness of the Jewish people must come to an end.... Or we shall be doomed for generations to an ignoble existence and ultimate disappearance as a people."

[2] *Jewish National Home*, 26. See also ibid., 169. Silver elaborated that he didn't mean to imply that all Jews should move to Palestine "any more than that all Englishmen in all parts of the world should return to England, or all Frenchmen to France, or all Germans to Germany." But "just as there is an England, a France, and a Germany, so must there be a Land of Israel in order that the status of the Jewish people might be normalized throughout the world."

[3] Berman, 316-317. See also *American Zionism from Herzl to the Holocaust*, 401-402.

[4] Berman, 319. Time, energy, and resources are, by their very nature, limited.

[5] See, for example, Berman, 323: "American Zionists vehemently opposed the [proposal to set up] emergency refugee shelters" in Palestine because they "feared that the opening of Palestine refugee centers, without recognition of the refugees' right to remain permanently in Palestine, would raise serious questions about the legitimacy of the Jewish claim to Palestine."

[6] Ibid., 329. See also ibid., 330: "Silver and other American Zionist leaders were ideologically incapable of distinguishing between the rescue issue and the statehood issue. They saw Nazi extermination as just another link in the chain of suffering which had been the Jewish destiny for two thousand years. The fulfillment of the Zionist dream would break the chain. Zionist leaders were willing to do anything to rescue European Jewry as long as it did not undermine the future establishment of the state. To do so would condemn future generations to a death sentence."

[7] See ibid., 320, 321, 324, 326, and 327.

[8] *Jewish National Home*, 1.

[9] American Zionists considered the White Paper a form of appeasement to Arab terror and a betrayal of the promise of the Balfour Declaration. As Lord Harry Snell said in the House of Lords, "What does a National Home [as promised to the Jewish people by the Balfour Declaration] mean? ... Does it mean when a people are petrified, as a minority amid a majority of hostile people? Is it a home where you are an unwelcome lodger in the house of somebody else who hates and tries to injure you? If so, then the Jews already have their national home in several places: in Germany, Poland, Russia and elsewhere." Appendix to *Jewish National Home*, 425. See also ibid., 473.

[10] On several occasions, Bloom claimed partial credit for this decision, maintaining that it stemmed from a suggestion he made at the Bermuda Conference. See ibid., 227; Appendix, 391; *Autobiography*, 296; *Problems of World War II*, 52, as well as Bermuda Conference Minutes, 115, and post-Bermuda Conference report to Eden, 3. This claim seems highly exaggerated judging from the November 23, 1943 letter from W. G. Hayter of the British Embassy to Bloom in NARA, RG-233, Box 67.

[11] Memorandum from Assistant Secretary of State Adolf A. Berle, Jr. to Secretary of State Cordell Hull, January 28, 1944 based on a telephone conversation between Berle and Bloom. *Foreign Relations of the United States: Diplomatic Papers, 1944, The Near East, South Asia, and Africa, The Far East, vol. V*, available at https://history.state.gov/historicaldocuments/frus1944v05/d610 (accessed April 16, 2021).

[12] In an interview with The Voice of San Francisco, Bloom said he held the hearings because the American Council for Judaism – a group representing the anti-Zionism position of classic Reform Judaism – opposed the resolution. Appendix, 498.

[13] Murray Frank, "Washington News Letter," *The National Jewish Ledger*, in *Jewish National Home*, 499. A Yiddish paper, The Day, anticipating opposition by Bloom, ran an editorial on February 2, 1944, arguing that it was his "duty" to facilitate the resolution's passage considering the "overwhelming" support for it among his constituents and American Jewry and the "ideals and aims of the present war." A clipping of the editorial and an English translation appear in NARA, RG-233, Box 68.

[14] "Washington News Letter."

[15] February 12, 1944 memo from Mr. Luxford to Mr. Marks at the FDR Library, available at www.fdrlibrary.marist.edu/_resources/images/wrb/wrb0144.pdf (accessed December 15, 2021). Bloom evidently sent this booklet to the editors of many major newspapers. See his February 11, 1944 letter to the editor of The New York Times in NARA, RG-233, Box 66.

[16] *Jewish National Home*, 277. See also ibid., 384. In his autobiography, Bloom mentions as a point of pride in relation to hearings on a different bill: "One of the things I insisted upon was that the committee of which I was chairman should never have to meet the accusation that any pertinent argument had not been presented. I wanted the full truth to be known to all. I was sure that the truth would win in the end." *Autobiography*, 241-242.

[17] Stevens, 41. Indeed, Bloom probably had already planned to display his pro-Zionist leanings several days before the hearings even began judging from a letter he sent Alexander Brin, editor of The Jewish Advocate of Boston, on February 4, 1944. In it, he writes, "Why don't you send a man to Washington to write up the hearings on the Palestine Resolution beginning next Tuesday? I personally will pay all expenses." SB Papers, Box 32.

[18] *Jewish National Home* 350. See also ibid., 254-255, 287, and 144, where he draws the attention of an anti-Zionist witness to a pro-Zionist statement made by President Woodrow Wilson.

[19] Ibid., 285 and 293-294.

[20] Ibid., 253, 256, and 312.

[21] Ibid., 359.

[22] Ibid., 186. For another example of Bloom trying to make the Zionist case stronger, see ibid., 99. See also ibid., 114, where Bloom comments on the transformation of Palestine to a Zionist leader: "You have done...marvelous work."

[23] Ibid., 162 and 2.

[24] February 19, 1944 letter in Abba Hillel Silver Papers in the New York Public Library. The documents cited in this chapter from these papers come from Reel 100, Box 35, Folder 31; Reel 102, Box 35, Folder 131; and Reel 108, Box 37, Folder 411.

[25] Qtd. in Appendix, 500. Stephen Wise was reportedly also very happy. See the

February 28, 1944 letter from E. I. Kaufman to Bloom in SB Papers, Boxes 60-61. Bloom received complimentary letters from some of the anti-Zionist witnesses as well. See ibid.

[26] *Autobiography*, 295.

[27] *Congressional Record,* 80th Congress, Second Session – Appendix, volume 94, part 12, p. A5238.

[28] He was scheduled to go in 1927. See "Congressmen Urge More Fast Liners," *The New York Times*, July 3, 1927, pg. 8. The article reports that Bloom planned on visiting Palestine as part of a summer trip, but Bloom doesn't mention visiting Palestine in his autobiography or in any of his discussions of Zionism. Perhaps, he later altered his itinerary and never made it to the region.

[29] "$82,000 Raised for United Palestine Appeal," *Jewish Daily Bulletin*, February 16, 1926, pg. 3. The article identifies Bloom as the honorary chairman of the Appeal's Harlem-Yorkville Division.

[30] "Louis Strauss, Noted Belgian Statesman, Dies," *Jewish Daily Bulletin*, November 24, 1926, pg. 6. The article identifies Bloom as the chairman of its Building Fund Committee.

[31] "Jews and Gentiles to Participate in N.Y. Maccabean Celebration," *Jewish Daly Bulletin*, December 10, 1933, pg. 3, and "Church Activities of Interest in City," *The New York Times*, December 9, 1933, pg. 12.

[32] "Sponsors Named for J.N.F. Concert," *Jewish Daily Bulletin*, October 9, 1934, pg. 2. Bloom was a member of the JNF musical festival's "citizen's committee."

[33] "Appeal to Britain for National Home," *The New York Times*, August 5, 1930, pg. 8.

[34] "Legislators Make Plea on Palestine," *The New York Times*, November 1, 1938, pg. 18.

[35] "All Diplomatic Steps to Alter Britain's Policy Taken, Congressman Told," *Jewish Telegraph Agency*, May 24, 1939, and *Congressional Record*, A5239.

[36] *Autobiography*, 144.

[37] Cohen, 11.

[38] Letter from Bloom to Max Klipstein, SB Papers, Box 8. See also "Bermuda Conference Did a Lot for Refugees, Says Delegate Sol Bloom," *The Forward*, May 24, 1943, pg. 1. Bloom also didn't believe Palestine could absorb very many Jews. In his autobiography, 297, he writes, "It simply isn't big enough. Even if there were no resistance on the part of the million Arabs who now inhabit the land....it is doubtful whether Palestine ever could be big enough to support an additional three or four million inhabitants – and as for a population of eleven or twelve million, the idea is nothing less than fantastic."

[39] So did American Jewish Committee president Joseph Proskauer. "We regard it as inappropriate to press the Zionist demands at a time when we are in the midst of war," he wrote to Bloom in a December 3, 1943 letter. NARA, RG-233, Box 67. This attitude perhaps also explains Bloom's failure to sign a pro-Zionist statement by 68 senators and 194 representatives in 1942 on the occasion of the 25th anniversary of the Balfour

Declaration. A copy of the statement, "The Common Purpose of Civilized Mankind," is in ibid., Box 68.

[40] *Foreign Relations of the United States*, available at https://history.state.gov/historicaldocuments/frus1939v04/d817 (accessed April 21, 2021). Bloom believed these tactics wouldn't work. The memo's author writes, "He felt that far more assistance could be rendered the Jews by quiet and reasonable discussion with the Department of all problems that might arise."

[41] Blum, 193-194. Bloom helped Berlin secure permission to return to Palestine in middle of the war and spent "many pleasant hours" with him, according to a thank-you letter Berlin sent him on the eve of his departure. December 8, 1943 letter in SB Papers, Box 61.

[42] "Conversation with Congressman Sol Bloom," September 22, 1943, in Central Zionist Archives, Z6/282.

[43] *Problems of World War II*, 23.

[44] Ibid., 225. See also ibid., 43 and 71, and the testimony of Rabbi Morris Lazaron in *Jewish National Home*, 329: "Should some consideration, ladies and gentlemen, not be given to the fact that we are at war? ... Can our government commit itself while we are at war to a policy deeply involving our ally Great Britain; to one side in a controversy that raises the bitterest feelings and holds the possibility of disaffection behind our own lines?"

[45] *Foreign Relations of the United States*, available at https://history.state.gov/historicaldocuments/frus1943v04/pg_799   and   https://history.state.gov/historicaldocuments/frus1943v04/pg_800 (accessed April 22, 2021).

[46] Ibid., https://history.state.gov/historicaldocuments/frus1943/d357 (accessed April 22, 2021). Ultimately, it wasn't issued thanks, ironically, to the War Department. According to Hull, Secretary of War Henry Stimson thought "the security situation in Palestine was not so serious as to warrant any action." Ibid., https://history.state.gov/historicaldocuments/frus1943v04/pg_803 (accessed April 22, 2021).

[47] *Jewish National Home*, 109. An additional 15 congressmen sent Bloom letters expressing their views, which they asked to be incorporated in the official record. Not a single congressman opposed the resolution.

[48] Ibid., 106. See also ibid., 91-92.

[49] See ibid., 104, 109, 112, 157, and 269 (featuring testimony of Emanuel Neumann): "What contribution have the Arabs made to the democratic cause during this, its greatest crisis? Where did they stand when Rommel stood at the gates of Alexandria? What Arab banner was carried to the field of battle to defend, not only the cause of democracy but their own...freedom and independence which had been so dearly won for them with the lives of Britons and Frenchmen and Americans, during the First World War? ... The leader of the Arab extremists in Palestine, the notorious Mufti, was commuting between Rome and Berlin doing the Fuehrer's work."

[50] *The Memoirs of Cordell Hull, vol. II* (New York: Macmillan, 1948), 1534-1535.

[51] *Jewish National Home*, 505. Bloom may have had a hand in drafting this letter. See

Stevens, 51, and an earlier draft of this letter (dated March 2) with edits in SB Papers, Boxes 60-61.

[52] *Foreign Relations of the United States*, available at https://history.state.gov/historicaldocuments/frus1944v05/pg_563 (accessed April 18, 2021).

[53] Ibid., available at https://history.state.gov/historicaldocuments/frus1944v05/pg_567 (accessed April 16, 2021).

[54] Ibid., available at https://history.state.gov/historicaldocuments/frus1944v05/pg_573 (accessed April 18, 2021).

[55] Ibid., available at https://history.state.gov/historicaldocuments/frus1944v05/pg_574 (accessed April 18, 2021).

[56] Ibid., available at https://history.state.gov/historicaldocuments/frus1944v05/pg_581 (accessed April 18, 2021).

[57] McCloy wrote on February 22, "I feel we should be most reluctant to express any view" on an alternative text for the Palestine resolution. "What is provocative [to the Arabs] or not provocative in the Palestine problem is a political matter on which the State Department rather than the War Department should speak." Ibid., https://history.state.gov/historicaldocuments/frus1944v05/pg_576 (accessed April 18, 2021).

[58] Memorandum from Elihu D. Stone to Abba Hillel Silver in AHS Papers, p. 4.

[59] Confidential memo from Stone to Silver in AHS Papers.

[60] Qtd. in *The Jews Should Be Quiet*, 240.

[61] Qtd. in Stevens, 53-54.

[62] "House Foreign Affairs Committee Announces Shelving of Palestine Resolution," *Jewish Telegraphic Agency*, March 19, 1944, and *Jewish National Home*, 505.

[63] May 8, 1944 letter in SB Papers, Boxes 60-61.

[64] May 10, 1944 letter in AHS Papers.

[65] May 17, 1944 letter from Lipsky to Bloom in ibid.

[66] May 25, 1944 letter from Lipsky to Silver in ibid.

[67] June 2, 1944 letter in ibid.

[68] June 9, 1944 letter in ibid.

[69] See the editorial "An Important Zion Document" (editorial), *The Morning Journal*, May 23, 1944; Bloom's July 5, 1944 letters to Dr. Goldstein and Max Manischewitz; his July 13, 1944 letter to J. I. Fishbein, editor of The Sentinel in Chicago; and the May 31, 1944 letter of thanks from the executive secretary of Mizrachi, Rabbi Max Kirshblum. SB Papers, Boxes 2, 10, 39, and 60-61, respectively. The Zionist Organization ordered 500 copies from Bloom's office in November. Letter from Isidore Cooperman to Boyd Crawford; the letter is dated November 1, 1944 – "One Day Closer to Victory." Ibid., Box 51.

[70] June 9, 1944 letter.

[71] "Brief note of Conversation with Congressman Bloom," June 26, 1944; letter from Goldstein to Silver, June 12, 1944; and memorandum from Arthur Lourie to Silver, June 22, 1944 ("he emphasized repeatedly that whatever his own opinion might be he would be guided with regard to action on the Resolution by ourselves"). All three documents are in AHS Papers.

[72] "Brief note of Conversation with Congressman Bloom."

[73] "War Department No Longer Objects to Palestine Resolution; Congress to Resume Hearings," *Jewish Telegraphic Agency*, October 16, 1944.

[74] *Foreign Relations of the United States*, available at https://history.state.gov/historicaldocuments/frus1944v05/pg_637 (accessed April 18, 2021). Bloom subsequently postponed consideration of the resolution. "See Hearing on Palestine Resolution Postponed; Bill on Restoration of Property Introduced," *Jewish Telegraphic Agency*, November 15, 1944.

[75] Stevens, 61. See also Rabbi Israel Goldstein's statement in *Brooklyn Jewish Center Review*, January 1945, p. 6 and 8.

[76] Qtd. in Stevens, 94.

[77] See the December 13, 1944 letter from Bloom to Dr. Goldstein, Central Zionist Archives, 4364/1656-b.

[78] November 27, 1944 letter from Silver to Bloom, NARA, RG-233, Box 68.

[79] "House Foreign Affairs Committee Approves Palestine Resolution; Amends Text," *Jewish Telegraphic Agency*, November 30, 1944 and the transcript of telephone conversations between Dr. Goldstein and Bloom on December 13 and 19, 1944, Central Zionist Archives, 4364/1656-b.

[80] "House Foreign Affairs Committee Approves Palestine Resolution" and "Congressional Committee Asked to Bring Palestine Resolution to Floor of House," *Jewish Telegraphic Agency*, December 6, 1944. See the transcript of Bloom's plea before the House Rules Committee in NARA, RG-233, Box 68.

[81] A copy of Roosevelt's letter to Wagner is in NARA, RG-233, Box 68. In a long letter to Stettinius on December 2, 1944 (in ibid.), Bloom again claimed the resolution had Roosevelt's support and even argued that Stettinius therefore could not possibly oppose it. Bloom was apparently prevaricating once again. (See also the transcript of the Goldstein-Bloom telephone conversations.) Other possible explanations are: 1) the November 15 memo is inaccurate; 2) Bloom didn't believe the information he had been given about the president's view.

[82] See *Foreign Relations of the United States*, available at https://history.state.gov/historicaldocuments/frus1944v05/pg_641 (accessed April 18, 2021).

[83] "The recent pro-Zionist statements in this country...gave rise to a wave of shocked disillusionment and protest in the Near East," Stettinius wrote in a memorandum to Roosevelt. Ibid., available at https://history.state.gov/historicaldocuments/frus1944v05/pg_648 (accessed April 21, 2021). After listing examples of the Arab

reaction, the secretary of state advised, "If this trend should continue, it would seriously prejudice our ability to afford protection to American interests, economic and commercial, cultural and philanthropic, throughout the area." Ibid.

[84] Ibid., available at https://history.state.gov/historicaldocuments/frus1944v05/pg_643 (accessed April 18, 2021).

[85] Ibid., available at https://history.state.gov/historicaldocuments/frus1944v05/pg_646 (accessed April 18, 2021).

[86] See "Zionist Meeting Supports Silver; ZOA Head Outlines Essence of Wise-Silver Dispute," *Jewish Telegraphic Agency*, December 12, 1944.

[87] See *A Voice That Spoke for Justice*, 344. Bloom evidently was happy at this outcome. See his December 29, 1944 letter in SB Papers, Box 26. The grassroots, however, were not. See Louis J. Gribetz, "The Need for Dr. Silver's Leadership," *Brooklyn Jewish Center Review*, January 1945, p. 1. See also "Zionist Meeting Supports Silver" and Mark A. Raider, "Where American Zionism Differed: Abba Hillel Silver Reconsidered," in *Abba Hillel Silver and American Zionism*, eds. Mark A. Raider, et al. (London: Frank Cass, 1997), 118. Articles by Goldstein and Rabbi Silver giving their respective sides of the story appear in *Brooklyn Jewish Center Review*, January 1945, p. 5-12. Neither article has anything negative to say about Bloom.

[88] Transcript of the Goldstein-Bloom telephone conversations. See also the concluding sentence of Bloom's December 13 letter to Goldstein: "[E]veryone knows my only thought is to do what I think is the right thing to do and to be guided, and informed, and instructed by the people who are supposed to know how to guide me."

[89] It's also possible that Bloom figured the administration could always kill the bill in the Senate if it wanted to, so it wasn't necessary for him to stand in the way.

Chapter 10 *(pages 131-147)*

[1] "Hull Will Attend Security Parley," *The New York Times*, February 14, 1945, pg. 1, and *Autobiography*, 3. The formal invitation from Roosevelt is in SB Papers, Boxes 60-61.

[2] For the minutes of the 77 meetings of the United States Delegation, see *Foreign Relations of the United States: Diplomatic Papers, 1945, General: The United Nations, Volume I*. Secretary of State Edward Stettinius wrote that Bloom "contributed greatly to [the country's] success...at that historic congress." Inscription of Stettinius in Bloom's copy of *Charter of the United Nations*, SB Papers, Box 62.

[3] "Nation After Nation See Era of Peace in Signing Charter," Lawrence E. Davies, *The New York Times*, June 27, 1945, pg. 1. Testimonials to Bloom's service in San Francisco appear in SB Papers, Boxes 60-62.

[4] Qtd. in Nasaw 108-109.

[5] "Truman Said to Aid Jews on Palestine," *The New York Times*, September 22, 1945, pg. 17.

[6] Program for "Testimonial and 77th Birthday Dinner in Honor of Congressman Sol Bloom," in SB Papers, Box 62. Bloom had written the secretary of war the previous year "concerning the possibility of sending Kosher food and clothing to Jewish displaced persons in the American zone of Germany." December 9, 1946 letter in SB Papers, Box 37. See also a similar request in a May 28, 1947 letter to Colonel Tyler Wood. Ibid. For Bloom's efforts on behalf of Agudath Israel Youth Council of America to send kosher meat to Jewish personnel in the U.S. armed forces in 1944, see the letters between Bloom and Tress, the organization's chairman, in Mike Tress Papers, Amud Aish Memorial Museum archives.

[7] Approximately 132,000 displaced Jews found a home in Israel by 1951. Nasaw, 404.

[8] The text of the resolution appears in *Problems of World War II*, 363. "The emotional reaction to the Holocaust and to the plight of the survivors strengthened the Zionist cause." Cohen, 71.

[9] *Problems of World War II*, 330.

[10] Ibid., 320 and 322.

[11] Ibid., 311-312. At the earlier hearings, Bloom estimated the number of telegrams and letters opposing the resolution at 10. *Jewish National Home*, 274.

[12] "House Adopts Palestine Resolution; Identical with Resolution Adopted by Senate," *Jewish Telegraphic Agency*, December 20, 1945.

[13] *Problems of World War II*, 366.

[14] "Truman Withdraws His Support from Wagner-Taft Resolution on Jewish Commonwealth," *Jewish Telegraphic Agency*, November 30, 1945.

[15] *Foreign Relations of the United States: Diplomatic Papers, 1945, The Near East And Africa, Volume VIII*, available at https://history.state.gov/historicaldocuments/frus1945v08/d824 (accessed April 25, 2021).

[16] Joseph B. Schechtman, *The United States and the Jewish State Movement: The Crucial Decade – 1939-1949* (New York: Herzl Press, 1966), 13.

[17] Ibid., 15-17.

[18] Ibid., 14, and Cohen, 72.

[19] Many in the government believed – in the words of a 1945 memorandum to President Roosevelt – that "Zionist activities in this country will remain the gravest threat to friendly relations between the United States and the countries of the [Middle] East until a solution to the [Palestine] problem is found." "Memorandum by the Acting Secretary of State to President Roosevelt," *Foreign Relations of the United States: Diplomatic Papers, 1945, The Near East And Africa, Volume VIII*, available at https://history.state.gov/historicaldocuments/frus1945v08/d662 (accessed April 25, 2021).

[20] "White House Receiving Favorable Reaction to Palestine Report, Says Truman Aide," *Jewish Telegraphic Agency*, May 2, 1946.

[21] "Bevin Unwilling to Open Palestine for 100,000 Jews," *The New York Times*, June 13, 1946, pg. 1.

[22] "Bloom Asks House to Act," *The New York Times*, June 14, 1946, pg. 6, and "House Foreign Affairs Committee to Start Hearings on Palestine; Bevin Criticized," *Jewish Telegraphic Agency*, June 16, 1946. In a long May 7, 1948 letter to Ted Thackrey, editor of The New York Post, Bloom claimed that he had wanted to introduce this resolution in 1944, but Wise, Silver, and others asked him "not to do anything about it; that [he] should leave this matter in their hands." When he introduced it in 1946, he said he received the same message. "I was again told practically to mind my own business; that the Jewish leaders have charge of this." SB Papers, Box 52.

[23] "House to Take Up British Loan Today," *The New York Times*, July 8, 1946, pg. 3.

[24] "26 Leaders Back Loan to Britain," *The New York Times*, July 11, 1946, pg. 8, and "British Loan Halts Trade War Rise," *The New York Times*, July 14, 1946, pg. 69. The Jewish War Veterans of the United States sounded a similar note. "As much as we are disheartened by Great Britain's unjust and illegal handling of the Palestinian issue, we are not opposed to any measure which will help promote world peace and international cooperation," it said. "Proskauer Says 'No Jewish Question Involved' in American Loan to Britain," *Jewish Telegraphic Agency*, July 12, 1946. See also Stevens, 117.

[25] For a very different view of this vote, see Israel Eldad, *The First Tithe*, trans. Zev Golan (Tel Aviv: Jabotinsky Institute, 2008), 337-343.

[26] April 16, 1948 letter to Howard I. Mantell, SB Papers, Box 10. If this evidence existed in his papers, it no longer does. See also his February 23 letter to the same person, ibid., plus his May 21, 1948 letter to Jack London, SB Papers, Box 43, and his August 23, 1948 letter to Harold I. Panken, SB Papers, Box 13 ("I think that I can safely say that if it had not been for my efforts last fall with members of the United Nations, the vote in favor of partition would not have gone through").

[27] *Autobiography*, 296-297.

[28] *Congressional Record*, 80th Congress, Second Session – Appendix, volume 94, part 12, p. A5238.

[29] SB Papers, Box 48. Cuba voted against partition. The text of the telegram sent to these presidents is in SB Papers, Box 48.

[30] February 22, 1948 entry of Forrestal's unpublished diary, p. 2095, in James V. Forrestal Papers, Princeton University Library, available at https://findingaids.princeton.edu/catalog/MC051_c05060 (accessed November 11, 2021).

[31] Ignacio Klich, "Latin America, the United States and the Birth of Israel: The Case of Somoza's Nicaragua," *Journal of Latin American Studies*, volume 20, issue 2 (November 1988), 406, footnote.

[32] See Peter L. Hahn, *Caught in the Middle East: U.S. Policy Toward the Arab-Israeli Conflict, 1945-1961* (Chapel Hill, University of North Carolina, 2004), 41. See also Hal Lehrman, "Partition in Washington: An Inquiry," *Commentary* (March 1948), available at www.commentarymagazine.com/articles/hal-lehrman/partition-in-washington-an-inquirythe-factors-guiding-our-governments-policy/ (accessed April 22, 2021), who writes that Liberia's president sent Bloom a telegram informing him that Liberia would

vote "yes" on partition.

33 2003 e-mail from William V. S. Tubman, Jr., as cited in D. Elwood Dunn, *Liberia and the United States During the Cold War: Limits of Reciprocity* (New York: Palgrave Macmillan, 2009), 73. The vote for partition at the UN apparently paid off; Tubman writes that "the Israeli government has never forgotten this."

34 Carlos Ramulo, *I Walked with Heroes: The Autobiography of General Carlos P. Romulo* (New York: Holt, Reinhart and Winston, 1961), 287. See also "Washington Mourns Death of Rep. Bloom; Flags Fly at Falf-Mast; Funeral Tomorrow," *Jewish Telegraphic Agency*, March 9, 1949.

35 Qtd. in Mary Ann Glendon, *A World Made New: Eleanor Roosevelt and the Universal Declaration of Human Rights* (New York, Random House, 2002), 104.

36 Romulo, 288.

37 Schechtman, 255. If Secretary of Defense James Forrestal is to be believed, Bloom was also less than enthusiastic about the Zionist cause at this point. According to Forrestal, Bloom told him that he was "in violent disagreement with the attitude of the Zionists on Palestine" and that the "recommendation of the General Assembly [to partition Palestine] was completely unworkable." He then proceeded to make several additional derogatory comments about Zionism to Forrestal and concluded that he only lobbied countries like Haiti and Liberia because he wished to advance U.S. policy in support of partition. See the February 22, 1948 entry of Forrestal's unpublished diary, p. 2094-2095.

38 Schechtman, 256, and Cohen, 90. Roosevelt had also been concerned about bloodshed. He wrote in December 1944: "There are about a half a million Jews [in Palestine]. Perhaps another million want to go.... On the other side of the picture there are approximately seventy million Mohammedans who want to cut their throats the day they land." Qtd. in Stevens, 85.

39 Qtd. in Schechtman, 266.

40 See his April 6, 1948 letter to Morris Engelman, SB Papers, Box 37, and his April 14, 1948 letter to E.I. Kufman, SB Papers, Box 7.

41 The sheet is in SB Papers, Box 51. The request to make the copies (dated April 14 and sent to Sauls Lithograph Co.) is in ibid., Box 49.

42 April 15, 1948 letter in SB Papers, Box 41. The other copies were presumably intended for a similar purpose.

43 "41 Democrats Spur U.S. on Palestine," *The New York Times*, March 12, 1948, pg. 7.

44 "Javits Says U.S. Abandons U.N.," *The New York Times*, March 20, 1948, pg. 3.

45 John Snetsinger, *Truman, the Jewish Vote and the Creation of Israel* (Stanford: Hoover Institution, 1974), 104. See also "U.S. Moves Quickly," by Bertram D. Hulen, *The New York Times*, May 15, 1948, pg. 1, *Congressional Record*, 80th Congress, Second Session – Appendix, volume 94, part 12, p. A5239, and Drew Pearson's May 23rd "Merry-Go-Round" column in The Washington Post, qtd. in *Congressional Record – House*, May 24, 1948, p. 6502, in SB Papers, Box 34. The week he died, The American Hebrew

editorialized, "Sol Bloom played a very real part in smoothing the diplomatic way for the establishment and recognition of the State of Israel, for which generations to come will remember him with deep gratitude." *The American Hebrew*, March 11, 1949.

[46] Letter to Ethel Meyers, SB Papers, Box 5.

[47] "Friendship Train Planned," *The New York Times*, May 24, 1948, pg. 5.

[48] In SB Papers, Box 40.

[49] Bloom asked for these actions in an August 3 letter that he handed to Truman during their meeting. The letter is in the Truman Library, "Palestine File." See also "In Washington Yesterday," *The New York Times*, August 5, 1948, pg. 6, and "State Dept. Denies That Marshall Threatened to Resign over Truman's Pro-Israel Plan," *Jewish Telegraphic Agency*, August 11, 1948.

[50] The plan is in SB Papers, Box 43. See also "Truce Observers to Go to Palestine," *The New York Times*, August 19, 1948, pg. 7.

[51] July 1, 1948 letter from Bloom to Arthur Szyk, SB Papers, Box 22.

[52] Full-page ad, *the New York Times*, October 19, 1948, pg. 23.

[53] Copy of telegram SB Papers, Box 52.

[54] SB Papers, Box 52.

[55] April 6, 1948 memo, in AHS Papers.

[56] Letter to Oscar F. Igersheim, May 24, 1948, SB Papers, Box 43.

[57] "Wallace Accuses Truman of Leading to Russian War," *The New York Times*, February 25, 1948, pg. 1.

[58] "Bloom, 78, Waging a Brisk Campaign," by Douglas Dales, *The New York Times*, October 27, 1948, pg. 17.

[59] *Statistics of the Presidential and Congressional Election of November 2, 1948* (Washington: United States Government Printing Office, 1949), 28.

[60] "Bloom, 78, Waging a Brisk Campaign."

[61] Bloom's record in helping immigrants was actually part of his very first re-election campaign in 1924. A campaign letter to Bloom's constituents states that he "is the only congressman...who will go to the front for any poor friendless immigrant who may be a victim of the present harsh and discriminatory laws and will use all the time, energy and legitimate influence to bear, to see that the immigrant gets a speedy and impartial hearing." SB Papers, Box 35.

[62] See the November 22, 1946 letter from Samuel K. Beier to Bloom, SB Papers, Box 3, and the many letters concerning his case in Box 42.

[63] See the May 20, 1948 letter from Bloom to the American Consul in St. John, New Brunswick, Canada, and the thank-you letter from the Rebbe to Bloom dated August 3, 1948. These letters, plus additional letters related to these cases, are in SB Papers, Box 42. According to a story that has circulated in recent years in Orthodox Jewish circles

(see here, for example: https://jewishgirlsunite.com/the-lawbreaker – accessed November 21, 2021), Bloom even helped the Bobover Rebbe bring Jews to America illegally after the war. The story is hard to accept at face value since Bloom insists in several letters over the years that he won't break the law to help people. But Ephraim Stein, a political activist, said he heard the story directly from the Bobover Rebbe, who made an emotional appeal to Bloom that apparently touched him (personal conversation with the author, 2019). Perhaps Bloom changed his stance after the horrors of the Holocaust or perhaps the details of the story were inaccurately conveyed or repeated in the course of transmission. (This author recently discovered a similar story in "Rebuilding the Glory of Bobov," *The Jewish Observer*, October 2000, pg. 14, by Rabbis Aaron and Benzion Twerski. According to their account, the person who responded to the Bobover Rebbe's emotional appeal and played loose with American law was an Undersecretary of State, *not* Bloom. The Rebbe secured a meeting with the undersecretary in the first place, however, thanks to Bloom.)

[64] See the March 24, 1947 letter from Bloom to the American Consul General and the July 21, 1947 thank-you letter from Rabbi Mendel Schneerson to Bloom in SB Papers, Box 18 and 23, respectively.

[65] The ad, which appeared in the November 4, 1946 issue of the newspaper, is in SB Papers, Box 31.

[66] See the Associated Press news story "Woman Doctor Saved From Deportation by Truman; Foiled Nazis" and a January 28, 1948 letter to Bloom from his secretary with background details on Perl's case. Both are in SB Papers, Box 58.

[67] February 26, 1947 letter from Eleanor Roosevelt and undated letter from Rabbi Moshe Teitelbaum to Bloom in SB Papers, Box 58.

[68] See the September 26, 1947 letter from Bloom to Rabbi Abba Abrams, SB Papers, Box 58. The first letter Bloom wrote on Dr. Perl's behalf is dated June 18, 1946 and was sent to Edward J. Shaughnessy, Deputy Commissioner of Immigration. Numerous other letters and documents related to her case are in Box 58.

[69] December 2, 1948 letter, SB Papers, Box 58.

[70] See the March 1, 1948 letter from Kornel Bernatsky to Bloom; the August 14, 1947 letter from James R. Wilkinson, the American Consul General in Munich Germany, to Bloom; and "Hungarian Couple Arrives at New Windsor Three Years After Flight From Budapest," newspaper clipping, all in SB Papers, Box 1.

[71] Her April 5, 1948 thank-you letter to Bloom, plus several other letters related to her case, are in Box 1.

[72] For details of the case, see the May 13, 1948, letter to Bloom from his secretary; the June 2, 1948 letter from Bloom to Rabbi Ch. M. Braun, chairman of the Association of former Yeshiva Students of the Old Hungary; and the June 8, 1948 thank-you letter from Rabbi Braun. All three letters are in SB Papers, Box 38.

[73] January 3, 1947 letter, SB Papers, Boxes 60-61.

[74] "New Book Covers Career."

[75] Approximately 900 people filled the synagogue while another 2,000 stood outside.

"Political Leaders at Rites for Bloom," *The New York Times*, March 11, 1949, pg. 25.

Appendix *(pages 148-149)*

[1] See *The War Diary of Breckinridge Long*, 110.

[2] *The Politics of Rescue*, 195.

[3] Melvin I. Urofsky, *A Voice That Spoke for Justice: The Life and Times of Stephen S. Wise* (Albany: State University of New York, 1982).

[4] *The Politics of Rescue*, 195.

[5] See *Problems of World War II*, 212.

[6] Appendix to the Congressional Record, 78th Congress, First Session, p. A2154.

INDEX

Made in the USA
Monee, IL
06 September 2023

cd5451e0-540f-41ef-9acd-3e5ecfd741f3R01